Welcome To...

Desktop Publishing

by David Browne

MIS:
PRESS

**A Subsidiary of
Henry Holt and Co., Inc.**

First Edition—1993

ISBN 1-55828-295-5

Printed in the United States of America.

10 9 8 7 6 5 4 3 2 1

MIS:Press books are available at special discounts for bulk purchases for sales promotions, premiums, fund-raising, or educational use. Special editions or book excerpts can also be created to specification.

For details contact: Special Sales Director
MIS:Press
a subsidiary of Henry Holt and Company, Inc.
115 West 18th Street
New York, New York 10011

Trademarks

DEDICATION

To F.W. Thurston,

who introduced me to a tin lizzie of a computer a long time ago,
and hooked me for life.

And to those people everywhere who struggle with computers,
knowing deep in their marrow that all things are possible, yet not
knowing where to begin, nor how to get there.

ACKNOWLEDGEMENTS

A book of this sort is only possible with the help and generosity of a number of people and organizations—mine is no different. Microsoft was most supportive, plying me with information and Windows applications relating to desktop publishing. In particular I want to thank Alex St. John, Dave Perry, and Dave Glenn for their attention and quick response to my inquiries. Thanks also to Adobe Systems for providing whatever applications and fonts I requested. Spinnaker Systems was kind enough to supply me with PFS Publisher for Windows. Kodak contributed their Photo CD images and software; my thanks to Paul McAfee and to Eastman Kodak for permission to use the photographs you see on the color pages. Aldus liberally plied me with their applications as well—my thanks, as always, to Freda Cook.

I would be remiss if I failed to thank publisher Steve Berkowitz who asked me to write *Welcome to Desktop Publishing*, and allowed me the time to do it right and the freedom to say what I believe is important. As usual, the production staff at MIS:Press did its professional best at turning my words into the beautiful pages you have opened before you. In particular I'd like to thank Laura Lewin for her help with the manuscript, Laura Specht for creating the page design and layout, and Amy Carley for her tireless efforts with revisions.

Last, but certainly not least, a most special thanks to my wife Sally, who proofreads my words, doles out criticizm and praise in mostly equal proportions, and generally keeps me on.

CONTENTS

Chapter 3: Using Page Composition Software

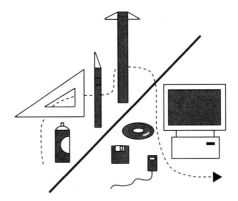

Preface

This book explains desktop publishing. If you have a Windows computer and seek to improve the look of your documents, you've come to the right place. If you have artistic talent and want to use a computer to automate many of the tiresome chores of document composition, read this book. If you're on the brink of deciding whether this desktop publishing thing is something to get involved with, this book will help you come to a decision. But *Welcome to Desktop Publishing* is a lot more; really three books in one.

- **This book is a guide to using Windows publishing software on your computer.** I explain how to publish documents, newsletters, stationery, and mailing labels using the software you probably already own, without buying a thing more. I tell you about the publishing capabilities of Word for Windows and WordPerfect for Windows, and show you how to use simple drawing programs to dress up all your documents. And I take you through the in's and out's of four of the most popular desktop publishing programs, including PageMaker and QuarkXPress.

1

- **This book is a handbook of graphic design techniques.** Even if you know absolutely nothing about graphic design, I explain the principles of design and typography so you can understand them and actually communicate with artists and printers! You'll learn everything you need to know about fonts, space, balance, graphics, and printing. And you'll get practical tips for designing professional documents that are good-looking and easy to read.

- **This book is a how-to cookbook with secret recipes to creating dozens of documents.** From memos to magazine ads, letterhead to literature, business cards to brochures, and logos to labels, I give you the steps, tips, and strategies you need to produce all your own professional-quality business communication tools.

Plus you'll pick up juicy tidbits, like creating publishable reports with Microsoft Access, saving money using Kodak's new Photo CD image service, printing in color for the cost of black and white, and sources for clip art, type fonts, and inexpensive utilities that will make your life easier and your documents better looking.

WHY IS DESKTOP PUBLISHING SO IMPORTANT?

Personal computers are roaring down the road at us; developments and innovations come at a pace that is inevitably faster each year. Some of the most startling advances are surely the technological leaps of desktop publishing. There is now a wealth of sophisticated software available for personal computers. Macintosh and Windows computers have gained wide acceptance as viable platforms for creating and preparing art work. Windows is in fact multiplying at an incredible rate—about one million copies are sold each and every month (during 1993), affording one million more people each month easy access to a number of important desktop publishing tools. Since the Windows applications that these new computer owners buy contain many standard features for document publishing, it is clear that the presentation of information is now just as important as the words themselves. The easier it becomes for us to add design elements—graphics, pictures, fonts, colors, and shapes—to documents, the more influential our documents become, and the more important desktop publishing becomes to us.

This is a book of words, graphic illustrations, photographs, and occasional flourishes. The words were put down on paper using a word processing program on a computer. That's the way most manuscripts for books are written; however, here is where the similarity to traditional book publishing ends. This book was created on computers using *desktop publishing software*—it was designed, edited, typeset, laid out, proofed, corrected, and produced electronically on Windows and Macintosh computers using a page composition program called PageMaker. All the graphic images in the book were created with off-the-shelf software, all the color photos were composed electronically using software readily available to anyone.

Nothing was handled in the traditional sense of preparing art work for printing. Graphic artists did not lay out the pages on drafting tables; color photos were not sent out to an expensive color seps house for preparation; type for the pages was not set in long galleys, cut apart and pasted down to art boards. Instead, the work was done by computer software, directed by the clicks of a mouse. The software and computers did all the mundane, boring things that artists used to have to do, while author and editors did the creative things—an efficient partnership of humans and machines, each doing their level best to create this book.

How Desktop Publishing Began

I witnessed the first stirrings of desktop publishing in 1982, when sales people from Apple arrived to show off their new Apple Lisa. At the time, I worked for an aerospace company as one of hundreds of writers and editors employed to communicate information. The Lisa was the grandmother of the Macintosh and it had a similar look and feel. The most startling thing we saw was presented on the screen; little icons, or graphic symbols, of tools showed the various functions—typing, drawing, filing, printing, etc.—and the screen itself, which was called the *desktop*. You used a mouse to open folders on the desktop and worked on multiple projects in those folders, much as we did at our own desks.

Apple wanted to give us Lisas to use and evaluate at no charge. A group of us watched as the sales staff demonstrated how you could open several software applications at once, and copy and paste information among the programs. This was pretty amazing stuff back then, when dedicated word processors from Lanier were considered pretty much state of the art.

Even though the Lisa was unbelievably slow and a bit awkward to use, it became clear to me and others that it would render the company's art department (which employed several hundred designers, artists, and drafts people) as obsolete as a dinosaur—we viewed the machine as a writer's tool that would allow us to do our own art work. Representatives of the art department silently watched the demonstration and figured it would bring about an end to all the writers and editors (the bane of their professional lives). They saw the machine as an artistic tool that could be used to add words as well. We were all new to computers in those days and guessed at only the threats of automation, without seeing the promise of efficiency and productivity. The drawback that kept my employer (and just about everyone else) from buying Lisas was a lack of both software and a printer that had graphic capabilities equal to the machine (there was no such thing as desktop publishing software, nor PostScript laser printers in 1982).

Then, several years later, the Mac Plus became available and Apple introduced the LaserWriter, the first PostScript laser printer with thirteen PostScript fonts in permanent memory. Adobe Systems (who had invented the PostScript language) released a limited number of fonts—actual typesetter's fonts, like Bookman, Palatino, Garamond, and Optima—identical to what photo-mechanical typesetting equipment could produce. And Aldus Corporation rolled out a new program called PageMaker that displayed circles, lines, and type in practically any size, exactly as pages would look when printed on the shiny new LaserWriters. By modern standards the hardware and software was fairly crude, but in 1985, it was downright miraculous.

Around the same time Adobe granted the Linotype Corporation, a phototypesetter manufacturer, an exclusive license to install PostScript in its typesetters, overnight the desktop publishing service bureau industry was born. The technology of graphic design and printing jumped through a millennium that day, for graphic composition changed as radically as if aliens from another galaxy had shown us the secrets of the future. Suddenly the separate acts of design, layout, drawing, writing, typography, and printing merged into one fluid, creative force.

WHERE DESKTOP PUBLISHING IS GOING

Today's progress begets tomorrow's traditions. More than 500 years ago, Johann Gutenberg figured out the concept of printing from moveable type—one master set of characters could be used over and over to produce different documents—and changed forever the traditions of publishing. Books proliferated with Johann's printing press. The cost of publishing dropped steadily and printed documents became readily available. Less than ten years ago the traditions of publishing were changed again, by the introduction of the personal computer, the PostScript laser printer, and the PostScript page description language. Once again the costs of publishing plummeted; once again more and more people were swept up in a wave of publishing technology.

Desktop publishing has become a mature, refined system of document production. It generates much of the junk mail that vies for our attention, yet it also creates the exquisite pages of *The New Yorker*. And, while we have computers and intuitive software to do most of the actual work of publishing, we are still tied invisibly to five centuries of experience as printers, typesetters, and artists cultivated the processes of publishing into traditions of design and typography. Today we can use computer software to handle the mundane tasks of publishing, leaving us with the more important responsibility of applying the legacy of those five centuries in the design of publications. *Welcome to Desktop Publishing* explains the software and the design principles, and tells you how to mix the two together to produce great-looking documents.

Having started out in document design and publishing long before the beginning of personal computers, I've had the opportunity to actively participate in desktop publishing as it struggled for a foothold in the graphic arts industry and exploded into the mature, sophisticated hardware and software systems we see today. Writing *Welcome to Desktop Publishing* has been a journey for me back to the roots of computer publishing. Writing about what is available now took me back to the days when there was so little, when there were only 100 or so PostScript typefaces to choose from—now there are tens of thousands—when a PageMaker document could have no more than 128 pages—now it can have more than 9,000—and when there was no such thing as scanned photos and computer clip art.

I hope you too will find a journey in *Welcome to Desktop Publishing*, one that will take you confidently into a future of faster computers and innovative software that will make your job easier and your designs even more appealing.

— David Browne
1361 Queen Elaine Drive
Casselberry, Florida 32707

A Quick Look at Desktop Publishing

Windows and desktop publishing are synonymous terms in many ways. Your Windows computer stands ready to handle many of your publishing needs fresh out of the box, with just a word processing program installed. So, wait a few minutes and read the chapters in Part I before you run out and begin buying software applications. You're about to see how effective the software you already own is at publishing documents, and you will learn some of the in's and out's of specialized page composition software.

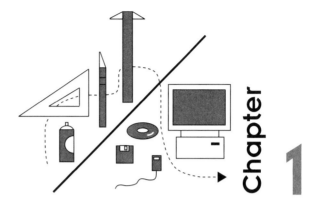

Chapter 1

Using the Computer's Desktop

▼**T**here is a quiet revolution going on among people not normally accustomed to document design and composition. It has spread across the country and around the world, changing forever the way many of us think about creating documents. Designers, artists, drafts people, printers, writers, editors, and folks who until recently have always shied away from drawing boards, have taken up personal computers and are using desktop publishing software to churn out beautiful black and white, and color documents. Brochures, fact sheets, newsletters, business cards and stationery, invitations, slimjims, presentations, proposals, magazines, books, product packaging, company logos, and anything else you can think of, roll out of laser printers and PostScript typesetters literally camera-ready.

Fueling this revolution is a new generation of publishing-sensitive software for personal computers that understands layout, typography, and color—issues that only a few years ago were reserved for only the most expensive and technically complex programs. Unlike the word processing, spreadsheet, and database software of the 1980's, today's programs for Windows (and in some cases for DOS), be they WordPerfect, Word, Excel, Lotus or Access, are tuned for appearance, presentation, and publication, as well as accuracy in their particular specialization. All allow you to specify type fonts in particular sizes and styles; all allow *WYSIWYG* (what-you-see-is-what-you-get) formatting—the *page* you create in the application looks like the page you print with your laser printer. All work with one another to help you build the structure and content of pages to your liking. Used singly or together, Windows software and your laser printer can give you the tools to design and produce professional-looking documents.

WHAT IS DESKTOP PUBLISHING?

Desktop publishing means preparing documents for printing on your own computer instead of preparing the work manually for publishing. There is no actual desktop involved (other than what your computer rests on). Rather, Windows programs simulate a creative work place (or desktop) on your computer's screen. The fact that the programs provide a multitude of tools for you to use in writing, drawing, painting, and coloring your documents, is the analogy to a desktop. Just as you have tools you use in your daily job arranged on your desk at work (a calculator, telephone, note pad, pens, pencils, appointment calendar, Rolodex file, and the like), so can you arrange publishing tools for instant access with desktop publishing software.

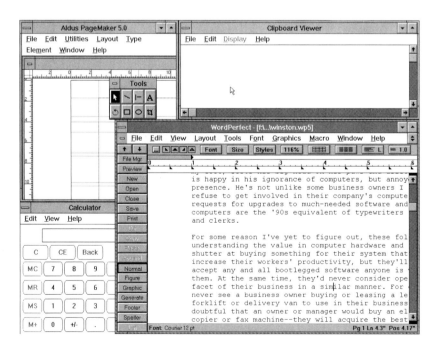

You can find desktop publishing systems everywhere, and with the advent of laptop and notebook computers, desktop publishing has moved off the desk. You can now find desktop publishing systems on the kitchen table, in the kid's room, the school library, and the study hall. They're on the manager's credenza and the CEO's conference table. It's used on airplanes, in autos, on the commuter train, (it even follows me onto my sailboat). You'll find the software in church offices, film studios, ad agencies, public relations firms, yacht brokers, car dealerships, grocery stores, schools, libraries, throughout corporate America, and across Europe and Asia—literally anywhere someone wants to say something attractively.

Desktop publishing has evolved from dedicated page composition systems like PageMaker and QuarkXPress to most Windows applications: from word processors like WordPerfect, to spreadsheets like Microsoft Excel, to database managers like Microsoft Access. Just about all Windows software gives you publishing features you may not realize exist and probably haven't tapped.

Desktop publishing implies the act of printing. While the printed results are surely the fruits of our efforts, but the term doesn't do justice to the capabilities of what I call *desktop composition*. With the mobility and diversity of desktop publishing comes a uniform need for graphic treatment. By that I mean desktop publishing affords us instant creativity never before possible in printed communication. Now we can affect words (in subtle shades of meaning) by controlling how the words look as well as choosing what they say. Whether we are generating a report in a database, graphing the results of a spreadsheet, or producing a four-color brochure, the size and style of type used will contribute to the overall meaning. The layout of the page will help or hinder comprehension. Colors and graphics will enhance or fog the conclusions we hope readers will draw from our publications.

If you already know some of the basic rules of typography and composition, you're ahead of the game. If not, later chapters of this book will give you a solid grounding in the do's and don't's of design. One word of warning: The advent of scalable fonts and laser printers has changed the emphasis in written communication, from words to image. It is easy to be lulled into time-consuming composition of what would otherwise be simple letters and memos. Desktop publishing is so easy and interactive, it can seduce you into wasting time laying out and composing documents that really require speed, not good looks, to get results.

MAKING BETTER-LOOKING DOCUMENTS

Probably the single biggest advantage desktop publishing gives you is better looking documents. Instead of simply typing a document in a word processor, you publish it, adding flourish, style, emphasis, and importance to your words. Mind you, there's nothing wrong with churning out a trip request memo to your boss on the old word processor, printed with a dot matrix printer (as shown below); however, the impact can be less than conclusive.

```
Date:     6 August, 1993
To:       Will Jacobs
From:     Len Carlyle
Subject: Adjuster93 Conference and Trade Show

1.        I have tentatively scheduled us to attend Adjuster93,
in Orlando the week of 10 January, 1994. This is the largest
conference on our profession and I think it's important that
we attend. All the new interstate regulations will be covered
as well as revisions to self insurance fund provisions. The
conference should save a lot of calls to get answers.

2.        We are slated to be housed at the Sheraton near the
convention center. We should probably rent a car for the
duration of our stay as nothing is close to the convention
center, least of all the airport.

3.        Travel budgets for next year's accounting must be set
by this month, so we should try to include this trip. I expect
$2k for travel and expenses. |
```

In business, attractive documents look only as useful as the speed with which they are produced. It's all very well to say a dressy memo has convincing power that the utilitarian Courier font version doesn't. But if it takes all day to lay out and compose a memo, its success is doomed before it is even drafted. Desktop publishing lets you draft the content of the memo and the appearance of the memo simultaneously, as in the example shown.

Time-Critical Memo

6 August, 1993

TO: Will Jacobs
FROM: Len Carlyle

SUBJ: Adjuster93 Conference and Trade Show

What
I have tentatively scheduled us to attend Adjuster93, in Orlando the week of 10 January, 1994. This is the largest conference on our profession and I think it's important that we attend. All the new interstate regulations will be covered as well as revisions to self insurance fund provisions. The conference should save a lot of calls to get answers.

When
The trade show actually runs from the previous Saturday (the 8th) until Friday the 14th. Conference days are Jan 10 - 13. I think we should arrive Saturday and leave Wednesday evening (to get the best air fares).

Where
We are slated to be housed at the Sheraton near the convention center. We should probably rent a car for the duration of our stay as nothing is close to the convention center, least of all the airport.

Why
Let's face it Will, we both need a break, and we always get a lot for the money at these conferences (if two from the same company go, the second goes for half price). Travel budgets for next year's accounting must be set by this month, so we should try to include this trip. I expect $2k for travel and expenses.

While the message is the same in both memos, the second is more pleasing to the eye, easier to understand, and more attractive in presentation. It commands professional consideration and makes a stronger case for its author. Desktop publishing gives you instant control over the content of your message and its underlying subtleties of meaning.

Desktop publishing can dictate the reaction to your message by controlling its appearance. The style of a document is as important as the document's message. Just as wedding invitations tend to use soft, cursive typefaces, an IRS invitation to the gala audit of your tax records will invariably have a strong official appearance. With desktop publishing, you can set the tone of your document interactively while you create it. Experiment with spacing, type fonts, and styles; try adding more emphasis with lines, boxes, and graphics. It's a simple matter to pick and choose from the ideas that work and throw away the ones that don't.

Desktop publishing allows you to combine individual documents into persuasive, interactive publications. For example, a typical technical report produced on a word processor might come with an addendum of Xeroxed graphics, an appendix of printed backup data from a financial spreadsheet, and a folder of copied drawings and photographs under separate cover. With desktop publishing you can combine all elements of information into one concise report whose pages contain text and graphs, charts, pictures, drawings, spreadsheet calculations, and so forth. It will look like a professionally published report because you have indeed published it instead of merely throwing together and three-hole punching a stack of disassociated pages.

MAKING DOCUMENTS EASIER TO PRODUCE

Before desktop publishing, improving the appearance of documents was reserved for high-priced publications. They were expensive because of the amount of handwork necessary to make them attractive. Type had to be set by a typesetter, cut apart and pasted down on art boards by an artist. Any color at all involved intricate, delicate work with X-acto knives on overlays of acetate. Color photos required expensive color scanning and separation by a color separation specialist.

So we divided documents into those the word processing center typed (or that we produced with a word processing program); and those that were taken to the art department (where the art director would smile gleefully and tell you not to bother waiting). It seemed everyone (but you) spoke a different technical jargon, while you stood in the middle, nodding but not really comprehending; and trying, often in vain, to keep things from falling through the cracks. Is it any wonder that sprucing up documents was usually reserved for only the most important publications? Displaying all the intricate steps in a flow chart shows the number of decisions and pitfalls, like Figure 1.1.

Notice that at every decision point there is a bomb symbol. I've tried to depict the feeling that developed in the pit of my stomach every time I went through this process. At each ticking bomb you'll see that someone else enters the chain of responsibility—if they don't do their job correctly, your job won't be finished. The more important and expensive the job, the more people become involved in its completion, and the more dependent you become on the good intentions of others (and the explosions are likely to occur). If, on the other hand, you look at the flow of tasks for a desktop-published document (in Figure 1.2), the only ticking bomb is the approaching deadline. You are in charge of all aspects of the job, at least up to the point of delivering it to your commercial printer.

Figure 1.1   *Flow chart of traditional page composition.*

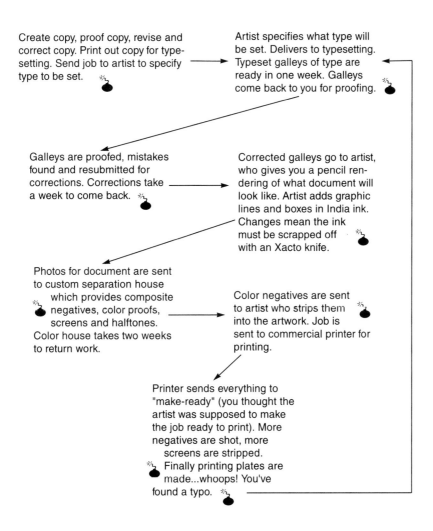

Figure 1.2 *Desktop publishing flow chart.*

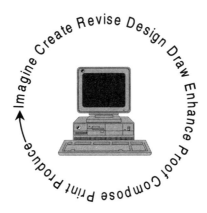

If the number of meetings, decisions, interruptions, and mistakes inherent in designing, composing, and producing documents doesn't convince you of the efficiencies of desktop publishing, consider this: You'll save enormous amounts of time and money.

HELPING YOUR COMMERCIAL PRINTER

Your commercial printer will certainly be one of the happiest beneficiaries of your desktop publishing efforts. That's because the final printed *mechanical* that you deliver is ready to print, without any additional work. The printer simply creates printing plates of each page and each color separation in your document, plates up the printing press, and prints your job. Less handwork for the printer means the job is completed sooner and less expensively. We'll cover the handling of separate colors, and exactly how color is printed in Chapter 6, *Graphics: Adding Lines, Boxes, Photos and More.*

A *mechanical* is all the pages of your publication, with the color and graphic elements that the printer needs in order to create the printing plates to print the job. All this stuff came to be called

GLOSSARY

the mechanical because each page of the publication was created on a separate art board. Type is pasted to the board and the color and graphic elements pasted to clear acetate (or velum) overlays and taped to the back of the board so they hinged into alignment over the type (or *down art*). Since every color needs to be separately printed, each overlay contained only items in a particular color. To put the whole thing together required a mechanical engineering degree.

Using Windows desktop publishing software, the results of your work will be completed documents rolling out of a high resolution PostScript-compatible typesetter (generally called an *imagesetter*). Unlike typesetters that traditionally set only the type for a page, imagesetters set an image of everything on the page, including type, graphics, and photographs. The pages will exactly reflect the formatting, typography, and design you created on the screen. There will be little, if any, preparation for your commercial printer to do other than create the printing plates and print the job.

GLOSSARY

Resolution is a term that's bandied about in desktop publishing, but what does it mean? The **resolution** of a printer is the degree of smoothness with which the elements are produced on the page. The higher the resolution, the more the page looks like it was created by a typesetter; the lower the resolution, the more it looks like you used a dot matrix printer (the edges of type and graphics look rough and *stair-stepped*). Generally, resolution for a printer is measured in dots-per-inch—the more dots to the inch the crisper the image, the smoother the edges of graphics and type, and the better looking the page. Laser printers typically print 300 dots to the inch, while high-priced PostScript imagesetters have as much as ten times higher resolution.

NOTE

Some imagesetters and high-resolution laser printers, like LaserMaster, can print your documents on electrostatic plate material, and all the printer has to do is mount the plates on the printing press and start printing. Ask your printer if electrostatic plates are acceptable, and check with your service bureau to make sure they can supply the work on plates. You'll find more information about service bureaus in Chapter 8, *Be Your Own Printer*.

GLOSSARY

If you haven't heard about PostScript yet, you will learn all about its magic in the chapters to come. For now, you only need to know that **PostScript** is the programming language that allows you to print beautiful typefaces, any graphic shape, or photograph to a low-resolution laser printer, or a high-resolution imagesetter. PostScript fonts are covered in Chapter 5, color separated photos are discussed in Chapter 6, and PostScript printers are explained in Chapter 8.

GLOSSARY

A **service bureau** is a business that houses expensive, high-resolution typesetters that can print your desktop publishing files at a minimal cost. One of the many benefits of desktop publishing software is the wide variety of printing devices you can use. While you probably own a low-resolution laser printer, which does a very nice job with office correspondence, you probably want your desktop publishing documents to have a higher print quality. Simply send the files (through the mail or through the telephone lines with a modem) to a PostScript service bureau and you'll get back gorgeous, high-resolution pages ready for your commercial printer to print.

A less obvious way that you'll help your commercial printer is when it comes time to revise and reprint your job. It's as simple as making any needed changes in Windows, then ship the file to your service bureau to have new negatives or plates made, and ship that to the printer. Compare this to the stacks of dusty art boards, scratched negatives that have been collecting dust for the past year, and you'll really appreciate the ease of revision desktop publishing affords you.

Saving Money

This is the part I like. If you design and produce your own documents you save the cost of paying a designer and a layout artist or drafts person to prepare your document for printing. You also save on the cost of typesetting and the camera shots used to convert photographs into halftones that can be printed. Over the course of a four- or eight-page document, that's a considerable sum of money.

For years, one of my professional duties was producing a little four-page monthly newsletter for a trade association. Before I jumped into desktop publishing, a designer/artist friend used to charge $800 merely to typeset and lay out the document after I had written the stories. Since the designer needed two weeks to work the job into her schedule each month, it left me only a week to write the stories and have the newsletter printed, so that it could be distributed during the fourth week. In other words, the part of the job that should take the least amount of time—that of setting type and laying out four pages—took the largest chunk of time in the schedule! Seems a little backwards, doesn't it? That same newsletter now requires only one evening to design and lay out on my computer; proofs are printed and corrected using my laser printer; and the computer file is transmitted through a modem to a commercial printer. Total costs, including printing, have dropped to about $250.

You also save money when it comes time to revise and reprint the job. Instead of having to pencil changes on the art boards and have a designer, typographer, and drafts person make the changes, you simply open the file on your computer and make the changes you want. Then reprint the master pages and deliver them to your commercial printer. There is an efficiency that goes beyond just the economy of working with a computer file. There are no longer great stacks of art boards cluttering up filing cabinets; no longer drawing boards and the associated mess that goes along with the traditional processes of document composition.

THE PRODUCTION COMPONENTS OF DESKTOP PUBLISHING

Producing a document with your computer is an act of wrapping your imagination in a blanket of precision and control. Unlike the traditional drawing board approach, you have complete freedom in the way you wish to create a document, and you can begin your desktop publishing project wherever you are most comfortable. For some projects, you may want to start by writing the words, then lay them out in an attractive format. For other projects you might come up with the overall design first, create and add graphics and photographs, and fill in with words at a later point. Or you may want to take the basic design from an existing document and use it to create (or clone) another document. The concept of cloning, which uses a *template* of the document to provide a design framework for future documents, is explained fully in Chapter 7, *Making Your Work Easier with Templates and Styles.*

GLOSSARY

A **template** is merely a shell of a document. It can hold as little or as much information as you like. For example, it could simply have the overall size and typographic specifications for a document, or it could also contain boilerplate text that can be easily changed to fit the need of the new document. A useful template would hold all the basic information about a monthly newsletter. Then, each month you would save the template as that month's issue and add the necessary stories and art to flesh out the issue.

Regardless of the order that text, graphics, and pictures are added to the page, you follow the same basic steps:

- Set up the overall format for the pages.
- Compose the pages.
- Proof your work.
- Make changes to the pages if neccessary.
- Print the final pages.

Choosing the Form and Specifying the Page

Just as you roll blank paper into a typewriter, or tape a blank sheet of paper down to a drawing board, so you start with a clean sheet of paper in most desktop publishing applications. The first step in any project, big or small, is to define the publication you want to create. What form will the document take? What is its overall size? Is it folded? If so, what is the size of the unfolded page, and what is the folded page size? You can create just about any type of printed document that you can dream up with desktop publishing, including menus, invoices and shipping instructions, mailing labels, wedding invitations, certificates, calendars, the list is limited only by your imagination.

The overall format of the document page can have a significant impact on the reader. The page margins alone offer many options depending on your communication goals for the document. For example, should the margins be narrow or wide? Wide margins give the page *eye appeal*, inviting the reader to read on; while narrow margins can give you more room for wider text lines and more words to the page. Wider margins allow you to add margin notes, shown in Figure 1.3. Wider margins give you room to add headers and footers; yet too much white space can ruin the simplicity of a small document by drastically increasing the page count. Clearly, the seemingly small matter of margins is really very important to the document, and considerations involving margin notes and headers, footers, as well as a wider binding edge, and handling page numbers, must be balanced against the constant need for visual relief through white space on the page. All of these margin issues, and much more, are covered in Chapter 4, *Choosing a Page Design to Compliment the Message.*

GLOSSARY

Headers and *footers* are simply text or graphics that are repeated at the top and bottom of document pages. For example, the header on the pages of this chapter alternately show the book's title on left-hand pages, and the chapter title on right-hand pages. A useful footer for a mail order catalog might be the toll-free telephone number to place an order.

Figure 1.3   *Adding a margin note and a header to a document.*

22

> If you think you might have trouble qualifying for a standard construction loan, consider buying down the mortgage, or paying for some percentage of the materials out of pocket. A lender will only be interested in your project if you are already financially committed.

Financing the construction loan can take many forms; especially with today's competitive market and rock-bottom interest rates. But you should be prepared to have located and secured the site for your house prior to qualifying for the construction loan. Owning the property is the equivalent to a cash down payment of from 20 to 30 percent. You should also ask if the construction loan is convertible upon closing to a conventional mortage. The advantages are that you save two closings (including two title searches, to appraisals, two pest inspections, and duplication of all the vertification statemetns). Of singular importance is having to pay origination fees and points on both mortgages. With a convertible construction loan, at the time the certificate of occupancy is issued, the loan converts to an agreed-upon conventional mortage with a significantly lower interest rate.

While you can specify basically any size page you need for a particular project, the physical page size can't be larger than your printer can handle. For example, an 11-by-17 inch page folded to 8.5-by-11 inches makes a standard four page brochure. Yet most laser printers can only handle 8.5-by-11 inches (or 8.5-by-14 inches) as the maximum paper size. On the other hand, most imagesetters can handle page sizes of 11-by-17 inches. So, to proof the pages in your laser printer, you may have to specify 8.5-by-11 and simulate the larger page size. Figure 1.4 shows the difference in page arrangement for the two sizes.

 The page size is always determined by the outside edges of the page, not by the margins. The margins denote the limits of text on the page although many programs allow you to add text outside the margins.

N O T E

Figure 1.4 *Two sizes of pages arranged for a 4-page, 8.5-by-11 inch brochure.*

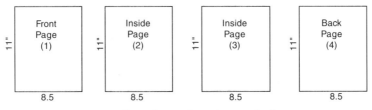

Page size configuration to print from
300 dpi laser printer
(4 8.5-by-11 pages)

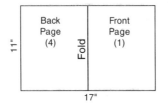 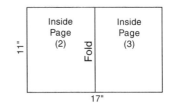

Page size configuration to print from
high-resolution imagesetter
(2 11-by-17 pages)

For smaller formats such as business cards, you may find it helpful to fit several on an 8.5-by-11 inch page. With trim marks noting the trimmed edge of each page, your commercial printer can print several cards per page, saving both time and money (printing 250 pages yields 1,000 cards). Figure 1.5 shows an example of a business card setup on larger page format.

Figure 1.5 *Four business cards set up to be printed on 8.5-by-11 inch pages.*

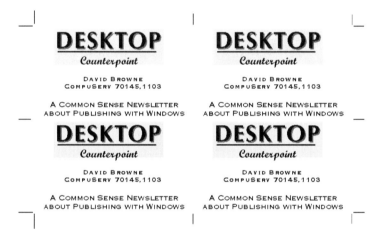

Composing the Page

Composition is the act of deciding where things go on the page—text, lines, graphic accents and flourishes, boxes, clip art, illustrations, photos—as well as the act of balancing the page so it's attractive and appealing. Once the overall size of the page and the text margins are decided, you can pretty much do whatever you want to do in designing and composing the page. (Unlike simply typing text with a word processing program, text can be added wherever you want.) While I offer a number of basic guidelines for page composition in Chapter 4, there are no hard and fast rules, and sometimes the most pleasing design is one that purposely ignores the guidelines. Generally speaking, whatever appeals to you will probably look good to your readers (unless you have an acute astigmatism and tend to create very tall, thin, out-of-kilter documents). Here are some questions to ask yourself that may help define the composition you're looking for:

- **What is the publication about?** Is the subject matter text-oriented, like a technical proposal, or is it picture-oriented, like a marketing or sales brochure? Proposals, by definition, tend to have more words and less pictures because you must be more careful what you promise to do and exactly how much it costs. Sales, on the other hand, is more emotional—a good sales person weaves a successful scenario for the prospect's imagination, and a good sales brochure should do no less with the right mixture of words and pictures.

- **Who is the audience for this publication?** Design the document to the targeted reader. If that person has a lot of time to study your publication, you have more leeway for added details. If the reader will only skim the document, you'll need a more novel design and more color, or illustrations to attract and hold attention.

- **How much attention will the reader devote to the publication?** If the publication is sent out to blind, unknown mailing lists, it may hold little importance to the readers. However, if this is a church newsletter going to the congregation, it will be scrutinized cover to cover.

- **What is the production budget for the publication?** You can create highly professional documents on your laser printer for pennies a copy. If you want to add color, or photos, the cost of printing can increase significantly. It's a good idea to decide on the budget before you begin composing your document.

- **How many copies will I need printed?** If you need a small amount and you're not using color, you might be able to use your laser printer. Unless you own a color printer, you'll need to seek out a commercial printer if you are composing a color document. However, for small printing runs consider the services of a color copier.

- **What is the life of the publication?** This question is really related to the previous question concerning the number of copies. You may be thinking about the immediate, short-term needs to get something out; when in fact the publication may be used for the next six months. To avoid costly reprints, consider the total needs and print accordingly (which, of course, affects your budget).

- **How will the publication be distributed?** If it will be mailed without an envelope, then it must be of a size and material acceptable to the post office. If it will be enclosed in an envelope, make sure it fits in a standard size envelope (custom envelopes are extremely expensive).

Printing Proofs

The very best thing about laser printers is instant access to exact proofs of your document. I'm a firm believer in printing proofs as you develop, enhance, and refine your document; it's the best way to gauge the effect of your work. As you build the page by adding elements, frequent proofing will often tell you when to stop. By using your laser printer, you can see the exact placement of text and graphics. You'll be able to confirm the alignments and measurements that you specified in your desktop publishing program. And, you'll have a printed record of each stage of composing your document. So print proofs as you go.

If you find that the time to print proofs is slowing down other phases of your work, consider some of these tips to speed up printing:

- **Lower the resolution of graphics.** Graphics are the monsters that slow down printing—the higher the resolution of the graphic the longer it takes the printer to process and print. Consider adding high resolution graphics at the end of the page's composition so your proofs for layout, alignment, and text accuracy won't be affected by the large graphic files.

- **Print the graphic boxes but not the graphics.** Again, consider adding boxes where graphics will be placed later, but indicate in the box for position only and leave the box blank for the time being. Some desktop publishing programs, like QuarkXPress, allow you to flag a graphic box to suppress the printing of the actual graphic and just print the box. For not so sophisticated programs, you can draw another box on top of the graphic, color the box the same color as the paper, and the printer will ignore the graphic and just print the blank box.

- **Print the text in one pass, then print the graphics if you need to.** Different desktop publishing applications control the printer in different ways. If your application allows you to print text and graphics on the same page as separate passes through the printer, by choosing just the text pass you again eliminate the slow printing required by high-resolution graphics. One such application is WordPerfect for Windows that allows you to choose whether you want to print text, graphics, or both, as shown in Figure 1.6.

Figure 1.6 *By selecting* **Do Not Print** *in the Graphics Quality list box, WordPerfect will only print the text on your pages.*

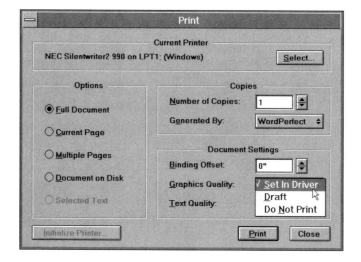

- **Download all the fonts at the beginning of the print job.** If you use a large number of different fonts for your text, consider loading them all first to the printer, which may ultimately speed up printing the document's pages. There are any number of programs that download fonts, including a nifty little shareware program called Downwind, as shown. You can get Downwind from Craig Harding (72010,1550) on CompuServe. The difference between fonts you download and the fonts that are resident in your laser printer is covered in "How Fonts Work in Your Computer and Printer," in Chapter 5.

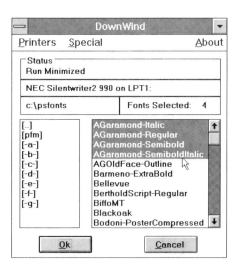

◆ **Use the Windows Print Manager to gang-print your pages.** You'll learn more about the Windows Print Manager in Chapter 8, but basically, Print Manager is a program that manages the job of sending the individual pages of your document to the laser printer in the background, while you return to your desktop publishing program and continue working. You can send Print Manager as many documents as you want to print, like the example shown on the next page, and they'll be queued up and printed in order.

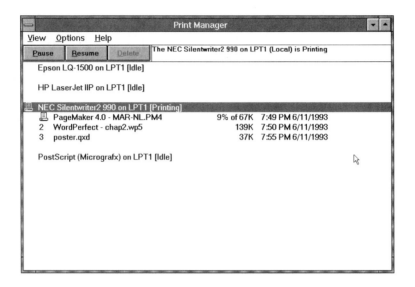

Editing Proofs

The editing step in the evolution of your publication is perhaps the most important—from a cost standpoint you will be forced to reprint pages with typos, or graphics and colors defined incorrectly. But editing also makes you cast a critical eye over your work. To proof the work accurately, you must look at it from the viewpoint of the first-time reader. Now is the time to step back from the job and give it the same appraisal as your audience, and honestly evaluate the work.

Take a look at the overall image of the page without worrying about the details of words, paragraphs, lines, or graphics. Hold the page at arm's length and squint your eyes. Look at the relationship of ink to white space. Are the margins inviting? Is there enough room to read the text comfortably or do the words look shoe-horned onto the page? Is the placement of graphics logical, is the page symmetrical? The answers to these questions are just as important as correct spelling and punctuation. You are considering the reading appeal of the page, and if there is little appeal your correctly spelled words may not be read.

Luckily, desktop publishing is just the tool to create that attractive page. As a matter of fact, most Windows applications, be they spreadsheets, word processors, or page composition programs, offer the same arms-length view of the page. For example, WordPerfect and Excel both let you see the entire page as a preview to printing, shown in Figures 1.7 and 1.8.

Figure 1.7   *WordPerfect's Print Preview screen.*

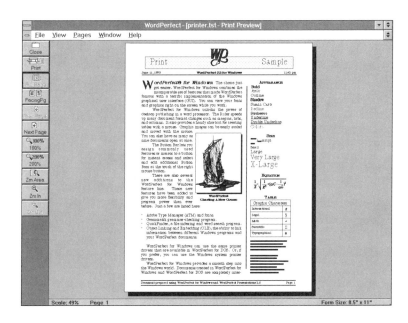

Figure 1.8   *Microsoft Excel's Print Preview screen.*

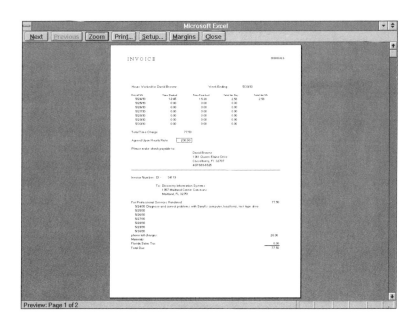

Several applications, including QuarkXPress and PageMaker, allow you to view the page in *thumbnail* size (a smaller, but still recognizable view of the full-page view, shown below), as well as print pages in the same thumbnail size. Thumbnails, like the ones shown here, are a great way to judge the reading appeal without getting bogged down by words and pictures.

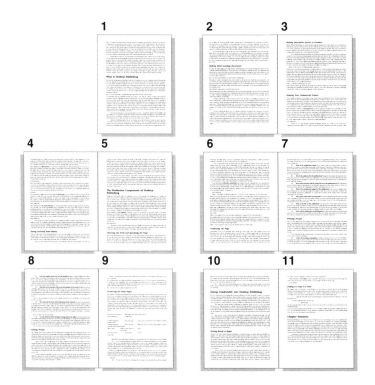

Producing the Final Pages

The manner of printing determines how the final, edited pages will be produced. If you plan to send the job out to a commercial printer (or to the print shop if your company has in-plant printing), you'll want the final pages produced at the highest resolution possible. A service bureau's high resolution imagesetter (like a Linotronic 330, or Agfa Selectset 5000) can produce the pages for you on either paper or film. The paper positives are much like what you get from your laser printer, only better. If you give your commercial printer the final pages on paper, the printer will have to create negatives of the pages so that printing plates can be made. However, if you request film from the service bureau, your commercial printer can save the step of shooting negatives (the film is the negative). You save money and your printer saves time. If this all seems a bit complicated, the various final page options are shown in the table below.

If sets of your document will be printed by:	Final pages should be produced by:	In the form of:
Commercial printer	Service bureau	Paper-the printer has to shoot negatives to make printing plates
Commercial printer	Service bureau	Film-you save the cost of shooting negatives; the printer can make plates from the film
Office copier	Either service bureau or laser printer	Paper
Laser printer	Laser printer	Paper

Regardless of the material the final pages are produced on, here are some points to keep in mind:

◆ If you are producing the final pages and the sets of printed documents are to be trimmed to a smaller size, add trim marks so you or the commercial printer have the references for trimming. All page composition software, such as PageMaker, QuarkXPress, and Microsoft Publisher, add trim marks automatically. While word processors and spreadsheets are not able to print them automatically, you can add them manually to the page.

If the program you're using can't create trim marks, use a graphics program, like Paintbrush that comes with Windows, to create just

NOTE

the marks in the proper location. Print the number of pages you need for your document in PaintBrush, then put the printed pages back in the paper tray of your printer and print the final pages using your word processor or spreadsheet on the (now) trim-marked pages.

- If your service bureau is producing the final pages, you will probably send the computer file to the service bureau on floppy diskette. Be sure to include the graphic files that are used in the document. For example, if your document contains the graphic LION.PCX, be sure to copy the file LION.PCX to the floppy disks as well. (Some desktop publishing software will save the graphic as a part of the document file, but to be safe, send all the graphics as well.)

- If the publication is to be duplicated on an office copier, print the final pages on your laser printer using as smooth a paper stock as possible—the smoother the paper, the sharper and clearer the laser printing.

EASING COMFORTABLY INTO DESKTOP PUBLISHING

If you've done much investigating into desktop publishing, you have probably learned it is a massive industry touting specialized hardware, high-resolution printers, video monitors, expensive software, and differing opinions. You may have been told that desktop publishing requires huge amounts of disk space and memory, or that hundreds of fonts and clip art graphics are needed before you can publish your own documents. It's understandable if you feel slightly overwhelmed; but you needn't be discouraged.

The main idea behind desktop publishing is simplicity. While it's nice to have the added horsepower of a high-performance computer loaded with fonts, graphics, tools, and special applications, it isn't required, nor needed for most of the real-world documents you will shortly begin designing and producing. Actually, everything you need to begin is included with Windows 3.1. In all likelihood, you can use the computer you're presently using and upgrade to the tools or accessories you want when you need them.

The software is easy to learn and use; the Windows work place is friendly and inviting. You may find desktop publishing as familiar as sinking into a well-worn arm chair—the software feels like a natural extension of your fingers. Once you get started, Windows and Windows desktop publishing applications will seem so intuitive that you will find yourself initiating creative steps before you've read how to do them. Whether you are working with WordPerfect for Windows, Microsoft Publisher, Aldus PageMaker, (or even creating fancy reports using Microsoft Excel, or Borland's Quattro Pro) you will discover similar commands and functions, a familiar feel to the applications, and a synergy of effort using the shared resources of Windows.

Getting Ready to Begin

The first step on the road to desktop publishing is to stop throwing away all that junk mail that fills your mailbox. Yes, that's what I said. Start sorting through the flyers, leaflets, brochures, fact sheets, magazines, and newspapers, and save the pages that give you ideas. Some of the finest design ideas are inside the covers of corporate annual reports, mail-order catalogs, and ads for software upgrades. I'm sure every successful design artist has a desk drawer full of *ideas*; start developing your own. Cast a critical eye over pages you like and try to decide why you like them. It may be the use of complimentary colors, the placement of art and text, the clever way a brochure unfolds, or a unique blend of typefaces. Compare the relative size of type and start getting a feel for the scale of a composed page. Use these good examples to stimulate your creative juices!

Now go back over your favorite examples and look for more subtle touches; these will often be seemingly small enhancements that carry more impact than their overall size might indicate. For example, a line or shadow added to a company logo; a photo rotated out of place to the surrounding text, or a graphic *bled* off the edge of the page—these design elements can have a stronger eye appeal and make a stronger statement than glaring type and bright colors. As you begin to study good designs and compositions, you realize the importance small, subtle effects can have. Chapters 4 and 5 show you some concrete examples of subtle versus blaring composition.

To *bleed* a photo or graphic off the page is to run the item over the margin and off the edge of the paper. The item prints over the margin and bleeds off the page.

GLOSSARY

Taking it a Step at a Time

The biggest step you will take is to get Windows 3.1, if you haven't already, and try out the Program Manager, File Manager and the accessories. Open the Games group and fire up Solitaire to get comfortable using the mouse. Windows 3.1 comes with an excellent computer-based tutorial that will teach you everything you need to know about Windows. To use the tutorial, follow these steps:

1.   Open the File menu in the Program Manager and choose the Run command to open the Run dialog box.

2.   In the Command Line text box type:

     `WINTUTOR`

     and the program starts.

3.   Once you are in the tutorial, press Esc at any time to quit and return to the Program Manager.

Once you have played around with Windows for a little while you'll be surprised how comfortable it feels, how easy and natural the mouse is to use. Windows is addictive, made doubly so by the beautiful things you can do to your documents and publications.

CHAPTER SUMMARY

Desktop publishing is a revolutionary idea. It empowers you to take charge of your own communication needs instead of entrusting what you want to say to the skills of someone else. Desktop publishing is ecologically sound: you eliminate the waste of dozens of products needed to create documents by hand (the least of which are neither recycled nor biodegradable). It is economical and saves you money, which is pretty revolutionary for an era when everything we use (with the exception of computers) rises in price without rising in functionality. And, desktop publishing is good for you: it saves you time and energy that can be directed at more important issues; pulls your boss out of last-minute jams, which makes you look good; and stimulates your creative energy which helps focus and direct your communicative skills.

Producing a professional-looking document is not the expensive, time-consuming chore it once was. With a little help from this book, a little practice with your computer, and a little imagination you can churn out in an hour the kinds of documents that used to take weeks to get out of a commercial artist, at a fraction of the cost. As you'll see in the next chapter, you don't necessarily need any more software than you already own to begin publishing your own documents.

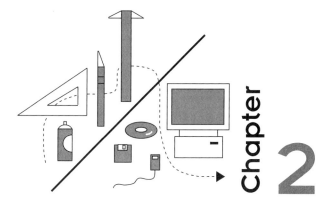

Using Whatever Software You Have

▼ **Y**ou can begin publishing your own documents right now and you may not even realize it. Perhaps you use your Windows word processor for merely office correspondence, your spreadsheet just for simple financial calculations, or your Windows database to store names and addresses. However, any of these programs, and most applications contain a powerful variety of tools that let you turn mere words and numbers into dynamic documents that sell, communicate, train, persuade (and make you look good).

Scratch almost any Windows application and you'll find desktop publishing capabilities. Most allow you the freedom to select a size and style of font (even a program like the lowly Cardfile lets you create custom headers and footers). Most have the ability to add graphics (either with their own commands, or by cutting and pasting from other programs, or linking the graphic using Object Linking and Embedding). And, since Windows controls the printer, you can print almost any type of document to a PostScript laser printer and get realistic-looking fonts (Chapter 5 explains how to print fonts in virtually any size to just about any printer).

So, before you rush out and buy a specialized page composition program, let's first look at what you probably already have running in

Windows—word processors, like WordPerfect for Windows or Microsoft Word for Windows, spreadsheets like Microsoft Excel, and drawing programs like Microsoft PaintBrush and Micrografx Draw. Then we'll look at a price range of composition programs, including Microsoft Publisher, PFS Publisher, Aldus PageMaker, and QuarkXPress for Windows.

PUBLISHING WITH WINDOWS WORD PROCESSORS

Word processors have one distinct advantage over dedicated page composition software: they manage the creation of words better than just about anything else. While programs like PageMaker and QuarkXPress offer search and replace, and spell checking features, they lag behind in the spelling, grammar, and thesaurus functions of high-powered word processors. Likewise, developing the text for long documents—a difficult task at best—is often faster with a good word processor. A word processor's weak suit is its lack of easy integration of text and graphics. That's where a page composition program, like PageMaker, shines.

Windows has made all software easier to use—word processors have undoubtedly benefitted the most from Windows' graphical user interface. What seemed clumsy and awkward with a DOS word processor now seems easy and natural using the Windows version of the same product. Adding any level of graphics with a DOS word processor was shooting in the dark. With Windows word processors you work with a realistic, accurate image of the page. Using a word processor to get the perfect effect with text and graphics has never been easier.

In computer years, WordPerfect has been around forever. It has been my principal word processor for the past 10 years, and it was in version 3 when I first learned how to use it. There are versions of WordPerfect that run on PCs, DEC and Data General and IBM minicomputers; there's even an IBM mainframe version. The non-Windows versions all look alike, all operate the same way (version 5.1 for DOS is shown in Figure 2.1). It's little wonder that WordPerfect can be found just about everywhere, used as a business tool to generate office correspondence. And, until the Windows version of WordPerfect, office correspondence, reports, and other text documents were what WordPerfect was best at.

Figure 2.1 *WordPerfect 5.1 for DOS shows a dull document page that doesn't exactly ignite one's creative imagination.*

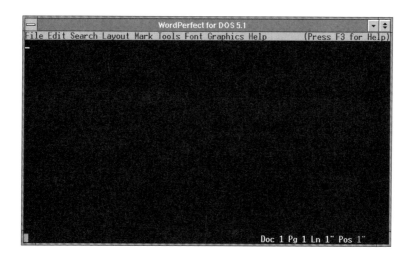

Although the DOS version of WordPerfect touted some cryptic desktop publishing features, to actually use them in a document, with any kind of precise formatting, was an act of extreme patience and faith. If you tried to add more than one or two fonts to a document, for example, you were flying blind, with no real idea of what the finished piece looks like until it was printed. Similarly, while you were supposed to be able to add graphic boxes on a page, WordPerfect for DOS wouldn't actually show you what your graphics look like—again, you were flying on instruments, never knowing exactly what the page looked like until it printed. Using Microsoft Word for DOS as a desktop publishing program was just as difficult. The two programs remained powerful word processors, but of little use in designing and producing creative pages on your computer. That is until Windows came along.

WordPerfect and Microsoft have been duking it out in a head-to-head battle over Windows customers ever since the Windows versions of the two products appeared on the market. Both are extremely powerful and sophisticated. Both sport all the bells and whistles you expect of word processing software, and both do a good job of arranging words on the page. While neither product is a page layout program, both have some color capability, both come with extensive graphic clip art files, and both can produce a wide variety of publications you might otherwise send out to the local graphic artist to do by hand. The two applications are shown below.

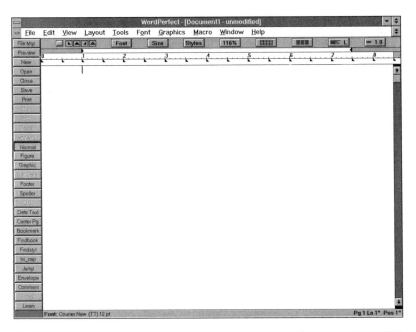

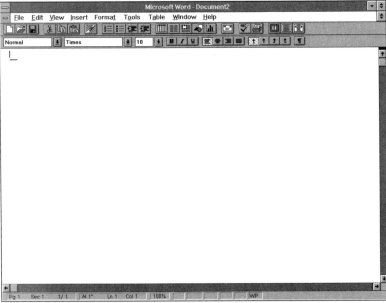

So, now that WordPerfect and Word are available in a format that is conducive to desktop publishing—one that allows you to see the actual formatting you specify and the changes you make—let's look at how to begin using the software for some creative endeavors.

The very first step to creating a good document is to add white space to open up your page, making it more inviting and more comfortable to read. White space is an important design tool that's described in detail in Chapter 4. It is added with word processing software differently than with page composition software, as I explain below. Once we've added some white space to the page, we'll look at adding elementary lines and boxes to the page. Finally, we'll see how easy it is to edit graphics that have been added to your design, and how to preview the pages of your document prior to printing.

How Word Processors Understand Space on the Page

Learn more about...

Using white space as a design element	See Chapter 4, "Improving the Look of the Page" and "Remember the White Space."
Handling spacing on the page	See Chapter 4, "Understanding Horizontal and Vertical Space."

There is one chief difference between working with a dedicated page composition program and a Windows word processor: the word processor forces you to stick to invisible lines on the page, while a page composition program gives you the freedom to add text or graphics wherever you want. Word processors see the page in much the same way as you do when you write on a lined tablet—you can write anywhere you want to as long as it's on one of the lines. Now, to be fair, you can change the height of the lines to adjust the placement of text, but your creative energy is still constrained to these invisible lines. For example, try typing a few lines of text at the beginning of a new page in WordPerfect or Word for Windows. Let's say you decide you want to add some text two-thirds of the way down the page. To do so, you must press Enter repeatedly until you get the mouse pointer, or cursor, to the area of the page you want. In WordPerfect for Windows, the resulting document window looks like Figure 2.2.

Figure 2.2   *WordPerfect for Windows showing return codes added to move the sursor down the page.*

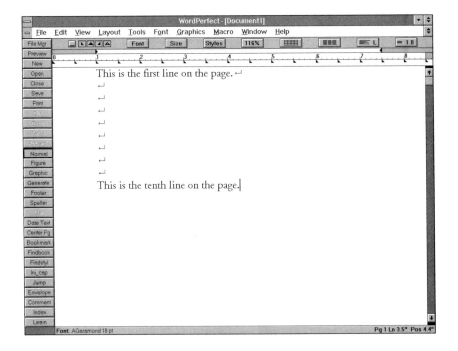

As you can see in the figure, the paragraph symbols mark the beginning of each line. It's necessary to create the line in order to move down the page (you normally move down the page of a word processor by typing text). If you want to add text or graphics below existing text and graphics you must repeatedly press Enter to force the insertion point down to the position you want. This concept of using the invisible 'lines' of a word processor is further complicated if you later go back and add some text to the blank space that you created by pressing the Enter key. The text you add *pushes* the original text or graphic further down the page. Notice in Figure 2.3 that the additional five lines of text in the center of the page has forced the text you added further down the page.

Figure 2.3 *Once a blank space is created with return codes, adding text forces adjacent lines further down the page.*

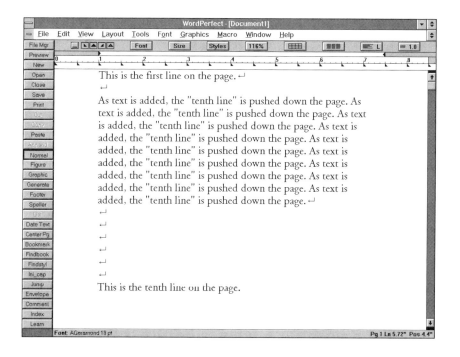

To keep the lines from *pushing*, press the Ins key to change to the *Typeover* mode in WordPerfect. The Typeover mode literally types over the existing characters and spaces, instead of creating new characters and spaces that push existing text further down the page. To use the same mode in Word (called the *Overtype* mode) open the Tools pull-down menu and choose the Options command. In the Options dialog box move to the General category and click on the Overtype mode check

NOTE

box to add an X. Choose OK or press Enter to return to your document.

There are a multitude of tricks WordPerfect and Word use to adjust text relative to those invisible page lines. In WordPerfect, for example, you can use the Line Height dialog box (choose Layout > Line), in the Line Spacing dialog box (select Layout > Line), in the Advance dialog box (on the Layout menu) and in the Typesetting dialog box (also on the Layout menu). Of all the choices in WordPerfect, the easiest to use is the Line Spacing dialog box, which allows you to adjust a line of selected text up or down by entering a line value. For instance, to adjust a line of text, in a group of single-spaced lines, open the dialog box and enter a value less than 1 to move the line you've selected upwards, or a value greater than 1 to move the line of text further down the page. In Word, you can use the superscript and subscript tools in the Character dialog box (in the Format menu), and the line spacing features of the Paragraph dialog box (also in the Format menu).

Since we've talked about positioning text and graphics vertically on the page, let's look at arranging items horizontally across the page. Just as word processors are limited to invisible lines up and down on the page, so too are they confined to character positioning along each of those lines. A common mistake that has carried over from the days of typewriters has been to use the Spacebar to move the insertion point across the line to the position you choose. Don't. Although the text you align using the Spacebar may look correct, it won't print correctly, and you'll have the devils's own time straightening it out.

Instead, use the Tab key to jump to the position you want. If there is no tab in the exact position, click on the text insertion point *before* the line and add the tab stop. In either WordPerfect or Word, you simply double-click on any Tab icon on the ruler bar to display the Tabs dialog box. Enter the exact position you choose for the tab stop and click on OK to return to your document. When you move the insertion point to the beginning of the line that you want to move across, simply press Tab to jump to that position.

Figure 2.4 shows the difference between aligning with the Spacebar and using the Tab key to align new text.

Figure 2.4   *The wrong way to align lines of type.*

This the first line

Now we have the secc

And now the third

In comes the fourth

While here is the fifth

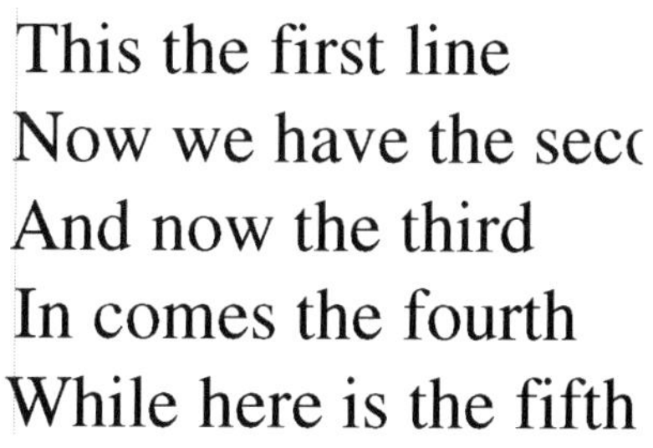

Figure 2.5   *The right way to align lines of type.*

This the first line

Now we have the se

And now the third

In comes the fourth

While here is the fif

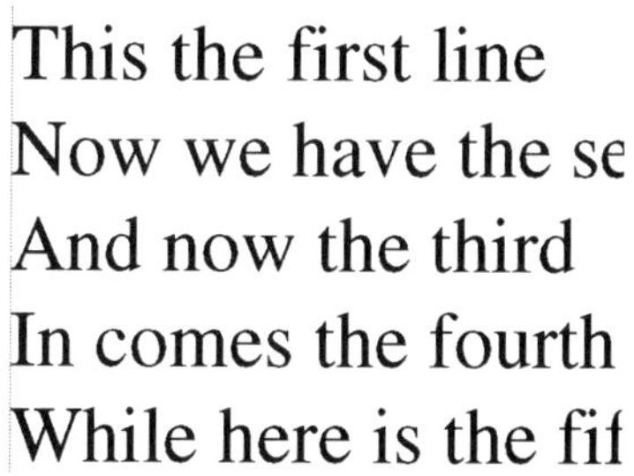

In Figure 2.4, the first letters of each line may look aligned when you type them, but when magnified they do not align. The different proportional width of the letters make it impossible for them to align properly. As shown in Figure 2.5, the tab key works well. When the page is printed, the disparity in alignment is obvious. If you need to align text to a number of columns on the page, consider setting up a table (described later).

The Correct Way to Add Lines

Learn more about...

Using lines in your design	See Chapter 6, "Adding Lines and Boxes for Emphasis."
How to add lines to a form	See Chapter 9, "Creating Forms."
Understanding baselines	See Chapter 5, "What is a Font?"

If you have ever typed using a word processor, you have undoubtedly used the underline character to create a line. While there's nothing wrong with this method, you are drastically limited in the positioning of the line relative to the surrounding text. The underline character, you see, acts like any other character you choose to type: it rests, like all characters do, on its *baseline*. To adjust the character above or below the baseline (or to the right or left) is a pain in the neck and rarely worth the effort. Luckily Windows word processors have separate line tools that create graphic lines as opposed to character lines.

GLOSSARY

The *baseline* is an invisible line on which type rests. You'll learn all about baselines in Chapter 5; for now just remember that all type in a line must rest on a collective baseline so that the type is even across the length of the line.

Things go better with ⟋ *baseline*

N O T E

There's actually a useful time to employ the underline character to create a line, rather than drawing a graphic line. In creating lines on a form (such as areas to write your name, address, and telephone number) it is often easier to align the lines to their associated text, rather than trying to adjust free-floating graphic lines. You'll learn more about this and other tricks to creating lines in Chapter 6.

Although it's not as easy as clicking on a line drawing tool in a page composition or drawing program, it's relatively simple to create a graphic line in WordPerfect. Position the insertion point in the general vicinity on your screen where you want the line and click on the Graphic menu. Choose the Line command in the Line submenu, choose a Vertical or Horizontal line. You will see the dialog box that controls graphic lines, as shown below.

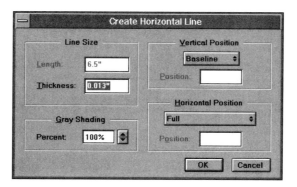

The default settings in the dialog box allow for lines the full width or height of the page (depending on whether you selected a horizontal or vertical line in the submenu). To draw a quick line that you can modify later, simply click on OK to accept the default line definition and add the line to your page. The line is displayed in relative position, like the example below.

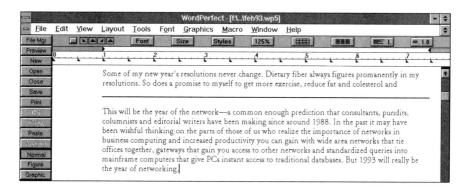

In Word, you can add lines by creating borders using the Border Paragraphs dialog box (choose Border command from the Format pull-down menu).

You can also insert a line as a graphic object by clicking on the drawing icon in the Ribbon above the ruler. You open the Microsoft Draw applet window. Choose the Line Drawing icon and draw a line to the desired length or height. Then double-click on the Control-menu box to close the applet, and the line is added at the present insertion point position.

Changing the Size, Weight, and Relative Position of the Line

Earlier, I said WordPerfect adds lines in *relative position* because, in all likelihood, you will have to make minute adjustments to its position after previewing the page. To adjust the line in WordPerfect, position the text insertion point over the line; you see the icon change to an arrow when you're directly over the line. Click the left mouse button to reveal sizing handles on the line, like this:

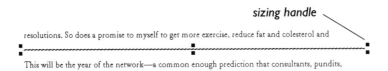

sizing handle

resolutions. So does a promise to myself to get more exercise, reduce fat and colesterol and

This will be the year of the network—a common enough prediction that consultants, pundits,

or click the right mouse button to display a floating edit palette. If you click on the command you'll see the Line Edit dialog box we looked at earlier. I find using the sizing handles much easier than fooling with the dialog box.

The sizing handles control the length of the line (either across the page if it is a horizontal line, or up and down the page if it is a vertical line), as well as the line's *weight* or *thickness*. For example, click on one of the end handles and drag the sizing handle to either lengthen or shorten the line. To increase the weight of the line, click on one of the middle sizing handles and drag it in the direction you want.

To adjust the weight of a border in Word, open the Border Paragraphs dialog box and choose a different weight by clicking on the format box you want. To change the color of the line, select a color from the list box. To change the character of a line you have created with Microsoft Draw, double-click on the line to open the applet and make the needed changes.

Creating an exaggerated line in WordPerfect looks like a solid box when you drastically increase its weight, as shown in the following example.

N O T E

Some of my new year's resolutions never change. Dietary fiber always figures promanently in my resolutions. So does a promise to myself to get more exercise, reduce fat and colesterol and

This will be the year of the network—a common enough prediction that consultants, pundits, columnists and editorial writers have been making since around 1988. In the past it may have been wishful thinking on the parts of those of us who realize the importance of networks in business computing and increased productivity you can gain with wide area networks that tie offices together, gateways that gain you access to other networks and standardized queries into mainframe computers that give PCs instant access to traditional databases. But 1993 will really be the year of networking.

To create this effect, drag one of the end sizing handles, or one of the corner handles in, to shorten the line creating a solid box:

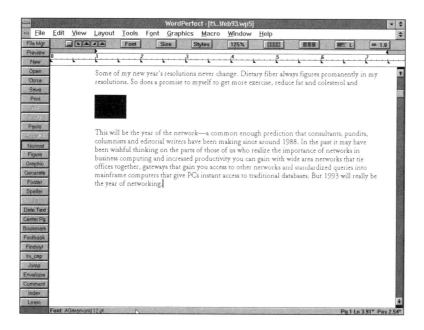

The box (line) is solid black because the default shading is set to 100 percent (of the printing color, which is black) in the Line Edit dialog box. To create a shaded box (or line) open the dialog box and change the setting in the Percent list box to the percentage of shading you want.

To move the line without changing its length or weight, click on the line to reveal the sizing handles and drag it to a new position. Using WordPerfect, position the insertion point anywhere over the line but not on a sizing handle. The insertion point changes to a four-pointed arrow, shown in the example below. Press and hold down the left mouse button and drag the line in any direction to its new position.

You can drag a line in this fashion anywhere on the page, or across multiple pages. You can also position lines across margins, up to the physical edge of the page, or stretch the line across both the page and the margins. In WordPerfect you are limited to horizontal or vertical lines—you can't create a diagonal line. If you are using Word, click the frame containing the line, and drag it to a new position.

Deleting Lines

Deleting a graphic line is simple: In WordPerfect, position the insertion point over the line so the icon changes to an arrow, and click the left mouse button to highlight the line. Once the line is highlighted, press Delete or Backspace to delete it. You can also go into the revealed codes in WordPerfect, find the line code, and then delete it. In Word, simply highlight the frame containing the line and press Delete to delete the frame and its line.

Lining Up Lines in WordPerfect

As mentioned earlier, the position of the line to surrounding text on the page in WordPerfect is slightly relative; in other words, when you print the page you may find that the line is misaligned in relation to text near that line. That degree of misalignment is WordPerfect's small margin of error in displaying text and graphics as accurately as it is able. You can correct the line's position, of course, by printing the page, gauging how much to move the line, repositioning it and reprinting the page as often as required to correct the misalignment. An easier way is to use WordPerfect's Print Preview feature. Print Preview shows you a rendering of what the document looks like when printed. Bear in mind that fonts are not displayed as they appear in your document—WordPerfect uses its own set of fonts to display type—however, the relative position of the type and lines is correct.

Let's walk through the steps required to check and adjust the position of lines on a document page. First, add a line under some text on the page, as shown in the letterhead below.

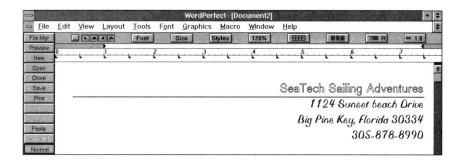

Open the File menu and choose Print Preview. You will see a representation of the actual page, with the letterhead and the lines of the page, as shown in the example below.

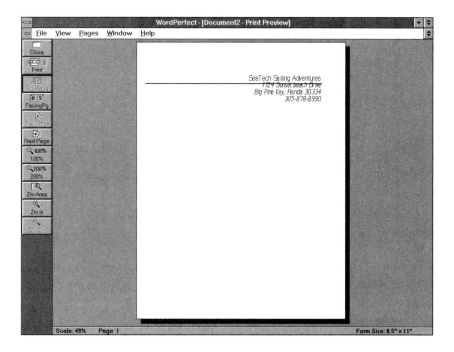

Choose a 100 percent view of the letterhead and note the exact position of the line. The line is on top of the second line of text, isn't it?

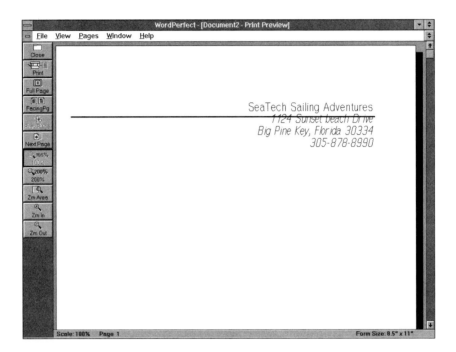

Next, click on Close to return to your document. Click on the line and drag it up slightly. On the document page, the line may seem to be too close to the type above it.

SeaTech Sailing Adventures
1124 Sunset beach Drive
Big Pine Key, Florida 30334
305-878-8990

But if you go back to the Page Preview, the line is adjusted perfectly (and prints correctly as well):

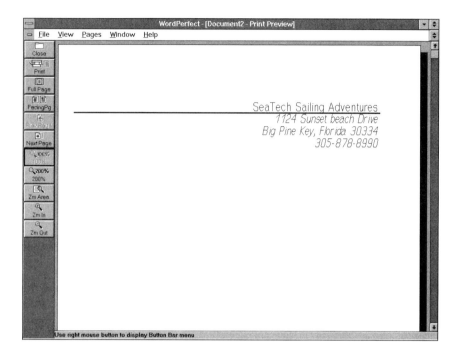

Unfortunately, neither WordPerfect nor Word has a perfectly accurate display of your laid out page, but by using the Page Preview features, you can make small, necessary adjustments to the positioning of text and graphics to get excellent printed results.

While most word processors don't provide crop or trim marks to use in trimming pages smaller than 8.5-by-11 inches, you can make them with graphic lines. Remember, lines can be positioned into the margins of the page. To add trim marks in WordPerfect, for example, simply create the graphic line, click on it to reveal the sizing handles, shorten it to about one-quarter inch, and drag it to its position on the page. Create three more lines the same way and you have trim marks for your document.

Express Yourself with Tables

Tables are a great way to display certain types of information (as a matter of fact, the best example of a table is probably a restaurant menu). Tabular data is easy to comprehend, and quick to reference. Having just told you how useful graphic lines are, I should point out a time when lines should not be used—if you use graphic lines to create a table, they will drive you crazy and you'll waste much valuable time and energy. Instead, use the Table command. To create a quick table with the click of the mouse, simply click the table button on the ruler in WordPerfect, or on the Toolbar in Word, and drag the arrow across and down the number of columns and rows you want:

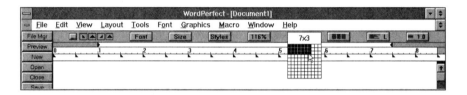

Release the mouse button and the table is created at the current insertion point position. The default WordPerfect table has a double line border around it and single lines inside, like the example in Figure 2.6. You can change the style of the lines by choosing the Layout menu, selecting Table and choosing Lines to display the Lines dialog box. You can choose line thickness and style for both the border of the table and the interior cell lines.

Figure 2.6 *Default table created with the WordPerfect Table button.*

Adding Graphics to the Page

Learn more about...

Rules for using graphics	See Chapter 6, "Working with Different Graphic Formats."
How to import any type of graphic	See Chapter 6, "Working with Different Graphic Formats."
Using commercial clip art	See Chapter 6, "Adding Clip Art Images"
Adding fool-proof color photos	See Chapter 6, "Preparing Color etc."

WordPerfect, as well as every other Windows word processor I know of, comes with a wide variety of graphic clip art images that are available for you to use in any document. The graphic files are loaded automatically when you installed WordPerfect on your computer. However, if you try to open any of the graphics as documents, you received an error message that the file type is incompatible. Take heart, you can open and use the graphic files, but there are only two ways that the graphics are accessible in WordPerfect:

- You can open any WordPerfect graphic in your existing document by positioning the insertion point where you want the graphic to appear, and opening the Graphic menu. Choose Figure and then the Retrieve commands to retrieve the graphic into your document. The graphic appears in a graphic box at the position of the insertion point. (If you try simply using the Retrieve command on WordPerfect's File menu, you'll see that incompatible file format error message again.)

- You can add a graphic to your document by first opening the Graphic menu, selecting Figure and then choosing Create. You will see the Figure Editor, shown in Figure 2.7 on the next page. Choose Retrieve to retrieve the graphic you want into the Figure Editor, and use the Edit buttons to modify the graphic. When you leave the editor the graphic is added to your document at the position of the insertion point.

Figure 2.7   *The WordPerfect Figure Editor lets you control and modify graphic tiles.*

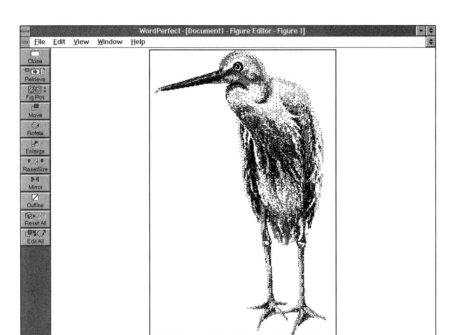

Word comes with a variety of import filters. It can understand graphics created by a number of different applications and saved in a number of different formats by filtering the *foreign* file. To add a graphic to your Word page, use the Picture command on the Insert menu. A dialog box appears that allows you to find the graphic you want. Click on Preview to see a preview image of the graphics. Choose OK to add the graphic to your document at the insertion point position.

Which Word graphic import filters do I have installed? You can see the installed import filters by choosing Options from the Tools menu, and select the WIN.INI category. Then choose MS Graphic Import Filters in the Application list box to see a list of the installed filters.

Previewing Your Pages

As I said earlier, the Page Preview feature has the final say in what your pages will look like. Often, with WordPerfect and Word alike, you will need to make minute alterations in the layout of text and graphics to get exactly the layout you want. Many applications, other than word processors, have Page Preview features including Excel, Microsoft Money, Microsoft Publisher, and others. One useful feature of WordPerfect's preview is your ability to enlarge or shrink the page. You have a choice of views, including the whole page, a 100 percent view or a 200 percent view—just the ticket for getting close to your work. While Word only shows you the whole page, Microsoft Excel lets you magnify specific portions of the page for detailed viewing. An example of Word's Page Preview is shown below.

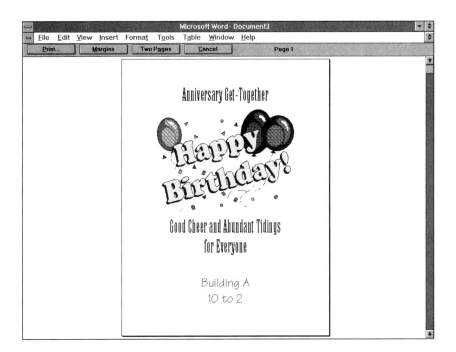

PUBLISHING WITH SPREADSHEETS

You might not think of using a spreadsheet program like Lotus 1-2-3 for Windows, or Microsoft Excel for Windows as a desktop publishing tool, and if you're dealing with a lot of words, you'd be correct. Often we need to present data in a more analytical format. A spreadsheet program that understands typography and graphic composition can be a huge help in preparing financial documents, proposals, sales reports, and the like.

For years, I consulted to a company whose employees used spreadsheets (Lotus, to be exact) for everything: why they'd likely as not do their shopping lists in Lotus. They wrote letters in Lotus; memos in Lotus; made lists, notations and everything else in Lotus. Of course, this was years before Windows, when the DOS version of Lotus could barely print a report. When I see the design features of Windows spreadsheets, I can't help but think back to that company struggling to communicate in a program that was intended purely for financial calculations.

There are a number of Windows spreadsheets, like Excel, Lotus, Borland's Quattro Pro for Windows, and Lotus Improv. All do a great job of crunching numbers, have the ability to chart the results of your spreadsheets, support scalable fonts, and print to PostScript printers. While there is nothing more boring (from a design standpoint) than your common, garden variety balance sheet, these spreadsheets can make an extraordinary impact in dressing up numbers and communicating their meaning.

Using Fonts to Enhance Your Spreadsheet

Dressing up a financial spreadsheet with some attractive fonts is an important step toward meeting the communicative needs of your financial data. As you learn in Chapter 5, fonts are a fundamental part of the design, organization, and structure of a professionally-composed document. For now, let's see how simple it is to add fonts to the spreadsheets you are already using.

Windows spreadsheets work with fonts in a similar way to word processors and other document-oriented applications. In Excel, for example, you have access to the same fonts as you do in Microsoft Word, or WordPerfect. You can specify any type size you want, any type style (italic, or bold, for example), and any paragraph formatting (such as left-aligned, right-aligned, centered, or justified text). To specify a font, or change its characteristics, open Excel's Format pull-down menu and choose Font to see the Font dialog box, shown in Figure 2.8. Here you find all of the attributes you can assign to a font, including size, style, and color.

Figure 2.8 *Font dialog box in Excel 4.0.*

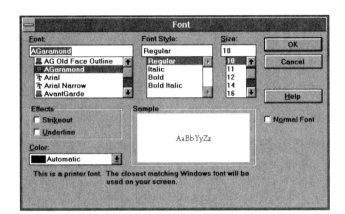

N O T E Using Excel's Font Formatting dialog box: In addition to the Font dialog box shown above, you can set up a special formatting dialog that is always visible and can give you no-wait access to font formatting. Open the Options pull-down menu and select Toolbars to display the Toolbars dialog box. Then choose Formatting Toolbar from the list and click on the Show button. The dialog box appears at the bottom of your screen:

To specify characters in different fonts, click the font list box arrow and choose the font you want. Then open the size list box and pick the type size you'd like. To change existing characters to a different font, select the characters with the mouse, then choose a different font specification.

Once you start using fonts in your spreadsheets the same way fonts are applied to text in your word processor, financial reports will never look the same.

Adding Headers and Footers

Learn more about:

Headers and footers   See Chapter 4, "Headers, Footers and Where to Put That Page Number."

Using headers and footers in large documents   See Chapter 12, "Keeping the Reader's Attention."

Headers and footers are text at the top or bottom of the page, respectively, that gives you information about what you're reading. The information can be as simple as a page number or the current chapter of a book. Creating and using headers and footers is covered in Chapter 4, but let's take a quick look at how to add them in Excel. Headers and footers can go a long way toward dressing up an otherwise bland spreadsheet, while passing on much-needed information to the reader.

If you scan the menus and commands of Excel you won't see anything about headers and footers. As a matter of fact, you must first open the Print dialog box, choose Page Setup, and then choose either the Header or Footer button to actually add a header or footer. Excel doesn't make the process very easy to get to, but it makes up for the deficiency by giving you a lot of flexibility in what can go in a header or footer. Let's take a look:

Figure 2.9   *Use Excel's Header dialog box to position text for page headers.*

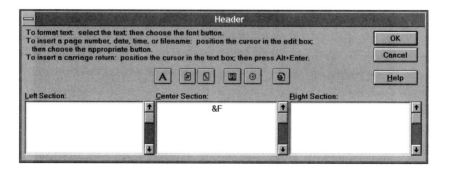

The Header and Footer dialog boxes look and act exactly the same. They are divided into three sections representing the left, middle, and right portions of either the top (for headers) or the bottom (for footers) of the page. Information you add to the Left Section box is automatically left-aligned. Likewise, text added to the Center Section is centered on the page and text in the Right Section is right-aligned. You can type virtually any information in any of the sections that you choose. For example, you could add a spreadsheet title to the Center Section, or create a date and time stamp in the Left Section by clicking on the Date and Time icons as shown on the left.

In the Right Section you could add a page number by typing the word *Page*, pressing the Spacebar once to add a space, and clicking on the Page Number icon as shown on the left.

To change the appearance of the text in a header or footer, click on the Font icon, as shown on the left.

When you either print the page, or use the Page Preview command, you'll see the header or footer you specified, with the date, time, and actual page number filled in.

WARNING

Beware of the size of the section list boxes in the Header or Footer dialog boxes. Their size is misleading as to how the header or footer looks. You would think that typing a lot of text in the Center Section, for example, centers the actual header on the page in a narrow column; the same would seem to apply to the Left and Right Sections, as well. But this isn't at all the case. If you add a lot of text to the Center Section, the actual header is expanded across the page, from margin to margin. If you also add a page number to the Right Section, the Center Section text runs on top of it, causing a real mess. The moral of the story is to be *careful* how much text you add to a header or footer, and be sure to preview the results of your work before printing.

Adding Graphics to Your Spreadsheet

Learn more about...

Using graphics on your pages   See Chapter 6, "Working with Different Graphic Formats."

Learn more about...

Using clip art images   See Chapter 6, "Adding Clip Art Images."

Graphics are easy to add to your spreadsheets. Regardless of what graphic capabilities an individual spreadsheet may have, you can always copy a graphic image from another program and paste it into your spreadsheet. Since we've been working with Excel, let's look at how to add graphics to Excel. As I mentioned earlier, Excel and Word come with a number of small, specialized graphic applications called *applets*. They can be found in the \WINDOWS\MSAPPS directory; but unlike normal Windows applications, they can only be started inside a Windows application like Excel or Word. When you open the applet, you establish an OLE connection between the applet and the application you're currently working in. In this case, Excel.

GLOSSARY

OLE (pronounced oh-LAY) stands for Object Linking and Embedding, which is a way (in both Windows and Macintosh System 7) of adding work from one application into the work of another application. You can, for instance, create a drawing (think of it as an object) in a graphic application, and link or embed the drawing, or object, in an Excel worksheet. The beauty of OLE is the ease with which you can make changes to the object. Say, for example, you decide to change the drawing: instead of opening the graphic application, then opening the drawing, making the needed changes, saving the changes, and copying and pasting the changed drawing back into your Excel worksheet, you simply double-click on the drawing in Excel. The parent application that created the drawing (called the *OLE server application*) will immediately open and present you with the drawing so you can make the changes you want. When you're through, close the server application and the drawing in Excel will be changed as well. To learn all about OLE, see your Windows User's Guide.

Some of Excel's graphic applets include MS Draw, MS Chart and MS Graph, as shown in Figures 2.10-2.12, respectively. Open any of these applets or any other OLE server applications by choosing Insert Object on the Edit menu. You will see the Insert Object dialog box, shown in Figure 2.13 . Double-click on the application you want to start. For example, if you want to add a graphic created with Aldus IntelliDraw, you would double-click on IntelliDraw in the dialog box.

Figure 2.10 *Microsoft Draw applet.*

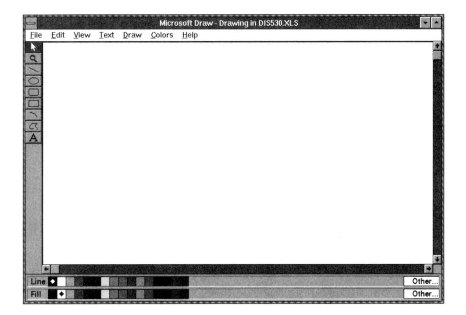

Figure 2.11   *Microsoft Chart applet.*

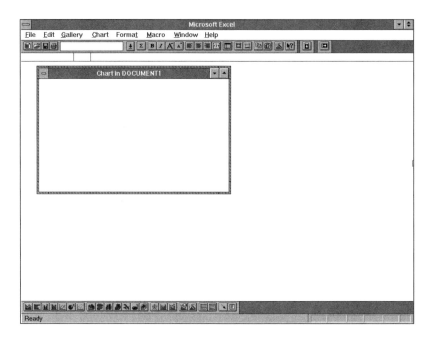

Figure 2.12   *Microsoft Graph applet.*

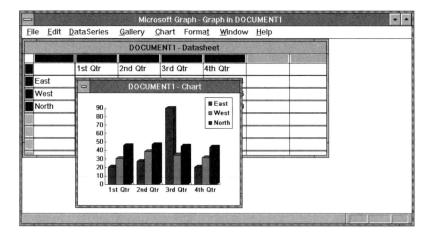

Figure 2.13   *The Insert Object dialog box displays a list of available applications you can use to insert OLE objects into your document.*

Learn more about...

Sharing a custom logo among business publications

See Chapter 9, "Creating Business Communications."

Creating your own shipping or diskette labels

See Chapter 9, "Mailing Labels and Diskette Labels."

Once you create a graphic and position it on an Excel worksheet, you can treat it like any other object on the page. In Figure 2.14 on the next page, a company logo is added to the beginning of a spreadsheet that will calculate projected sales. The Tiger Radio logo is a Micrografx clip art image added to Excel as an OLE object. Once you create a logo, you can add it to letters and envelopes that you create in WordPerfect or Word to create your own stationery, use it in a drawing or page layout program to create business cards, shipping labels, and forms.

Figure 2.14 *Graphic added to the top of an Excel worksheet creates a company logo.*

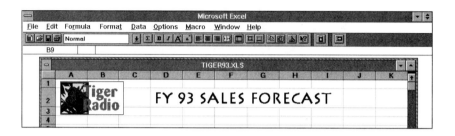

PUBLISHING WITH DRAWING PROGRAMS

You may not associate a painting or drawing program with desktop publishing. Sure, you can use it to produce art work to use in another program, but for the right kinds of jobs, a graphics program like Micrografx Windows Draw or Microsoft PaintBrush may be well suited for desktop publishing. Both can integrate text and graphic images, and both can import and export graphics in a variety of formats—PaintBrush is somewhat limited here, but Draw is extremely versatile, as you'll learn about in a moment.

A Look at Windows Draw

Micrografx Windows Draw easily combines text and graphics on a page, comes with a large number of clip art images, and can import and export a wide variety of graphic formats. At a street price of around $100, Draw is easy on your pocketbook and a welcome addition to your portfolio of desktop publishing software. Draw gives you a straightforward document window, shown in Figure 2.15.

 To start drawing, click on the Pencil button. You might want to also choose one of the drawing mode buttons, to draw squares, circles, curves, freehand lines, or polygons. To define the type of line you want to draw, click on the Line Definition button, as shown on the left.

Figure 2.15 *Micrografx Windows Draw document window.*

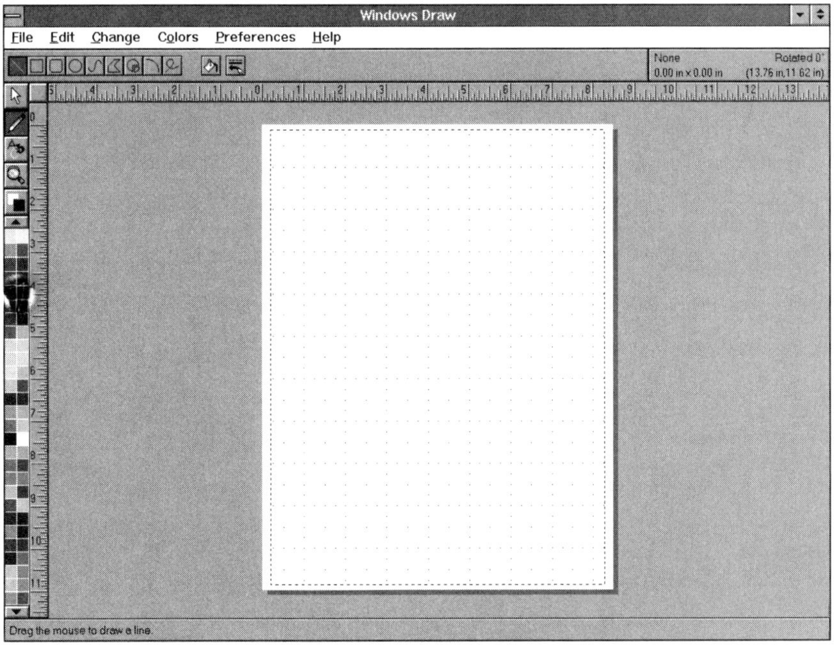

Learn more about...

When to use graphic boxes and lines for emphasis	See Chapter 6, "Adding Boxes and Lines for Emphasis."
Creating a visual foundation	See Chapter 4, "The Basic Steps of Design."

To change the width or line style, choose Width from the list to see the Line Width dialog box, as shown on the next page. Here you can decide how the ends and corners of lines should look.

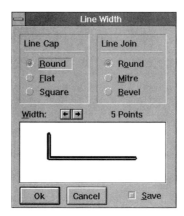

Draw gives you the usual graphic tools, aligned along the left side of your screen, plus color choices you can define, based on the capabilities of your color monitor and what you want to do. While you don't have the power-hungry capabilities of Adobe Illustrator with this package, you will find that Draw can do a number of very useful things. For example, in working with text, you can specify paragraph parameters by choosing the Change pull-down menu and selecting Paragraph to open the Paragraph dialog box, as shown below.

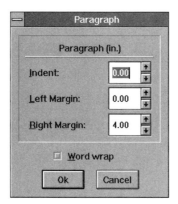

The key to using this dialog box is to understand that the values shown are not related to the ruler. For example, the paragraph's left edge doesn't start at the zero mark on the ruler. Instead the values are relative to the page. If you look at the example, the paragraph is four inches long—where the text is positioned depends on where you click the text insertion point to begin typing the text. To indent the first line of text in the paragraph, enter a value in the Indent text box. To create a *hanging indent*, leave the Indent text box set at 0.0, but enter a value in the Left Margin text box. All but the first line of the paragraph will be indented according to the amount you enter.

A *hanging indent* means that all lines of the paragraph but the first are indented. Or, you can think of it as the first line of the paragraph is outdented. Just remember that with a hanging indent the first line of a paragraph extends further to the left than the remaining lines.

One other item on the Paragraph dialog box merits attention. It is the Word Wrap check box. By default it is not active, which means that, regardless of the specifications you enter to determine the size of text paragraphs, the text you type will extend in a line off of the page, like this:

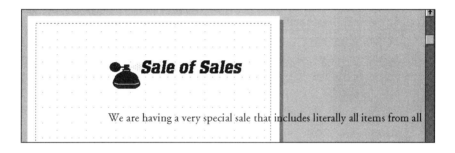

If, however, you click the Word Wrap check box to make it active, the words will wrap normally within the confines of the paragraph specification you set in the Paragraph dialog box, like this:

You can also set the alignment of text using the Change pull-down menu. Choose Justification to see a small submenu of alignment (what Draw mistakenly calls *justification*) choices. Ironically, the submenu does not include a choice for justified type (where both the left and right edges of paragraphs are aligned evenly). You can set paragraphs to left, right, or centered alignment.

One more feature about Draw worth mentioning is its ability to lay down type along a curve. This is a feature normally associated with more expensive graphics packages, yet it is just the sort of jazzy detail you can use to dress up a bland document. Here's how you do it:

1. First draw a curved line in the shape you want the text to follow.

2. Then choose the Text tool, select a font and size from the list boxes, and type the text you want.

3. Choose the Pointer tool, position the pointer icon to the upper left of the text and line, and click and drag the mouse diagonally down and to the right to enclose all the text and the line.

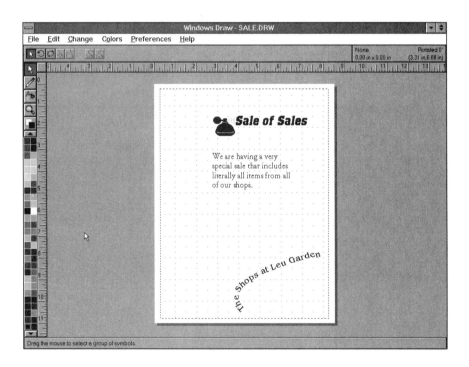

4. Open the Change pull-down menu and choose Fit Text to Curve. The text will reflow along the line you have drawn.

5. Finally, click just the line to select it (and display its sizing handles), and press Delete to remove the line but leave the text. The results might look like the example on the left.

A Quick Look at PaintBrush

If you are running Windows, you already own a copy of Microsoft Paintbrush. You'll find it in the Accessories group. Let's take a look. To open the Accessories group click on it (if it's visible in the Program Manager). If it's not visible, choose the Window command in the Program Manager and select Accessories from the list. You may have to click on the More Windows option to see a list of additional groups. Double-click on the Paintbrush icon to start the program. In a minute you'll see a window shown in Figure 2.16.

Figure 2.16 *Microsoft PaintBrush main window.*

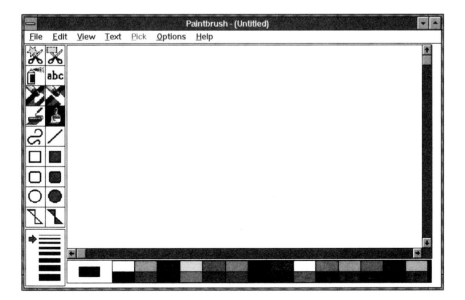

PaintBrush is a basic art package with enough text features to allow you to combine limited text and graphics on the page. PaintBrush does not come with predrawn clip art like Windows Draw; however, the desktop designs that you can choose for your Windows desktop (in the Control Panel) are PaintBrush images. You can open one of the desktop designs and customize it to your specific needs, or you can create your own custom desktop in PaintBrush. While PaintBrush lacks the textual controls of Windows Draw, it does one important thing that Draw doesn't allow: you can edit the actual *pixels* of a *bitmapped graphic* with PaintBrush.

GLOSSARY

A *pixel* is one tiny spot of an image on your computer's screen, and it is saved in much the same fashion in a computer file. The computer screen displays images much like a television does, in spots, or pixels of color. Pixels are small enough to fool your eyes into thinking that a line is curved or that the letter O is curved, when in fact the line or letter is made up of tiny square dots. The finer the dots the more that can fit on the screen, and therefore the higher the **resolution** of the screen. A standard Windows monitor displays images in 640 by 480 resolution. A PostScript laser printer can print the same image displayed on the screen in 300 by 300 dots per inch resolution. When the pixels comprise a graphic image, it is said to be **bitmapped**, because the computer maps (or remembers) the location of every pixel in the image.

If you draw a line in PaintBrush and enlarge the line by using Zoom In on the View menu, you will see the actual pixels that make up the image. You can add pixels of color, or remove pixels by coloring over them white, to change the shape of the image. To me, this is especially interesting when you add type instead of lines, and modify the shape of the type. Here's how:

1. Choose the font and type size you want and enter the characters in the PaintBrush main window using the text tool.

2. Enlarge the characters by choosing Zoom In from the View menu. Your characters look something like the following example.

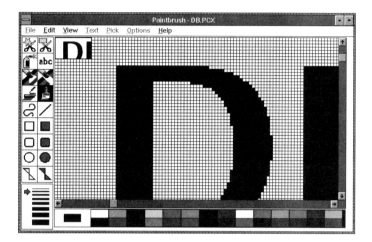

3. Now make a change to the character shapes. For example, you
    could shave off some of the upper left corner of each character to
    give them a unique appearance. Wherever you want to remove
    some of the character, choose the white color from the palette
    below, and click the arrow on the pixels of color to be removed
    (by coloring them white). Whenever you want to build up the
    shape of characters, click the black color from the palette, and click
    the arrow in the pixel squares that you want to color black. The
    finished characters might look like the example shown below.

The finished characters can be saved and imported into either another graphics program, into your word processor, or into your spreadsheet program.

Exporting Artwork to a Word Processor

Exporting your graphic file (or importing the file—same thing) into your word processor is one of the many wonders of Windows applications. Most—even the lowly Paintbrush—offer choices of graphic formats that you can save your work in, and recognize different file formats. For example, WordPerfect can import both Draw and PaintBrush files. Windows Draw has a powerful export capability that supports many graphic formats. To export a Draw file choose Export from the File menu. Open the Export dialog box, as shown in Figure 2.17.

Figure 2.17 *Use Draw's Export dialog box to pick the format for the file you want to export.*

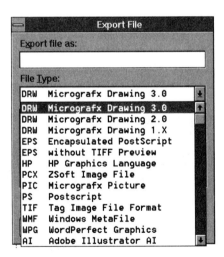

You'll learn about many of the formats listed in the dialog box in Chapter 6. For now just remember that Draw can import any of these formats, allows you to modify the files, and convert them to any other format—useful to keep in the back of your mind when you run into the inevitable problem of an unacceptable graphic file format. Then you'll recall, "Oh, that's right, I can convert this in Draw to the format I want."

PUBLISHING WITH A DATABASE

If you've ever struggled with a DOS database to squeeze out a seemingly simple report, you might find the idea of desktop publishing with your database a contradiction in terms. Fortunately, Windows has brought an end to bland reports and tempermental programs. Microsoft Access, for example, combines the search, query, and data-entry features of traditional relational databases, with graphics, fonts, and impressive publishing tools.

Publishing Data with Access

The most unique aspect of Access is its Wizards. Wizards are Microsoft helpers that do most of the design work for you—you tell a Wizard what you want done, and it does the rest. Access uses Wizards to help you design reports for your Access data. Simply press a Wizard button to activate the Wizard. Let's create a quick customer report:

1. Choose the **New report** button to display the ReportWizards dialog box. Choose which table or query you want to use to supply data to the report. Then click on the **ReportWizards** button.

2. The Wizard presents a choice of report formats; choose a single-column format and press **Next**.

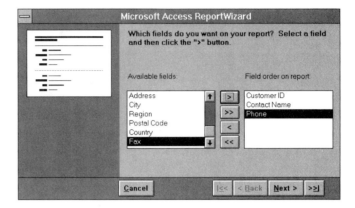

3. Choose the fields you want in the report. Let's include the customer number, contact name, and telephone number. To add the fields, click on each one that you want. Click the right-facing arrow to move it to the report column. Press **Next** to continue.

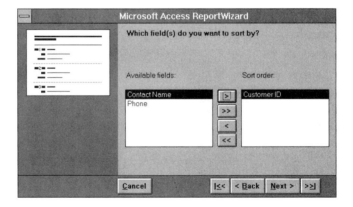

4. Decide which of the fields you want to sort the contents of the report. Let's sort by customer number. Click it, and click the right-facing arrow to move it to the sort order column. Press **Next** to continue.

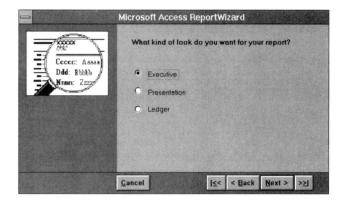

5. Click on the option button that describes the kind of report you want. For this example choose an executive report. Click **Executive** and press **Next**.

6. Fill in a name for this report. Click the **Print Preview** button to see what the finished report looks like, shown in the example on the next page.

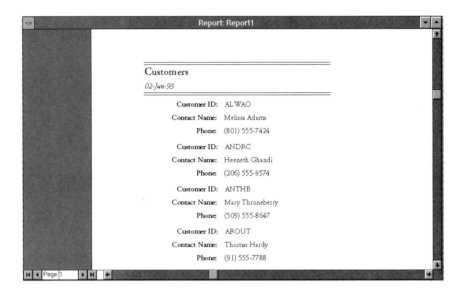

Adding Graphics to Database Reports

As you can see in the sample report above, its creation was simple and straightforward, giving you the foundation of a nice-looking report. Notice that the report title has been formatted automatically in a larger, bolder typeface, the date of printing is in italics, and the field names (Customer ID, Contact Name, and Phone) are bolded. Not bad for about six clicks of the mouse. Now let's dress up the report by adding a graphic in the header opposite the title. Open the Edit menu and choose Insert Object to embed an OLE graphic object. Pick PaintBrush from the list and create a suitable graphic (we'll add a company logo). Close PaintBrush, and the graphic is automatically added to the header, like the following example.

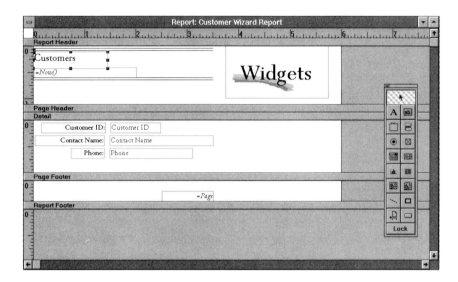

The finished report now looks like this:

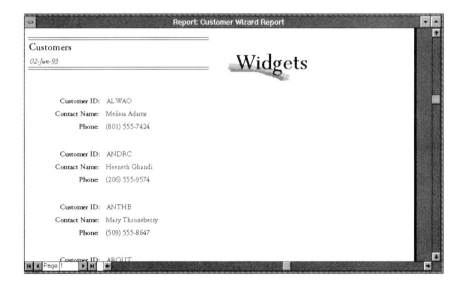

While the report looks better, it seems to be slightly out of balance on the right side. Let's add a vertical line (or rule) down the right side of the page to absorb some of that white space. To add a line, choose the line button on the Toolbox palette, shown below.

Click the *Line* button and draw a vertical line in the Detail area of the report design:

The report now shows an attractive vertical line on the right side of the page, shown in the following example.

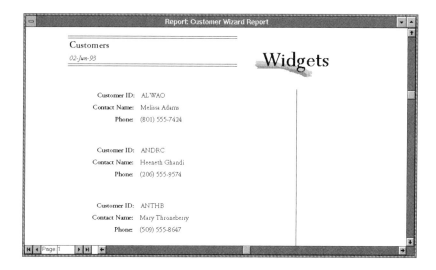

Here is one more step to finish balancing the report. Let's increase the size of the type for the report title, and change the font to a stronger typeface. For this example, let's choose 18 pt Friz Quadrata. To make the change, click the pointer on the report title—notice the font choices at the top of the Access window. Open the Font list box and scroll through the list to pick the font you want. Do the same for the size, increasing it to 18 points. Now click on the center alignment button to center the report title. Finally, here's our report one last time:

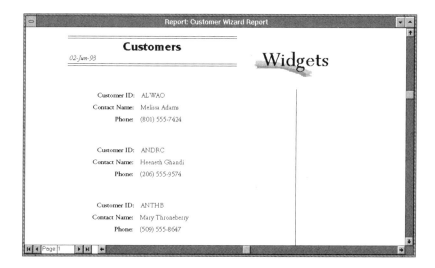

Obviously, this is just a brief glance at Access and its capabilities. Aside from the powerful editing, graphic and typographic controls in Access, you have a direct link to most, if not all of your other applications with OLE, and pasting from the Clipboard. While I'm partial to Microsoft Access, virtually all Windows databases have similar flexibility in adding a professional touch to reporting information.

CHAPTER SUMMARY

Whether you're working with a great bruiser of a word processor like WordPerfect, Word for Windows, or a simple application like PaintBrush, graphic finesse is just a mouse click away. There is a common efficiency in just about all Windows applications. But perhaps more important is the assurance that all Windows applications play to the same sheet music. All pull together to meet your creative ideas with a plate full of simple, intuitive graphic gadgets that make desktop publishing a breeze. Regardless of what Windows software you're currently using, you'll find easy ways of dressing up your documents and composing them instead of merely typing them.

In this chapter you've seen a number of elements common to many different types of Windows applications. Word processors, spreadsheet programs, graphic programs, and even database managers now share many of the same publishing tools, and allow you to customize the pages that your laser printer produces in ways never imagined in the days of DOS.

Using the Windows software you already have can make marked improvements to your documents, but in Chapter 3, you'll see why specialized page composition software is most appealing, if not downright addictive.

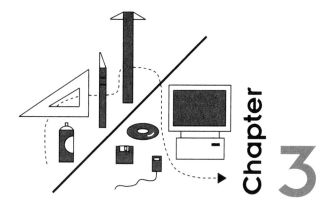

Chapter 3

Using Page Composition Software

Page composition software speeds up the chores of preparing documents for printing. In the time it takes to explain it, you can open a new document, specify all the page-oriented parameters including margins and columns, import text from a word processor, add some graphic clip art images, specify color, and print the job. You can do in minutes what takes hours to do by hand. If you add the changes and corrections that normally occur in the process of developing a publication, you can save days of work, and consume no materials other than a few sheets of paper. Gone will be the mess and confusion of X-acto knives, artist's tape, rubber cement, drawing boards, tee squares, rulers, compasses, art gum erasers, press type, non-reproducible blue pencils, India ink, and drooling wax machines. No longer need you suffer the time schedules of artists, photographers, typographers, and printers; or the delays of typographic corrections.

If you are serious about publishing your own documents, you will want to read this chapter and judge for yourself whether the cost of special page composition software justifies the features and increased efficiency.

PUBLISHING WITH PAGE COMPOSITION PROGRAMS

If you could boil down the features and usefulness of page composition software to just one item, it would be unlimited freedom to position text and graphics where you want them on the page. While text in a word processor is limited to the invisible *lines* of the page, page composition software allows you to click the mouse where you want the text to go and begin typing.

The second feature unique to page composition software is its ability to stack text and graphics on top of one another. This is a significant accomplishment, if you think about it. It means, for example, that color can be added behind a graphic by coloring a box, and positioning the graphic over the box. The graphic that blocks the color underneath is opaque. Position text on top of the graphic, which might be in a third color, different from the two layers below ... well, you see the flexibility inherent in stacked objects. When combined with the ability to print color separations, you begin to understand and justify the additional cost of page composition software.

GLOSSARY

Color separations are needed in order for your commercial printer to print a color job. To print color, each color you want on the page must be separated into the percentages of the primary colors that comprise that particular color. Thus four separations are produced, one for each of the primary colors—cyan, magenta, yellow, and black—with the percentage of primary color for each object represented by a screen, or dot pattern. The closer the dots are spaced in the screen, the higher the percentage of primary color. You learn more about color separations in Chapter 6.

If you want the results of your desktop publishing efforts printed in color, you will find that only page composition software is capable of printing the requisite color separations needed by your commercial printer. The costs saved from hand-separating alone pay for a page composition program. Color separation firms use exotic, laser scanners, and ultra-expensive computer systems to separate photographs often charging over $100 for a single photo to produce the separated color negatives needed by your printer. Page composition software like PageMaker and QuarkXPress can create the same separations. Chapter 6 shows you how to let Kodak both capture and scan the "Moments of Our Lives" with Kodak Photo CDs.

Page composition software generally breaks down into two groups based on price: under $200 and over $500. Price is used as the separation of low-end to high-end systems because, as you will see in this chapter, the supposedly entry-level systems share many of the same features as the high-end systems (and have some features the high-end systems don't have!). We will look at Microsoft Publisher and PFS Publisher (from Spinnaker Software) on the low side, and Aldus PageMaker for Windows and QuarkXPress for Windows on the high side.

Before we begin poking around inside page composition software, let's take a look at some of the features and define some terms you may not know.

Understanding the Drawing Board Analogy

Most desktop publishing software is alike in many respects; most provide a work space based on the analogy of the artist's drawing board, usually called the *pasteboard*.

GLOSSARY

The *pasteboard* represents the extreme edges of your electronic desktop; the pages of your document are shown on the pasteboard. Some page composition programs let you work on either the pasteboard (which extends past the edges of the page) or the page itself. You can store work on the pasteboard and add it to your pages at a later time.

When you open a new document, you see a blank page on the pasteboard, much as you would tape down a page to your drawing board. Anything we add to the pages is considered an object—text is generally added by designating a text box and typing text in the box. Once the box is created, you can click on it with the mouse and drag it wherever you want, even off the page onto the pasteboard. Graphics are added in similar graphic boxes and they too can be dragged wherever you want them. We will learn more about text and graphic boxes in a moment.

Using Rulers

Most desktop publishing programs have vertical and horizontal rulers so that you can accurately align text and graphics on the page. Some programs allow you to adjust the zero point of the rulers so that you can accurately measure anything on the page, while others have fixed ruler tick marks. Most programs give you a choice of different measurement systems that you can set for the rulers, such as inches, *picas* (there are 6 picas to the inch) or *points* (there are 72 points to the inch). You might want to change the rulers to picas when working on a page layout (since a pica is 1/6th of an inch, you will work in whole picas rather than fractions of inches). Changing the rulers to points can be useful when you begin adding type, since type is measured in points.

As you move objects on the page, you see corresponding alignment marks move along the rulers. The alignment (or tick) marks show the exact position of the object, relative to the page, like the example shown below. Notice the tick marks at the one-inch marks on both the horizontal and vertical rulers. This means that the current position of the mouse pointer is one inch down from the top and one inch in from the left side.

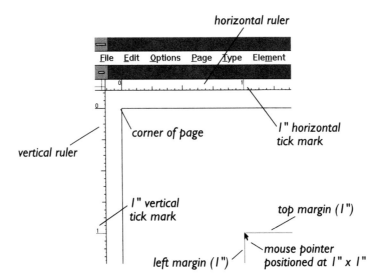

Using Guides

Desktop publishing programs generally have a guidelines feature. Guidelines are non-printing lines that you use to line up text and graphics on the page, shown at the top on your right.

You can generally use as many guidelines (or guides) as you need. And you can usually turn the display of guidelines on and off, so you can see what the page looks like when it's printed. In the days before desktop publishing, these lines were drawn with a special non-reproducible blue pencil, or pre-print *blank page frames* (pages preprinted with the non-printing blue guidelines). Unfortunately, since the lines were preprinted, you still had to use blue pencil marks to get accurate alignment. Today, desktop publishing guidelines make composing the page so much easier.

Using the Snap-To Feature

Many publishing programs allow you to activate a sort of magnetic field around guidelines. Whenever you drag text or graphics near the guide you want, this field takes over and pulls, or snaps, the object to the guide so that it is aligned exactly. The snap-to feature is useful because it does that final bit of aligning to the guide; you know that the snap-to alignment is exactly the same for all objects snapped to the guides. Sometimes the snap-to feature interferes with where you want to position an object. In these instances, you can turn the snap-to feature off and align the object the way you want.

Using Page Views

The ability to reduce or enlarge the page you're working on is fundamental to desktop publishing software. To get close to your work, most programs can enlarge areas of the page up to 200 percent (twice normal size)—an important feature when you are making fine adjustments to the alignment of objects. Many programs also reduce the page size so the entire page can be seen, called the *fit in window* size—useful when you want a bird's eye view of your design. The page view sizes are usually percentages of normal (25 percent is one-fourth normal size; 50 percent is one-half normal size, and so on).

Figure 3.1 *Typical Fit in window view of page (QuarkXPress).*

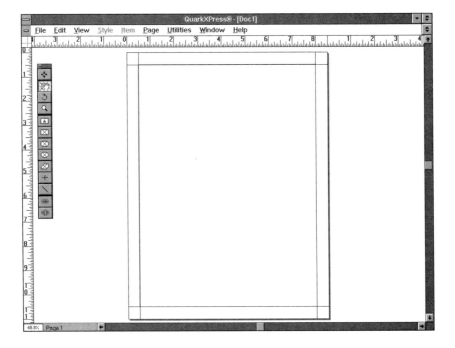

Using Scroll Bars

You undoubtedly have seen scroll bars, as shown in Figure 3.2, in other Windows applications. However, because of the magnified page view size choices you can have in publishing programs, scroll bars become your means of moving around the page. To move in small steps, click on the scroll bar arrow, to move in larger steps, click on the scroll bar itself near a scroll arrow. Or, you can click and drag on the scroll bar the exact amount you want.

Figure 3.2 *Parts of a horizontal scroll bar.*

scroll bar

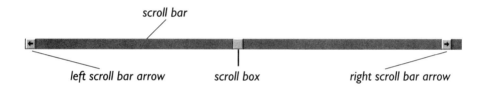

left scroll bar arrow   scroll box   right scroll bar arrow

Inserting and Deleting Pages

In a word processor, pages are added as you get to them, removed when you delete the material on them; their existence is an integral part of typing the words. Not so with page composition software which often begins with only one page. The reason for this is unclear; although, it is probably due to the fact that it's similar to the way you would lay out pages by hand—one at a time. When you are ready for page two, most programs have an Insert Page command that lets you add one or more pages to the open publication. A Delete Page command is used when you want to remove a page from your publication.

Changing the Stacking Order

A stack of objects—text and graphics—is much like a deck of playing cards. To see a card in the deck you must move it to the top. In most page composition programs, you use the Send to Back or Bring to Front commands to arrange the order of objects in the stack (you can only modify the top-most object). You may have a stack consisting of a graphic box in a color, another box on top, and text on top of the second box. In order to work on an object in the stack that you can't see, you must first bring it to the front (with the Bring to Front command), or move an object in front to the back (using the Send to Back command). By using these two commands you can rotate the order of objects in a stack.

Using Master Pages

If you took the concept of a page header and footer and extended the header and footer area to cover the whole page, you'd have a master page in a page composition program. The master page (some programs allow you to have multiple master pages) holds items that you want to appear on actual document pages—the master page, like headers and footers, repeats the items on all document pages. What do you put on a master page? Well, anything you want repeated on your document pages. For example, you might add vertical or horizontal lines to the pages of your document by placing them on a master page. Or, you might add a company logo in the margin of a master page and have it automatically appear on all document pages.

Using Trim Marks

Normally, a commercial printer prints your job on paper sheets larger than your laser printer can produce. There is an economy of scale in printing several of the document pages on one of these sheets and then cutting them apart into the page size you specified. Trim marks (or *crop marks*) tell your printer exactly where to cut. Most page composition software offers the option of adding crop marks to signify the exact page size—they are much more precise than you can possibly make by hand. However, you must remember that if your document page and paper size are 8.5-by-11 inches you will not see the trim marks. The trim marks are printed outside of the 8.5-by-11 inch dimensions. To see them you must slightly reduce the page size. Of course, if you print your final pages on a laser printer capable of handling 11-by-17 inch paper, you will see the crop marks.

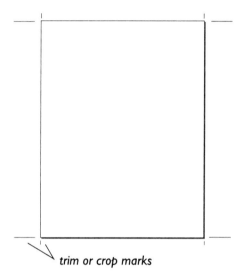

Figure 3.3 *Trim marks for a document page.*

trim or crop marks

Working with Facing Pages

When pages are prepared for publications, you must decide how the pages will be bound together. If they are bound, regardless of the method, and the final document will be printed on both sides of the paper, most page composition programs allow you to work on pairs of opened pages (just as the two open pages of this book comprise a pair of pages). They are called *facing pages*, and represent the opened left-hand and right-hand pages, bound in the middle. When facing pages are specified, you usually see that the left and right margin names have changed to inside and outside margins. For a left-hand facing page, the left margin is outside and the right margin is inside (left-hand pages are always even-numbered pages). For a right-hand facing page, the left margin is inside and the right margin is outside (right-hand pages are normally odd-numbered pages; chapters usually begin on right-hand pages). Figures 3.4 and 3.5 on the next page may help you understand the relationship of facing pages.

Figure 3.4   *A four-page, 8.5-by-11 inch newsletter printed front and back, showing a layout of facing pages.*

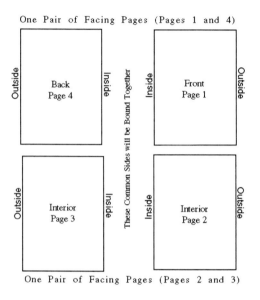

Figure 3.5   *Left and right margins become inside and outside margins when you specify facing pages.*

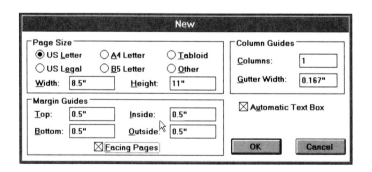

Linking Text Boxes

Most page composition programs apply the drawing board analogy to text and graphics by forcing you to create text boxes to hold text and graphic boxes to hold graphics. If you think about the word processor you are currently using, the pages that you type on are one giant text box; it expands as you add words, shrinks when you delete words. Page composition programs allow you to add more than one text box on the page. To keep straight which text is earmarked for which text box, the boxes are *linked* together. A series of linked text boxes is shown in Figure 3.6 below.

Figure 3.6   *Text boxes linked together in QuarkXPress.*

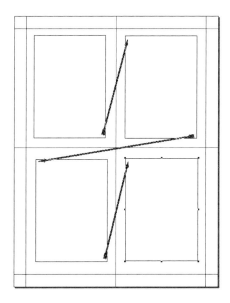

Different programs handle the task of linking text boxes in different ways, which I will explain as we look at specific publishing applications.

Paper Size Versus Document Size

In desktop publishing, there is often a difference between the size of the page you are designing and the size of the paper it is printed on—the sizes are relative, based in great part on what will be printing your document. Let's look at a typical example: You are preparing to design and produce an invitation card. Its final size will be 6-by-8 inches. The size of the text area you will be working with on the card is 5-by-7 inches, to account for a one-inch margin. The card will be printed on your laser printer, which handles 8.5-by-11 inch paper. It will then be given to your commercial printer who will print a number of cards on larger sheets of paper, and then cut the finished invitations apart. So what does page size mean, and which of these sizes do you specify when setting up the page in a desktop publishing program?

In printing documents that are smaller than the paper you have in your laser printer, you should specify the actual, finished page size when specifying the page. For instance, let's take the example above, and specify the page in QuarkXPress. Its page setup would look like Figure 3.7.

Figure 3.7 *QuarkXPress New (document) dialog box showing parameters for a 6-by-8 inch invitation card with one-inch margins.*

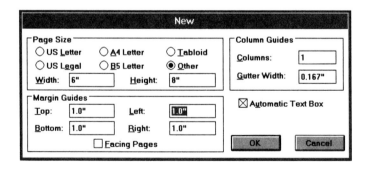

Notice that we did not specify a page size of 8.5-by-11 inches, even though that's what will be passing through the laser printer. With documents smaller than the actual paper size, specify the smaller size and the page composition system prints accurate trim marks for your commercial printer to use in cutting apart the printed invitations.

If this seems like overly complicating the small matter of trim marks, keep in mind that any work you save your commercial printer reduces the cost of printing the job; if you don't provide accurate trim marks, your commercial printer will have to add them before the work is printed.

USING LOW-COST DESKTOP PUBLISHING SOFTWARE

There are several low-cost desktop publishing programs for Windows, including Microsoft Publisher and PFS Publisher. Both come with clip art (something neither PageMaker nor QuarkXPress do) and both recognize and use the fonts you've already installed on your system and use with your other applications. Depending on the documents you want to prepare for your commercial printer, there is absolutely no reason why you cannot use an application like Microsoft Publisher or PFS Publisher. Both, as you will see, are entirely adequate for the job of publishing non-color pages, and in many ways are friendlier and easier to use than more expensive applications.

Some low-cost programs come with their own fonts that cannot be shared with other Windows applications. These fonts may work correctly only if you disable some of the standard features of Windows. Beware of such applications (you can usually recognize them by their invitingly low price), and realize that if you use one of them you may be missing many of the features that are otherwise standard with true Windows software. Let's take a look at two applications that are 100 percent Windows compatible.

Using Microsoft Publisher

Microsoft Publisher is an intriguing application: It looks to all the world like an entry-level beginner's package, but contains many interesting and sophisticated features. It comes packed with several kinds of help, including help from the Help menu; *Cue Cards* that prompt you through specific steps; dialog box *Helpful Hints* that clue you in to specific commands on specific dialog boxes; and the *Print Troubleshooter* that helps you solve potential printing problems. It offers an impressive *Check Layout* feature that looks through your publication for potential layout problems, such as objects which are completely covered by other objects, and text that has over-flowed a text frame (and will not print until the text frame is either enlarged or the text is linked to another text frame). The layout checker is a truly remarkable tool for a low-priced application like Microsoft Publisher—it is more usually found as an add-on tool in programs like PageMaker and QuarkXPress.

Microsoft Publisher is extremely easy to use. Beginners can be up and running in minutes thanks to its speed and the use of PageWizards and templates. Yes, I said Wizards, just like Microsoft Access used and we learned about in Chapter 2.. Wizards are a learning tool that I believe Microsoft will eventually incorporate into all of their Windows applications. Some day (perhaps by the time you read this book) you may be able to create your own Wizards in a programming language like Visual Basic, or modify the standard ones that come with Publisher; but for now you are restricted to only the Wizards that Microsoft has programmed for you. When you start Publisher, it presents you with a dialog box to immediately choose a PageWizard, as shown in the example below.

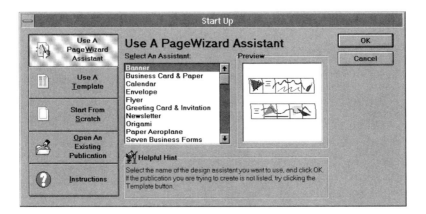

Choose the PageWizard button to select from a number of PageWizards that build specific documents for you. You will see a dialog box, like the example shown below, that lists the Wizards and shows you a small preview of the finished documents they produce.

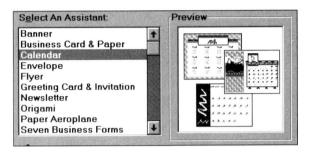

If you choose the Templates button, you will see a list of 35 professionally-designed templates, like the example shown below. (If you recall in Chapter 1, templates are preconfigured shells of documents that you use to clone specific documents.) Included in the list are templates to create labels on a number of Avery labels, business cards, brochures, letterhead, and much more. Again, a small preview window shows you a thumbnail view of the template.

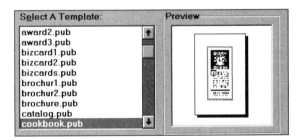

If you click the Start from Scratch button, the dialog box will display a list of page formats for you to choose from, including a full-page format, several folded-page formats, a business card format, and a banner page format that can produce a banner up to 20 feet long. Choose the format you want, and you will see the main document window, shown in Figure 3.8 on the next page.

Figure 3.8 *Microsoft Publisher's main document window.*

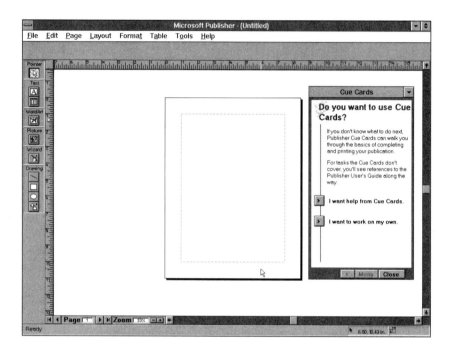

Like most page composition programs, Microsoft Publisher has rulers along the top and left side of the document page, and scroll bars along the right and bottom. In the lower left corner is the Page tool. Let's see how it works.

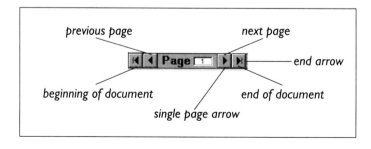

To move to a specific page in your document, click the current page number to highlight it and enter the page number you want. Press the Enter key and the page will be displayed. Alternatively, you can click on the single arrow or end-arrows. The single arrow moves you forward or backward one page at a time. The end-arrows take you to the last page or the first page of your document.

Another handy tool in the lower left corner is the zoom box. Click the box to display a list of magnification sizes, and choose the one you want, like in the example on the left.

To change the page size incrementally, click the plus button to increase the page magnification, or the minus button to reduce the page size.

Using the Tools

Notice the tool bar along the left side of the window. Use these tools, shown in Figure 3.9, to build each of the components of your document pages.

Figure 3.9 *Microsoft Publisher toolbar.*

To add text, click the Text Frame tool, draw a text frame (text box) where you want the text and begin typing. To add a graphic, click on the Picture Frame tool and draw a picture frame. Then import a graphic into the frame using the Import Picture command on the File menu (you can also call up the Import Picture dialog box by double-clicking the picture frame). The WordArt tool opens the WordArt application. Squares and rectangles with either sharp or rounded corners, and circles, and ovals are drawn with the three drawing tools. You can get help from Wizards by clicking the PageWizard tool.

Working with Text

Text is added to the page by first creating a text box (called a text frame in Microsoft Publisher). The Text Frame tool creates the box, and displays a blinking text insertion point (or I-beam tool). Here's how to put text on a page.

1.   Click the Text Frame tool and position the cross-hairs where you want the upper left-hand corner of the frame to be.

2.   Hold down the left mouse button and drag (click and drag) the cross-hairs diagonally down and across to create a box, like this:

When you release the mouse button you'll see your new text box:

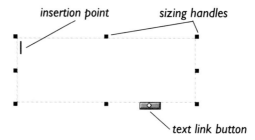

3. Notice the blinking text insertion point in the upper left-hand corner. The text you add is positioned at the insertion point.

N O T E   If you type some characters only to see nothing appear in the text box, remember this rule that is universally true for text boxes: The box must be tall enough to accommodate the height of at least one character in the size you specify. So, if you created a rather small text box and tried to add 48 point type, you might not see the characters until you enlarge the box. To enlarge the box, click the border to display the sizing handles. Then click and drag a handle to resize the box.

Learn more about...

Rules of typography   See Chapter 5, "Basic Typographic Rules."

Choosing a font style   See Chapter 5, "How Font Style and Size Can Add Meaning to Your Words."

When you create the text frame, you will see an additional text tool bar above the page. Use these tools to select the font and type size, plus type styles, such as bold or italics, in the Effects area.

The three Effects buttons apply bold, italic, and underline styles to the font you have selected. You can click on any or all effects for a given font. To undo the effect, click the same button again. Alignment (left, right, center, or justified) is controlled by the appropriate buttons. Styles are assigned to type using the Styles list box.

As you'll learn in Chapter 7, styles can save you enormous effort in reformatting and changing document specifications (and just changing your mind). If you tie the formats of paragraphs and text to specially-named styles, then to change from one typeface to another, all you need to do is specify a different typeface for that style; all the text assigned to the style instantly changes as well. Styles are an important efficiency tool that has long been associated with word processors and high-end page composition systems.

While both Microsoft Publisher and PFS Publisher allow you to assign styles to text formatting, one advantage Microsoft's application has is the ability to import styles from other documents, including other Microsoft Publisher documents and a variety of word processing files. To import a style, open the Text Styles dialog box, as displayed in Figure 3.10, and click the Import New Style button. You will see a file management dialog box to use in finding and choosing the document whose style you want to import. You can import WordPerfect, Word, and WordStar styles, as well as styles from other Microsoft Publisher documents.

Figure 3.10 *Microsoft Publisher's Text Styles dialog box lets you define, change, and import styles.*

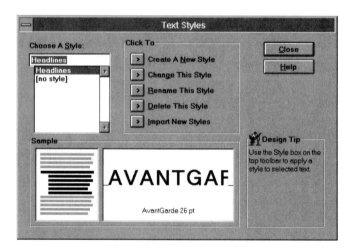

Another way to save time is to import text from another application, rather than retyping it in Microsoft Publisher. To do so, simply draw a text frame and choose the Import Styles command on the File menu. You will see the Import Styles dialog box, shown at the top on your right.

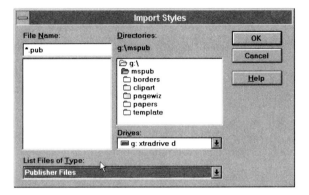

Use the List Files of Type list box to choose the file format you want to import, as shown in Table 3.1. Choose the file you want from the File Name list box and choose OK to import the text file into the text frame you just created. If you have trouble finding the file you want, choose the Find Files button to use Microsoft Publisher's powerful search capability (see "Using Microsoft Publisher's Search Feature," later in this chapter.

Table 3.1   *Text import formats supported by Microsoft Publisher.*

Word Processing Format	File Name Extension
Windows Write	.WRI
Word for DOS	.DOC
Word for Windows	.DOC
WordPerfect	.DOC
WordStar	.DOC
Works for DOS	.WPS
Works for Windows	.WPS
Rich Text Format	.RTF
ASCII (text)	.TXT
Other Microsoft Publisher files	.PUB

Working with Graphics

To add a graphic to your page in Microsoft Publisher, choose the Picture Frame button and draw a frame on the page. Double-click the frame to display the Import Picture dialog box, as shown in Figure 3.11.

Figure 3.11 *Microsoft Publisher's Import Picture dialog box.*

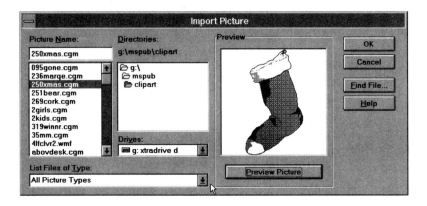

Choose the type of graphic file from the List Files of Type list box. The graphic formats Microsoft Publisher imports are shown in Table 3.2. Based on which format you select, the available files are displayed in the Picture Name list box. Click any file and choose the Picture Preview button to see a thumbnail preview of the graphic. Choose the Find Files button to have Publisher conduct extensive searches for you (see below). When you have the file you want, choose OK to import the graphic into the picture frame. As Publisher imports the graphic, it will pause and ask you whether you want to alter the dimensions of the picture frame to accommodate the height and width of the graphic, or whether you want to change the dimensions of the graphic to fit the picture frame. Based on how you answer, Publisher will do the necessary resizing and add the graphic to the frame.

Table 3.2   *Graphic import formats supported by Microsoft Publisher.*

Graphic Format	File Name Extension
AutoCAD	.DSF .PLT
HP Graphics Language	.HGL
Lotus 1-2-3 Graphics	.PIC
Computer Graphics Metafiles	.CGM
Windows Metafiles	.WMF
Tagged Image File Format	.TIF
Micrografx format	.DRW
Encapsulated PostScript	.EPS
PC Paintbrush	.PCX
WordPerfect	.WPG
Kodak Photo CD	.PCD

Using Microsoft Publisher's Search Feature

There are a number of search features, I could explain really too many to detail in this short chapter. One that bears mentioning is Microsoft Publisher's file search capability—it's one of the best—and certainly equal to Word for Windows and almost as good as WordPerfect's QuickFinder. Keep in mind that PageMaker and QuarkXPress, both priced at more than $800, have no file search capability. Yet here is a $200 application that can whiz through your disk looking for certain types of text and graphics files without you having to lift a finger (or click a mouse). Here's how it works:

Let's say you are looking for a certain type of graphics file that has the tagged image format file extension, TIF. Instead of you having to manually open each directory on your hard drive, you can have Publisher do it for you and display the names and paths of any TIF graphics that it finds.

1. Draw a picture frame and double-click to open the Import Picture dialog box. Then click on Find File to open the Find File dialog box, as shown in Figure 3.12 on the next page.

Figure 3.12 *Microsoft Publisher's Find File dialog box can search through all your directories for just the files you want.*

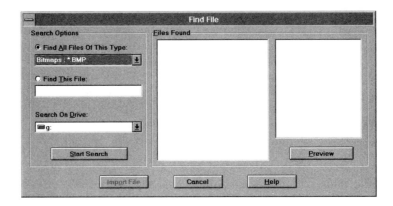

2. Now enter the type of graphic file you're looking for in the Find All Files of This Type list box. Let's look for encapsulated PostScript files (ending in the extension EPS).

3. Choose the Start Search button to search the drive listed in the Search On Drive list box. The files that are located are shown in the Files Found list box. Press the Preview button to see a thumbnail preview of the file you want:

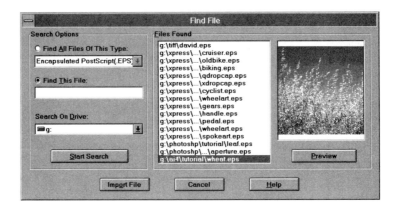

The Find Files feature is available when you want to import both text and graphics.

The speed and flexibility of this and similar low-priced applications only makes me believe that Aldus and Quark had better start looking over their shoulders.

Using PFS Publisher

PFS Publisher is a very well-designed, well-executed program. There is really nothing in this program I don't like other than its rather crude method of indexing, which I'll get to in a moment. PFS Publisher is a full-featured page composition program with several tools that neither PageMaker nor QuarkXPress can claim. For instance, like WordPerfect for Windows, it has active tab positions, visible at all times as tab icons on the ruler, as shown in Figure 3.13. That means that whenever you're adding or editing text, the actual tab stop positions are right there, aligned to the text. To change a tab stop, simply click on the tab icon and drag it to a new position. As you drag the tab icon, the text constantly reformats itself, indicating the changing tab position.

Figure 3.13   *PFS Publisher shows tab stop positions on the horizontal ruler.*

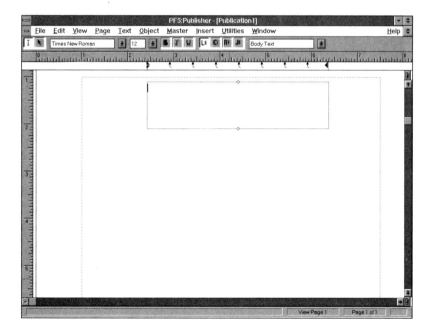

Another great idea is the QuickButton palette, shown in Figure 3.14. You can pick and choose buttons with recognizable icons for over two dozen commands displayed in a floating palette. Not only do the commands activate faster than choosing them from the pull-down menus, but for me, the palette is less of a distraction.

Figure 3.14   *PFS Publisher's QuickButton floating palette with all command choices displayed.*

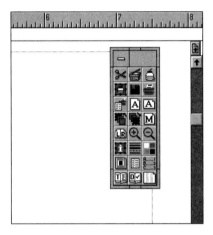

PFS Publisher gives you constant reminders of important information about the current page of your document. For example, in an information area to the right of the tools, PFS Publisher notes the measured position and dimensions of text and graphic boxes, as shown in the example below:

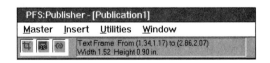

In the lower left corner of the document window, PFS Publisher constantly offers you polite hints and instructions based on what tool you have clicked. For example, if you click the picture frame tool, Publisher will display:

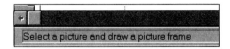

And, in the lower right corner, PFS Publisher displays the current page number and the total number of pages in your document.

Finally, PFS Publisher allows an unlimited number of guides to be positioned on the pages of your document. To add a guide, move the pointer onto either the horizontal or vertical ruler. Press and hold down the left mouse button and drag a guide onto the document page. Note that, for some unexplained reason, when you click in the horizontal ruler you get a vertical guide; clicking the vertical ruler creates a horizontal guide.

How PFS Publisher Works with Templates

PFS Publisher is highly template-oriented, and comes with a large number of templates designed for your use. If you like the concept of working with templates, you will find the template management tools in PFS Publisher to be extremely helpful. Let's take a quick look. First of all, the program makes it easy to open a template: When you choose the New command on the File menu, the New dialog box will display a current list of templates, as shown in Figure 3.15.

Figure 3.15   *PFS Publisher's New dialog box.*

To choose a template, double-click the template name in the list. To see a smaller view of the template, choose the View button. PFS Publisher will display a view template dialog box like this display of the invoice template:

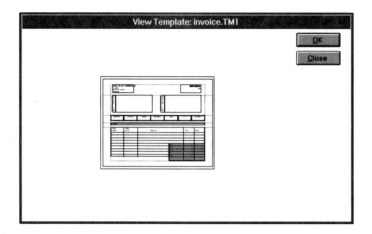

If you like the template displayed in the view dialog box, choose OK to open it. To go back to the New dialog box and see the template list again, choose Close. Finally, if you decide you don't want a template, just a new, blank document page, choose the Normal template, which is exactly that. To manage the large number of templates that comes with PFS Publisher as well as the ones you create, PFS Publisher uses a template manager called the *Template Catalog*. To see the catalog, choose View Personal Catalog on the File menu. You see the Template Catalog dialog box shown in Figure 3.16.

The Template Catalog dialog box is referred to as the Personal Catalog on the File menu because you can designate which catalog you want. For example, you could organize templates by clients or projects by creating a client catalog or a project catalog. Or, if you work for a large company, you might create a departmental catalog to hold templates for different departments. To change the default catalog to the one you want to automatically open, select the Preferences command on the View menu. In the Preferences dialog box, open the Template Catalog list box and choose the new default catalog you want.

Figure 3.16   *PFS Publisher's Template Catalog displays and organizes templates.*

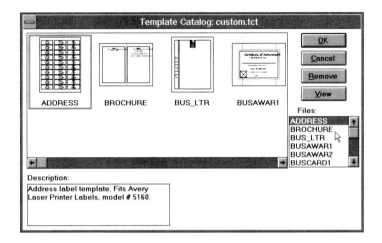

Here's how to create a specialized template catalog to hold client templates:

1.   Once you have created a document for a client, save it as a template by choosing the Save As command on the File menu.

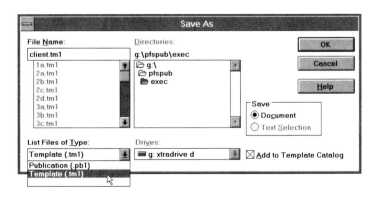

2. Open the List Files of Type list box and choose Template, which adds the correct PFS template extension to the file name. Then give the template a name in the File Name text box. Click on the Add to Template Catalog check box, and choose OK.

3. PFS Publisher will display the Add Template to Catalog dialog box, as shown in Figure 3.17. In the Description area, type a descrip-tion of the template. If this is a template for a client catalog, you might include information here about the client, printing runs, special colors used by the client, special corporate logos used, etc.

Figure 3.17 *PFS Publisher's Add Template to Catalog dialog box lets you create special-ized catalogs of templates.*

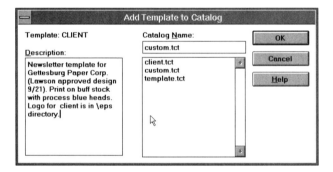

4. If you want to add the template to an existing catalog, double-click the catalog you want from the Catalog Name list box. However, since we want to create a new catalog, simply enter a new name in the Catalog Name text box. Let's enter CLIENT.TCT (TCT is the name extension required for all catalogs). Choose OK to save your new catalog.

5. Now open the Preferences dialog box on the View menu and choose your new client catalog as the default personal catalog for PFS Publisher:

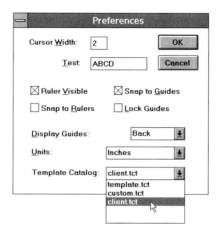

You can create as many template catalogs as you need, and make whichever one you want displayed as your personal catalog by choosing the catalog in the Template Catalog list box.

Working with Text

To add text to the page in PFS Publisher, you must first create a text frame. Choose the text frame tool from the tool bar, position the icon where you want the upper left-hand corner of the frame to be, then click and drag the icon diagonally to the right and down to create the frame, as in Figure 3.18.

Figure 3.18   *Creating a text frame in PFS Publisher.*

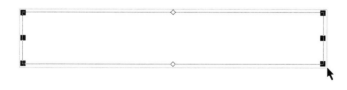

The selected frame displays sizing handles at its corners and sides, and link diamonds on the upper and lower lines (used to create links between text frames). Once the frame is drawn logic might dicatate that all you have to do is start typing. Sorry, you first have to go back to the tool bar and click on the Text tool (the I-beam icon). Now you will see the blinking insertion point in the text frame, and a number of text formatting tools will be displayed at the top of the window:

Add whatever text you want to the frame. Use the formatting tools to specify the font, size, and style of type. You can highlight the text with the insertion point, and click on one of the alignment buttons (displaying the letters L, C, R, J, for left, center, right, or justified alignment) to change the alignment of the text.

When you fill the text frame with text, the insertion point will stop in the lower right corner and blink. To continue, you must either enlarge the frame, or create another text frame and link it to the current frame. Once frames are linked together, text flows freely within them: If you delete text in one frame, text in all the linked frames will reflow to adjust itself within the boundaries of the frames. Similarly, if you add text to the first frame in the link, all the text will reflow, filling toward the last frame. Here are the steps to link two text frames together:

1. Create two text frames with the text frame tool. Click the first text frame to display the sizing handles and the link diamonds.

2. Now choose the Link tool shown in the margin; the pointer will change to a chain link icon. Use the Link tool to establish a link between the parent frame and the child frame. The *parent frame* is where the text comes from; the *child frame* is where the text is going. For example, if you have a frame at the top of page two that fills with text and you create a second frame to hold the overflow, the frame at the top is the parent and the frame that catches the overflow is the child.

3. Position the icon over the lower link diamond in the parent frame, and click the mouse. Now move the icon over the upper link diamond of the child frame and click the mouse again.

4. Press Esc to end the link session.

While PFS Publisher is capable of creating an index, the index it makes is less than useful. I suppose I should be satisfied that Publisher has any indexing tools at all for such a reasonably-priced application—QuarkXPress for Windows can't generate an index at all and costs many times more. However, the index features in PFS Publisher allow only one level of index entries, and without more specific subordinate entries the index is pretty worthless. Spinnaker Software gets around this by suggesting that you can manually edit the index after it's generated to add subordinate entries—if you're going to do that, you might as well create cross references, which you must add by hand as well. If indexing is an important consideration for the type of work you are doing, you should consider a program that has a more extensive index capability.

As with all page composition programs, PFS Publisher can import text files created with a number of different word processors. To import a word processing file, create a text frame on the page, click the Text tool, and choose Import Text from the File menu. In the Import Text dialog box, choose one of the formats PFS Publisher supports, as displayed in Table 3.3. When you have found the file you wish to import, choose OK to add the file to the text frame you just created.

Table 3.3 *Text import formats supported by PFS Publisher.*

Text Format	File Name Extension
ASCII (text)	.TXT
Rich Text Format	.RTF
PFS Windows Works	.WPD
PFS Write	any extension
PFS First Choice	.DOC
WordStar	.DOC
Word for DOS	.DOC
Word for Windows	.DOC

WordPerfect	.DOC
Professional Write	.DOC
Ami Professional	.DOC

Working with Graphics

It is especially easy to add a graphic to your PFS Publisher pages. Click the picture frame tool and Publisher automatically presents the Picture dialog box, as displayed in Figure 3.19. Use the dialog box to find the graphic you want to add. The program catalogs graphics in much the same way it catalogs templates.

Figure 3.19 *PFS Publisher's Picture dialog box offers you a catalog of graphic files.*

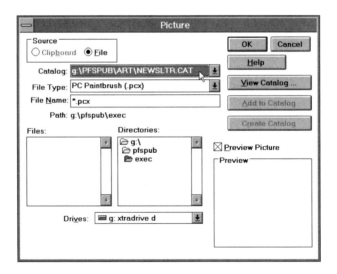

Choose the catalog you want from the catalog list box. To see the catalog, choose the View Catalogbutton:

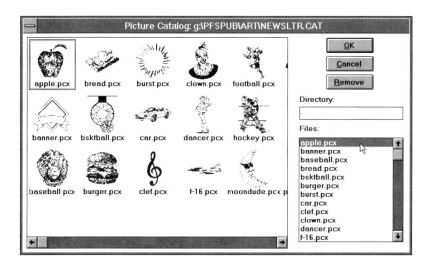

Move the highlight bar down the list of file names and the matching graphic is also highlighted. When you find the graphic you want, choose OK and the graphic is imported into the picture frame you just created. Table 3.4 displays the graphic formats.

Table 3.4 *Graphic import formats supported by PFS Publisher.*

Graphic Format	File Name Extension
Windows PaintBrush	.BMP
PFS Picture Catalogs	.CAT
CompuServe Graphics Interchange Format	.GIF
PC Paintbrush	.PCX
Windows Metafiles	.WMF
Windows Clipboard	.CLP
Tagged Image File Format	.TIF
Targa	.TGA
WordPerfect	.WPG

USING HIGH-COST, HIGH-POWERED DESKTOP PUBLISHING SOFTWARE

High-powered publishing programs are the personal luxury cars of page composition software: lots of horsepower with great handling and perhaps a few annoying quirks. The advantages to using PageMaker or QuarkXPress include added printing capabilities and complete control of the relationship of objects on the page. The disadvantages (besides costing upwards of $1,000 for either program) are the need for larger amounts of memory in your Windows computer and the need for possibly a faster Windows computer (or the programs will run very slowly). Since both PageMaker and QuarkXPress are fully color-capable programs, you may need a high-resolution monitor and a color graphics adapter capable of displaying as many as 16.7 million colors. (Appendix A details the hardware and software requirements for a Windows desktop publishing system.)

The biggest reasons to fork over the extra money for one of these programs is most likely to be the need to publish color. PageMaker, QuarkXPress, Ventura Publisher, and FrameMaker (in that order of popularity) are the programs most often used in serious publishing efforts. PageMaker was the first program to offer the composition features we now take for granted in any desktop publishing program. It and QuarkXPress, which followed closely behind PageMaker, began on the Macintosh and migrated to Windows (PageMaker has offered a PC version since 1987, but had little popularity until Windows 3.0 came out in 1990; while Quark has only offered a Windows version of QuarkXPress since early 1993).

PageMaker and QuarkXPress together comprise a huge percentage of the desktop publishing software market. Users of each program seem intensely loyal and generally opposed to the competing program. That's probably because the approach to page composition that each program takes is different. I have always considered PageMaker to be more of a designer's program, it offers you a clean slate to create new ideas from scratch. I think of QuarkXPress to be more of a graphic artist's program—more mechanical in its approach—offering less spontaneity in exchange for more precision and control. There are some other differences between the two programs. For example, PageMaker comes with a powerful indexer and can create multi-level tables of contents; QuarkXPress lacks the ability to create indexes and tables of contents. PageMaker also has an easy to use word processing mode that lets you type and edit text without worrying about page layouts; QuarkXPress doesn't. Quark, on the other hand, is more oriented to complex color art: expensive color brochures, color packaging, color advertising, and the like. Let's take a look at both and you can judge for yourself.

Using PageMaker for Windows

PageMaker is the granddaddy of page composition software. It was the first full-featured program and set the standard by which other programs were measured. The program has matured over the years to include full color capabilities, templates, and other features I'll explain in a moment. As you can see in Figure 3.20 its document window is simple and straightforward.

Figure 3.20   *PageMaker for Windows with a new document displayed.*

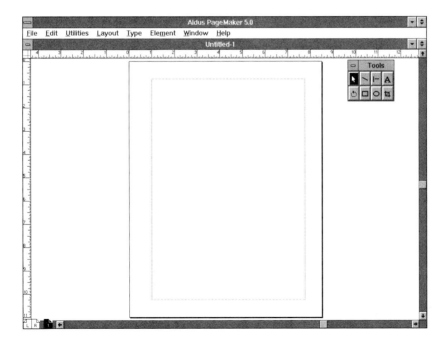

Right off the bat you will probably notice that there aren't as many tools, help boxes, and other aids on the document page as with Microsoft Publisher or PFS Publisher. PageMaker provides a toolbox shown in the upper right corner of the document window. Other tools, called palettes, can be opened by choosing the Window menu. They include a Color palette, a Styles palette, a Library palette (a storage area for objects you use on a regular basis, like a company logo), and a Control palette. The palettes are shown in Figure 3.21.

Figure 3.21   *PageMaker's floating palettes containing layout and design tools.*

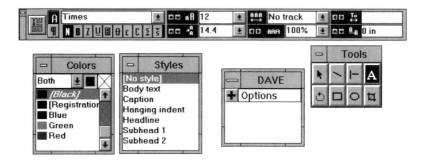

Working with Text

Unlike other page composition programs, you don't create text boxes or text frames in PageMaker to hold text. You simply click the Text tool in the Toolbox, click the insertion point where you want to begin typing, and type. When you click on the insertion point on the page, PageMaker creates a text block to hold the text. Text blocks are like text boxes in that they hold text, yet PageMaker saves you the added step of having to create the box before you begin to type.

Text blocks have sizing handles at each corner, as displayed in Figure 3.22, and top and bottom windowshade handles. The windowshade handles are used to thread text blocks together (*threading* text blocks is PageMaker's term for linking text boxes or frames). The notations in the handles tell you different things about the text in the text block. For example, an empty top handle means this is the beginning of a text block. A bottom handle containing a plus sign means this text block is threaded to other text blocks and text can flow among them. A bottom handle with a red down-pointing arrowhead means there is more text remaining to be placed on the page (the text is considered *overflow* text because it hasn't yet been added to a text block). A bottom handle with a pound sign (#) means that is the end of the text in the text block.

Figure 3.22 *Anatomy of a PageMaker text block.*

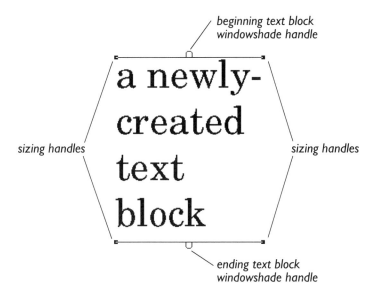

If you are confused the term *place* in the previous paragraph, Place is PageMaker's term for importing either text or graphics. To place text, you must first choose the Text tool from the Toolbox (this tells PageMaker you want to place text and not graphics). Then choose the Place command from the File menu. In the Place Document dialog box, as shown in Figure 3.23 on the next page, find the file you want to place, based on the import formats you installed with PageMaker. Table 3.5 lists all text formats PageMaker supports.

Figure 3.23 *PageMaker's Place Document dialog box controls importing both text and graphics.*

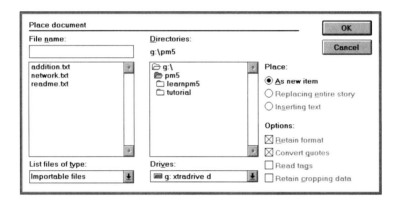

 Choose OK to import the file. You will return to your document and the Text tool will change to a loaded text icon, as shown on the left.

Position the icon where you want the text to flow and click the mouse; the text is placed on the page. Use PageMaker's Autoflow command (on the Layout menu) to automatically flow the text onto as many pages as are needed.

Table 3.5 *Text import formats supported by PageMaker for Windows.*

Text Format	File Name Extension
Ami Professional	.SAM
Document Content Architecture format	.DCA

Windows Write	.WRI
Word for DOS	.DOC
Word for Windows	.DOC
WordPerfect	.WP5
Revisable Form Text	.RFT
Rich Text Format	.RTF
WordStar	.WS, .WST
Ventura Publisher	.VP
Wang Word Processing	.1WP, .DOC
ASCII (text)	.TXT
dBASE III+, IV versions 1.11.5	.DBF
Excel 2.1-4.0 (Macintosh or Windows)	.XLS
Lotus 1-2-3 2.01-2.4	.WK1
Lotus 1-2-3 3.0-3.1+	.WK3
Lotus 1-2-3 1.1 for Windows	.WK3
Quattro Pro	.WK1, .WKS
R:BASE	.DBF
SuperCalc	.WK1, .WKS
Symphony 1.1-3.0	.WR1
PageMaker 4.0 files	.PM4
PageMaker (Macintosh) 4.2 files	.PM4
PageMaker 5.0 files	.PM5

Using PageMaker's Templates

PageMaker comes with a number of useful templates. You can also change any current document into a future template, so if you create a publication you like, by all means save it as a template. Here's how:

1. Choose the Save as command from the File menu.

2. When the Save Document As dialog box appears, click the Save As Template option box.

3. Give the template a name and PageMaker will save it with the template extension *.PT5* instead of the document extension *.PM5*.

4. Once a document is saved as a template, you can open the template and improve it or change it; or open it as a new document containing all the personality of the template.

PageMaker's own templates are available on the Additions menu. Open the Utilities menu and select the Aldus Additions menu. Then choose Open Template to display the Open Template dialog box, as displayed in Figure 3.24. Select the template from the list. The Preview window shows you a thumbnail view of what the template looks like. The Page size list box often has different page size options for the template. When you click on OK, the template will be opened as a new, unnamed document.

Figure 3.24 *PageMaker's Open Template dialog box lists the professionally-designed templates that come with PageMaker.*

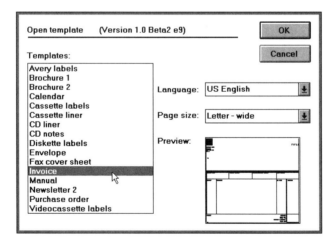

Working with Graphics

Graphics are placed (imported) in PageMaker documents in much the same way as text is placed: You use the same Place command on the File menu. Before choosing the command, you should decide whether you want an independent or in-line graphic. An *independent graphic* is added anywhere on the page, and can be moved anywhere on the page. It is not tied to any text, although it can be fitted into a text block that describes it. However if the text is reflowed on the page (for example, because you added some text earlier and pushed the text near the graphic further down the page), the independent graphic will not move with the text—you have to physically relocate it. An *in-line graphic* is anchored to the text around it. It looks and acts (and is handled) just like text in PageMaker—when the text reflows, the in-line graphic anchored to the text reflows as well. In-line graphics are used when the surrounding text describes them, such as how the graphics in this book are described.

Independent and in-line graphics are determined purely by the tool you select prior to choosing the Place command. To place an independent graphic, select the Pointer tool from the Toolbox. If you want to create an in-line graphic, choose the Text tool and click the insertion point in the text block where you want the graphic to be positioned. For example, if you want the graphic following a particular paragraph, click the insertion point immediately following the paragraph.

Once you have decided which type of graphic you want to import, choose Place on the File menu to open the Place document dialog box, as shown in Figure 3.23. Choose the graphic you wish to import. Table 3.6 details the graphic formats PageMaker recognizes.

Table 3.6   *Graphic import formats supported by PageMaker for Windows.*

Graphic Format	File Name Extension
Adobe Illustrator	.EPS
Aldus FreeHand	.EPS
Aldus Persuasion (Windows)	.CGM, .WMF

Aldus Table Editor (Windows)	.TBL, .WMF
Arts & Letters 3.01	.EPS, .CGM
AutoCad 9.1	.ADI, .EPS, .PLT
Computer Graphics Metafile	.CGM
CorelDraw	.EPS, .CGM, .TIF, .WMF
DXF	.DXF
Encapsulated PostScript	.EPS
Excel charts	.WMF .XLC
Excel spreadsheets	.XLS
Harvard Graphics	.CGM, .EPS, .PLT
HP Graphics Gallery	.TIF
HPGL plotter	.PLT
Lotus Freelance	.CGM, .EPS,
MacPaint	.PNT
Micrografx Designer	.CGM, .PIC, .PCX, .TIF, .WMF
PC Paint	.PIC
PC Paintbrush	.PCX, .TIF
Paintbrush Plus	
Publisher's Paintbrush	.PCX
Tektronix Plot 10	.PLT
Tagged Image File Format	.TIF
VideoShow graphics (NAPLPS)	.PIC
Windows Metafile	.WMF
Windows Paintbrush	.MSP
Windows Paintbrush 3.0	.BMP, .PCX

Using QuarkXPress for Windows

If PageMaker and QuarkXPress were personal luxury cars, PageMaker would be a BMW—powerful, yet subtle and steadfast without a lot of frills. Quark would be a Lexus or Infinity—raw power sporting every conceivable option, gadget, and gizmo. QuarkXPress is known for the minute control it has over page design. Its ability to control *trapping*, for example, is extraordinary; yet may well be more control than your commercial printer wants in the preparation of your publications.

Trapping is a complicated subject, and can seem at times like one of the many ageless mysteries of the printing profession. You sometimes trap an object, like type, for example, when it is printed over a background color. The outside edges of the type characters are enlarged slightly to overlap the white area underneath the characters (called the **knockout** because the colored background is knocked out for the type). The microscopic overlap accounts for the possible misalignment of the colors printed on the page. If they were misaligned without the trap, you might see the edge of the white knockout around part of the type characters.

QuarkXPress's main document window includes the requisite horizontal and vertical rulers, plus a page magnification box in the lower left corner like Microsoft Publisher. What is most surprising about Quark is the number of palettes you can have opened, as shown in Figure 3.25 on the next page—so many you may have trouble seeing the document page underneath all the palettes. Quark's tools include the usual toolbox palette, as well as a Measurements palette (what PageMaker calls the Control palette), a Library palette (a storage area similar to the PageMaker library), a Colors palette, a Style Sheets palette, a Document Layout palette (used to control the order of pages in a document), and a Trapping Information palette.

Figure 3.25 *QuarkXPress main document window with all palettes visible.*

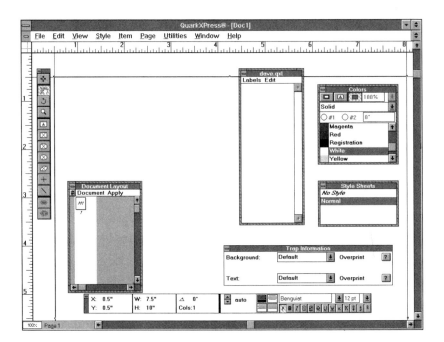

One of QuarkXPress's many features worth mentioning is its ability to search for specific typefaces and change them to other typefaces. The Font Usage dialog box (shown in Figure 3.26) on the Utilities menu, acts like a Search and Replace command; only in this case you are searching for typefaces and type styles. With this command you can change every occurrence of Helvetica bold italic to just Helvetica italic, or change Helvetica to Avant Garde bold italic. In a complicated or long document, this dialog box can save enormous time by eliminating a manual search and the risk of missing a change that you wanted to make.

Figure 3.26 *QuarkXPress's Font Usage dialog box finds typefaces and changes them to different typefaces.*

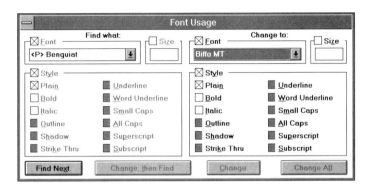

Another extremely useful command is Picture Usage on the Utilities menu, which shows you the name of each graphic in your document, the page it's on, the graphic format, and the status of the graphic. If the graphic is changed in the program that created it, you may need to re-import the graphic to get the up-to-date version—the graphic's status will so indicate. Also on the Utilities menu are commands to modify the *kerning* and *tracking* values of different typefaces (kerning and tracking are two ways to minutely adjust the space between letters and words—you'll learn more about this in Chapter 5).

Working with Text

Text is added to the QuarkXPress page by first creating a text box to hold the text (like both Microsoft Publisher and PFS Publisher); then actually typing or importing the text . Click the Text Box tool button in the tool bar.

Position the tool icon where you want the box and create the box. Then click on the Text tool (the one with the I-beam and the hand) and begin typing your text. To format the text, choose the Formats command on the Style menu, or you can use the Measurements palette, if it's visible.

QuarkXPress offers several type styles not available in the other page composition programs we've looked at: outline, shadow, and superior. The outline style creates an outline in the shape of the typeface, but leaves the middle white.

Outline

The larger and bolder you make characters in the outline style, the thicker and the more distinct the outline becomes. Note that you can apply any color to the characters, which changes the actual lines of the outline from black to a color, but the white middle of the characters always remains white. The shadow style adds a drop shadow behind the characters, offset slightly down and to the right.

Shadow

Like the outline style, the bolder and larger the characters are, the more distinct the shadow becomes. While you can change the color of the characters to any color you have defined in QuarkXPress, the shadow always remains a medium gray. The third interesting style is called superior, which reduces the size of the characters and raises them above the baseline of surrounding characters. The perfect use for the superior style is to add a trademark, registered trademark, or copyright symbol. Here's how the trademark symbol looks with Quark's superior style:

QuarkXPress™

The beauty of the superior style is that the characters are not only raised (like superscript characters) but they are significantly reduced in size, making symbols like trademarks and copyright bugs unobtrusive, yet still recognizable. (To do the same formatting as the superior style in another page composition program would mean changing the symbol manually, requiring a number of steps this style performs automatically.)

If you wish to import text into QuarkXPress, create a text box and choose the Get Text command from the File menu. In the dialog box, find the file you wish to import. Choose the Convert Quote box to change typewriter-style single and double quotes to real typographic *curly* quotes. Select Include Style Sheets to include any word processing styles that you have used in the file. The file formats QuarkXPress recognizes are shown in Table 3.7.

Table 3.7   *Text import formats supported by QuarkXPress for Windows.*

Graphic Format	File Name Extension
ASCII (text)	.TXT
Rich Text Format	.RTF
Ami Professional	.SAM
WordPerfect	.WP
Windows Write	.WRI
Word for DOS	.DOC
Word for Windows	.DOC
XyWrite III Plus	.XY3

Working with Graphics

 Graphics are added by first creating a picture box on the page. Choose the Picture Box tool from the tool bar.

Choose the Get Picture command on the File menu. Select the graphics file you want from the dialog box. The graphic formats QuarkXPress recognizes are shown in Table 3.8 on the next page.

Table 3.8   *Graphic import formats supported by QuarkXPress for Windows.*

Graphic Format	File Name Extension
Bitmap files	.BMP, .RLE
PC Paintbrush	.PCX
CompuServe Graphic Interchange Format	.GIF
Windows Metafiles	.WMF
Tagged Image File Format	.TIF
Encapsulated PostScript	.EPS
Macintosh PICT files	.PCT
Scitex CT files	.CT
Micrografx files	.DRW
HPGL Filter	.PLT
Computer Graphics Metafiles	.CGM

CHAPTER SUMMARY

Like a wine tasting party, this chapter has given you just a whiff of what four page composition programs are capable of doing. Two, Microsoft Publisher and PFS Publisher, cost one-fourth as much as the other two programs discussed, yet contain many of the same commands, and provide you with many similar features. The other two, PageMaker and QuarkXPress, are powerhouse products capable of producing practically anything you can imagine. Both produce magazines and newspapers that are read around the world. Both are used in book publishing, and to create color print ads, color brochures, annual reports, and complex product packaging. Yet, each has a very different personality and each can handle some tasks better than the other.

I've included the file formats each program recognizes for importing text and graphics. If you are working with a specific word processing program that one of the page composition programs supports, then you should probably consider that program more strongly than the others. I've also tried to give you a sense of how easy (or difficult) each is to add simple text and graphics to the page. But like fine wine, page composition software is also a matter of subjective opinion, and you may have to try several bottles before you find the one you like best.

PART II

A Design Primer

Why do some documents look better than others? Why do some magazine ads jump off the pages at you? Why are some technical manuals and computer books easy to read, while other books and manuals are never opened? What exactly is that professional touch we see in some brochures, newsletters, and magazines that sets them apart? If you think the common answer to these questions is great writing, lots of photographs, and expensive graphics, you would fall into the same black hole of mediocrity that swallows thousands of unremarkable documents.

While the words must be noteworthy and the photos striking, it is the document's design that wraps around the words and graphics, catching your eye and leading you to the author's conclusions. It is the design that embraces or rebuffs; extends welcome feelings of comfort to read on, or shakes you up with cluttered space, fragmented images, and confusing messages. And it is the design that creates thematic unity in which beautiful photographs and graphic designs can flourish. Designs can be simple or complex, subtle or obvious, straightforward or thought-provoking; but without a design the pages of your document will suffer and the best of messages will diminish.

Part II is a running start at Elementary Design 101. It gives you the basic foundation on which to build practically any document, and includes the help you need with designing pages, adding typography, and putting graphics, photos, and color to best use. The chapters in Part II won't make you an instant graphic designer, but they get you up and running with practical help, advice, and tips.

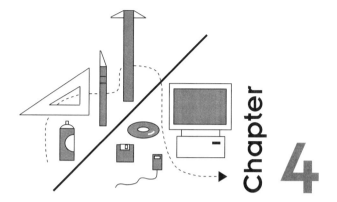

Chapter 4

Choosing a Page Design to Compliment the Message

J ust about any time words and graphics are arranged on paper, the design of the three becomes important to successful communication. It matters little whether you have created an Exit sign, a corporate brochure, or a label for a can of soup, the design of the page—the relationship between what is printed on the paper and the surrounding white paper—determines how the message will be received. This chapter offers help in marrying the overall page with the words and images it contains.

THE BASIC STEPS OF DESIGN

Think of the page design as directing the flow of information in the proper order. A successful page design helps communication by attracting the reader, holding the reader's attention, and helping the reader sort, categorize, and prioritize information. Based on what you want to say, some page designs are more effective than others. Take newsletters for example, which come in many shapes and sizes—as large as daily newspapers, tabloid size (11-by-17 inches), letter size (8.5-by-11 inches), and smaller.

The size you choose becomes a compromise of having enough paper to fit all the words you want to say, versus the cost of printing, and often the costs of distribution. A tabloid size holds a lot of words, and requires more creativity in its layout in order to hold the reader's attention. (Just because you have a larger page doesn't mean you can run long columns of small type down the page and expect the page to be read.) You need to balance the additional type with more creativity, interesting graphic effects, and an attractive use of white space. Once you have a basic mix of type, graphics, and white space, you face the challenging tasks of creating attention-getting headlines and subheads (and we haven't even written a word yet!). A smaller-sized newsletter may not hold all the stories you want to include; you may find yourself tempted to reduce the size of the type to squeeze in more words, close up white space, and eliminate a few graphics—don't. Add more pages if you need to, or save the least important story for the next issue. You'll learn more about squeezing the space and life out of pages later in this chapter.

Once you know the design, it's a matter of adding the framework in your Windows software, filling in each design element, creating or importing the text, and fitting it to the space provided by the design. Let's look at some of the ingredients that go into a page design.

Use Proportions to Create Scale

Regardless of the size of the page you choose, it will lend itself to some designs better than others. Use the proportions of the page to your advantage. This may mean accentuating the height of a narrow, tall page, or putting the emphasis on strong horizontal themes if the page is wide but not very tall. Don't try to stuff a vertically-oriented layout onto a wide page. For example:

- **Use narrow or condensed versions of fonts if you are working in a tall, narrow layout**. Narrow and condensed typefaces have less width and spacing between letters, so you can fit more characters in the same length line. Likewise, condensed fonts allow more height in the letters for the same size width. You might consider using Helvetica Condensed or Helvetica Compressed rather than Helvetica. Fonts such as Willow, used in the headline in the example shown below, may be a bit exaggerated, but works quite well in tight situations. Other tightly-packed fonts include Adobe Onyx, Latin Condensed, and ITC Machine.

Council: OK more student money

In a surprise move today, Orlando city council approved increasing apportionment of property taxes for the local school district. According to Sharon Watson, council staff worker, the additional resources would be earmarked strickly for student services, not for increased administration overhead.

Learn more about...

Using the best font for your design   See Chapter 5, "Basic Typographic Rules."

- **Rotate the headline to run vertically up the page.** Rotating text is a great attention-getter as long as you're frugal with the number of words that are rotated. If the subject for a page layout lends itself to rotated type, then by all means rotate away. Figure 4.1 shows a narrow page with an extremely tall photo. Vertical type is used to fit the number of words needed in the headline.

Figure 4.1   *Vertically-rotated headlines fitted to a tall, narrow photo in a newsletter layout.*

The proper way to handle vertically-rotated text is to run it up the left side of the page, or the left side of a graphic or photo, and down the right side, like this:

- **Run a double-truck across two pages.** If the page width isn't wide enough for the headline, run the headline across two pages (called a *double-truck*), shown in Figure 4.2, or create a two-page spread and use the full width of both pages for the headline.

Figure 4.2   *For a narrow page layout, a double-truck may be the only way of fitting words on the page.*

- **Use vertical graphics on vertical pages and horizontal graphics on horizontal pages.** If you are ordering a product shot for an ad or brochure, you should know in advance whether you want horizontal or vertical photos. Be sure to let the photographer know which format you need for your pages, like Figure 4.3 on the next page. Forcing a horizontal photo into a vertical space is like trying to shoehorn a size 10 foot into a size 8 pump—you might get it to fit, but it never feels comfortable.

Figure 4.3 Use graphics and photos that naturally relate to the page orientation.

Learn more about...

Using graphics on your page   See Chapter 6, "Adding Lines
and Boxes for Emphasis."

- **Leave the page blank and use the white space as the attention-getter.** There is no more startling a page design for me than a blank page with the smallest of copy in one corner. As an ad, such a page shouts, "We're so successful we can buy a whole newspaper page and not bother you with a lot of words." In a brochure, a stark, blank page contrasts nicely with a facing page of graphics and photos. The intelligent use of white space is a vital design ingredient and one we look at in more detail later in this chapter.

Use Lines to Control Attention

The world around us is full of lines: the straight lines of cities, buildings, streets, corners, poles, lamp posts; the soft curved lines of meadows, forests, trees, shorelines. There are lines of clouds, lines of waves, lines of people. Geese fly in lines of formation, flags fly in line with the wind. All around us lines catch and direct our attention, telling us where to go and where not to go. Use lines on the page in the same way, to catch our eyes and show us what's important, what's the order of the page. White lines are covered in Chapter 6, let's look at some ways lines can help your design:

- **Add lines to define columns of text.** Margins can be noted with vertical lines, like Figure 4.4. Headers above the body of text, or footers below the body of text, are often separated by horizontal lines. In complicated layouts requiring large amounts of text or numbers, lines are helpful to keep the eye moving down the columns, not skipping across to other information. By the same token, lines added to the rows of a table help the eye move across the page. If you add a line to the space between two columns (called the *gutter*), remember to widen the gutter space to accommodate the line or your page may look overly heavy with type.

Figure 4.4 *The left margin is marked by a column line (or rule) to separate the column of text from the margin note.*

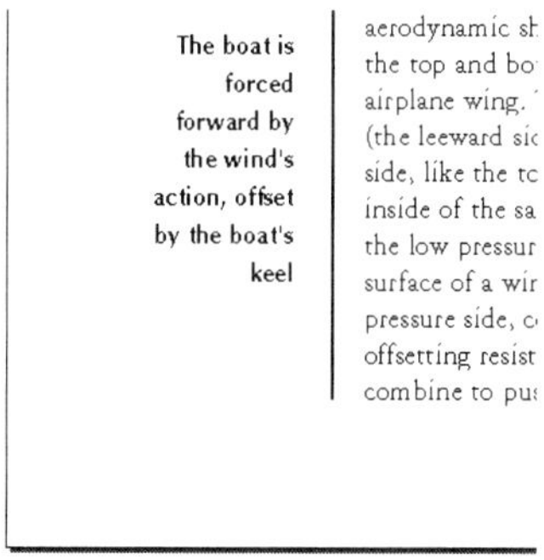

◆ **Use lines to emphasize words of importance and force them to stand out from surrounding text.** Underlining words must be done with care; have too many words underlined and you lose the impact of the underline. Reserve underlining for those times when words must truly pop out from the text. If you add underlines to words, be sure there is enough space between the word you're underlining and the words directly below on the next line. You may have to increase the space between the two lines to accommodate the underline. (The spacing of letters, words, and lines is detailed in Chapter 5, "Understanding Horizontal and Vertical Spacing.")

Figure 4.5   *The photo, without a lined border, loses its background on the page.*

Figure 4.6   *The border in the photo gives you the full impact of the image.*

- **Add lines around photos to sharpen light backgrounds.**
Often with black and white photos, the background in a photo is so
close to white that it is indistinguishable when printed on white paper,
like Figure 4.5. To correct the problem, the photographer should
select a darker background for the shot, but an acceptable fix is to add
a thin-lined box around the edge of the photo, as shown in Figure 4.6.

- **Use lines with arrowheads to emphasize the important
messages.** In ads and fact sheets that contain a lot of information, use
lines to point out the messages you want remembered. Exaggerated
arrows can be used in the background to move the reader through a
busy page to the conclusion you want.

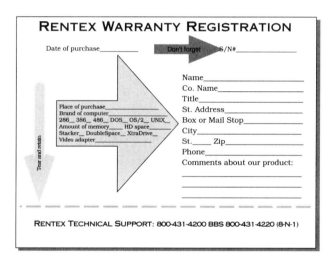

There are a number of graphic arrowheads included with dingbat-type fonts,
such as Adobe's Zapf Dingbats:

Examples of TrueType Wingdings:

Use Graphic Shapes to Add Dimension

Graphic shapes can add interest to the otherwise flat, bland plane of the document page. As with lines, we see the world in the context of shapes. You can use these universal shapes to add variety, interest, and an artistic relationship to the subject matter of your document.

- **Crop photos as recognizable shapes to emphasize the subject.** Create a stylistic car shape for an Autobahn Society brochure; or fish shapes for a GreenPeace flyer.

- **Design the document itself in a special shape that relates to the subject at hand.** Another way to handle this idea is to die cut just a flap or window in the front cover in a specific shape: open the flap and read a sales message or product summary.

- **Compose text in the shape of an object that the document relates to**. Before the days of desktop publishing, having text composed in specific shapes was a monstrously expensive undertaking, requiring hours and hours of a typesetter's time and expertise. Now, some programs, like QuarkXPress and PageMaker, can do the same work in seconds. Either program can wrap either side of a text block around the edge of a graphic shape. Delete the graphic and you're left with the shape, like the example below showing the points of a star in text.

Just about any time words and graphics are arranged on paper the design of the three becomes important to successful communication. It matters little whether you have created an Exit sign, a corporate brochure, or a label for a can of soup, the design of the page—the relationship between what is printed on the paper and the surrounding white (or colored) paper— determines how the message will be received. This chapter offers help in marrying the overall page with the words and images it contains. <a head>The Basic Steps of Design <body text 2>Think of the page design as directing the flow of information in the proper order. A successful   page design will help communication by attract- ing the reader to it, hold- ing the reader's attention and helping the reader sort, catego- rize andprioritize information. Based on what you want to say, some page designs are more effective than oth- ers. Take newsletters for example, which come in many shapes and sizes—as large as dailynewspapers, tabloid (11 by 17 inches), let- ter size (8.5 by 11 inches) and smaller. <body text 1>The size you choose becomes a compromise of having enough paper to fit all the words you want to say, versus the cost of printing, and often the costs of distribution. A tabloid- size holds a lot of words, and requires more creativity in itslayout in order to hold the reader's attention. (Just because you have a larger page does-

Add Depth by Adding Texture

Texture can be the most challenging element to add to a design. Let's face it, paper is a fairly flat, smooth surface (it has to be to run through a printing press). In spite of its basic flatness, there are interesting things you can add to give an appearance of texture.

- **Use a rough, textured paper for the printed document.** There are any number of high cotton-content papers and recycled papers that can add a real flare to your document. However, you must keep in mind that when using one of these papers, you may be limited in other design choices. For example, the rough surface spreads the ink more than a smooth or slick coated paper stock, so the edges of letters, lines, graphics, and photos won't be as crisp. In especially small sizes, type will have a tendency to break (italics in small sizes should be avoided entirely). The reproduction of photographs will not be as crisp as those printed on a smoother stock paper, and you will not be able to get as high a resolution of the printed photo as you can with smoother paper.

- **Consider embossing or foil stamping an area of the page.** *Embossing* is the act of making a metal die in the shape of whatever you want—text, logos, graphics—and pressing the paper onto the die, creating a raised impression in the paper (sort of like a notary public's seal). Embossing is expensive because of the steps required to make the metal die, but the die is yours to keep and can be used over and over again. You can further enhance the look of embossing by adding a color on top of the embossed area. You can also add ink in a shadow effect to one side of the embossed letters, which would further highlight the embossed effect. *Foil stamping* is normally used when you want to print gold or silver, or other metallic colors. The area to be printed is actually stamped with a metal foil. Foil stamping is slightly delicate (it can be scraped off) and also requires a metal die to be prepared. But the results can be unusual, eye-catching, and very impressive.

- **A few words of caution about embossing and foil stamping.** Not only are they expensive, but a little goes a long way. When you emboss a page, the backside of the page carries the indentation of the embossing as well (one of the reasons embossing is often reserved for the front cover of brochures, or for stationery and business cards). One idea to think about for embossing the interior pages of a document (where you will be printing on the backside of the embossed pages) is to emboss a margin line, or a line separating a header from the body copy. Since the line would normally be repeated on all interior pages, it looks natural to have it raised on one page and indented on the backs of those pages (the line is still obvious both ways).

- **Use varnish to accentuate parts of the page.** *Varnish* is just what the name implies: a clear coating applied over the ink. Varnish is traditionally used to prevent the ink from smudging and to give a gloss finish to the page. However, by specifying varnish for only certain parts of the page, like only over the photos, or the company's logo, or major headings, you can create an exciting contrast between matte and gloss finishes on the same page. It's easy to specify varnishing with page composition software: simply create a custom color called *Varnish* and use it like any other color in your document.

- **Use gradient color fills as a background to the text, or color the text itself with a gradient fill.** A *gradient fill* is a seamless blend of colors from light to dark, or from one compatible color to another. An interesting effect is to create text colored with one gradient fill over a background of an opposite gradient, as shown in the example below.

IMPROVING THE LOOK OF TEXT IN COLUMNS

Endless columns of text: Look over any home-brewed newsletter and you may see them—unfortunately you probably won't notice much else. It seems as though there is a natural tendency to add as many columns as possible. It must give the impression to those designers that you can fit more words on the page if you have more columns, so let's take an 8.5-by-11 inch page and put five columns on it. Actually, you can't fit any more words in five columns than you can in one column (probably less words will be found in the five column format because of the excessive hyphenation and word spacing the narrow columns require). The number of columns on the page should be determined by the length of the text line (called the *line measure*), not by some arbitrary need to have lots of columns so the newsletter resembles the daily newspaper.

Using the Line Measure to Determine Column Width

The proper length text line—the proper line measure—makes the line easier to read. If the line is too short there is little flow to the words, you're always having to move your eyes down to the next line. If the line is too long, it's easy to loose track of the beginning of the line, so you're not sure if the next line is really the next line, or if you skipped a line or two. Either way, your concentration is interrupted, and reading suffers.

The size of type used in the line also helps determine the correct line length. The smaller the type, the shorter the line length must be. However, as you increase the size of type you can comfortably read a longer and longer line. In Figure 4.7, you can see that there is a comfortable line length for any size type.

Figure 4.7 *Awkward and comfortable line measures for different type sizes.*

This is 11-point Palatino on an 11-pica measure. In order to justify the text properly   spacing between words must be exaggerated.

This is 9-point Palatino on an 11-pica measure. The distance between words is more uniform and because the type is smaller, the line measure is easier to read.

This is 8-point Palatino on the same 11-pica measure, but with the space between lines (the leading) increased to improve readability. Smaller type is easier to read with greater white space between the lines.

This is a comfortable line length for 11 point type. The eyes take in the length of the line without difficulty. The reader is able to find the beginning of the next line with ease. Notice the uniform spacing between words in the lines.

This   is   14-point   Palatino considerably   larger   than   the example above, and used to show the need for a longer line measure for larger-sized type.

This is a 23-pica measure for the same size Palatino. Notice that the line length seems to fit the type size more comfortably and is easier for the eyes to follow.

A comfortable line measure to start with is about 18 to 24 picas (let's work with picas—six to the inch—so we don't have to worry about fractions of inch). If you consider that a 8.5-inch wide page with one-inch margins has a single column measure of 39 picas, it's obvious we must add a second column to create a more reasonable text line. With two columns (and a one pica gutter between them) the line measure is reduced to 19 picas—right in the ball park. If we add a third column the measure would drop to a bit more than 12 picas (much too short). If the page is set with four columns the measure drops to a paultry 9 picas (half the length of the line should be for comfortable reading at 10 or 11 points of type size). So, with an 8.5-by-11 page, the most comfortable layout is a two-column format.

A tabloid page size (11-by-17 inches) gives you more flexibility in the area of columns. For example, with one-inch margins, the 11-inch width of the page equals 55.5 picas. Split with two columns (and a one-pica gutter), the line measure is reduced to a little more than 27 picas, a more manageable measure. If you add a third column the measure drops down to about 18 picas, a very comfortable line length. So you can readily see that there is really no place for pages of four and five (or more) columns. Stick with a decent line measure and don't worry about how many columns that equals.

Handling Graphics within Columns

Once you have determined your line measure for the document and thus how many columns you need, it's time to think about what graphics you want to use, and where to position them on the page. Graphics can include not only clip art and scanned photographs, but also boxes, dingbats, and other artistic elements that break up the monotony of the page. Use graphics in mod-eration, especially lines, boxes, shading, bullets, and other dingbats. A small amount added judiciously to the page gives a strong professional touch. Add too many and your pages take on the look of a high school class project.

When sizing and positioning graphics within your columns, keep in mind that wherever possible the graphics should be at least one column wide. If the graphic cuts partially into a column, it is a *runaround* (the text must run around the graphic). Figure 4.8 shows the results of a thin run-around—the line measure is so narrow that there is not enough room to properly space the text, resulting in wide gaps of space between words.

Figure 4.8   *Text that runs around the graphic is too narrow for proper word spacing.*

right now and you may not realize it. Perhaps you use your Windows word processor for merely office correspondence, your spreadsheet just for simple financial calculations, or a Windows database to store names andaddresses. However, any of those programs, and most otherapplications contain a powerful variety of tools that let you turn mere words and numbers into dynamic documents that sell, communication, train, persuade (and make you look good!).

Scratch almost any Windows application and you'll find desktop publishing capabilities. Most allow you the freedom of selecting a size and style of font (even the lowly Cardfile lets you create custom headers and foot-

with their own commands, or by cutting and pasting a graphic from another program, or linking the graphic using Object Linking and Embedding). And, since Windows controls the printer, you can print almost any document to a PostScript laser printer and get realistic looking fonts (Chapter 5 explains how to print fonts in virtually any size to just about any printer). So, before you rush out and buy a specialized page composition program, let's first look at what you probably already have running in Windows: word processors, like WordPerfect for Windows or Microsoft Word for Windows, spreadsheets like Microsoft Excel, and drawing programs like Microsoft PaintBrush and Micrografx Draw. Then we'll look at a price range of composition programs, including Microsoft Publisher, PFS Publish, Aldus

To cure the runaround and the poor spacing in Figure 4.8, move the graphic to completely fill the width of the column. If it is too wide for the single column, have it intrude as little as possible into an adjacent column. Figures 4.9 and 4.10 show some examples of good and bad graphic positions.

Figure 4.9   *A number of graphics positioned to prevent thin runarounds.*

You can begin publishing your own documents right now and you may not realize it. Perhaps you use your Windows word processor for merely office correspondence, your spreadsheet just for simple financial calculations, or a Windows database to store names andaddresses. However, any of those programs, and most otherapplications contain a powerful variety of tools that let you turn mere words and numbers into dynamic documents that sell, communication, train, persuade (and make you look good!).

Scratch almost any Windows application and you'll find desktop publishing capabilities. Most allow you the freedom of selecting a

own commands, or by cutting and pasting a graphic from another program, or linking the graphic using Object Linking and Embedding). And, since Windows controls the printer, you can print almost any document to a PostScript laser printer and get realistic looking fonts (Chapter 5 explains how to print fonts in virtually any size to just about any printer). So, before you rush out and buy a specialized page composition program, let's first look at what you proba-

size and style of font (even the lowly Cardfile lets you create custom headers and footers). Most have the ability to add graphics (either with their

bly already have running in Windows: word processors, like WordPerfect for Windows or

Figure 4.10 *A more amateurish treatment with poor results.*

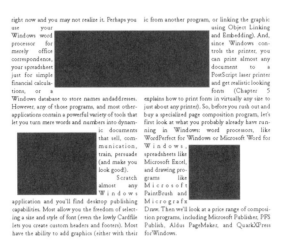

My advice concerning runarounds is to keep them to a minimum. Where possible, resize graphics so they occupy the full width of one or more columns, making them less intrusive to the reader's attention. One further problem with runarounds is that they increase the risk of a heading or sub-heading falling in the narrow area of the runaround line measure. Now you have to worry about the word spacing of the text, as well as how to fit a heading in larger type into the narrower measure. When you keep graphics the full width of the columns, you eliminate the problem of a narrow heading, as shown below.

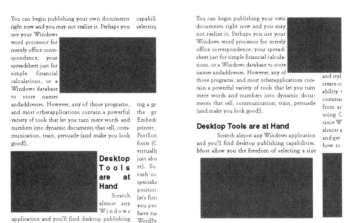

Adding Pull Quotes to Tease the Reader

When you get right down to it, much of what a good design does is to tease the reader, entice the reader, and try to get the reader to read further. One attractive way to do this in a full page of text is by using a *pull quote*. A pull quote is a sentence, or part of a sentence, taken from the columns of text on the page, that is enlarged and treated as a graphic. As readers glance at the page, the pull quote (which should be something witty, controversial, or inflammatory) gets their curiosity up and they continue reading to find out what was meant by the statement in the quote. Pull quotes (again, when not overdone) can add pizazz and a professional touch to the page.

To create a pull quote, first find a quote, copy it, and insert it into a suitable position in a column, or run it across two columns, as shown in Figure 4.11. Increase the size of the type in the pull quote to a size that is readable at arm's length, about 18 to 30 points. Play with the size to get the depth you like best (the larger the type, the taller it will be in relation to the surrounding columns).

Figure 4.11   A single column and a two-column pull quote.

now and you may not realize it. Perhaps you use your Windows word processor for merely office correspondence, your spreadsheet just for simple financial calculations, or a Windows database to store names and addresses. However, any of those programs, and most other applications contain a powerful variety of tools that let you turn mere words and numbers into dynamic documents that sell, communicate, train, persuade (and make you look good!).

Scratch almost any Windows application and you'll find desktop publishing capabilities. Most allow you the freedom of selecting a size and style of font (even the lowly Cardfile lets you create custom headers and footers). Most have the ability to add graphics (either with their own commands, or by cutting and pasting a graphic from another program, or linking the graphic using Object Linking and Embedding). And, since Windows controls the printer, you can print almost any document to a

In computer years, WordPerfect has been around forever

(Chapter 5 explains how to print fonts in virtually any size to just about any printer). So, before you rush out and buy a specialized page composition program, let's first look at what you probably already have running in Windows—word processors, like WordPerfect for Windows or Microsoft Word for Windows, spreadsheets like Microsoft Excel, and drawing programs like Microsoft PaintBrush and Micrografx Draw. Then we'll look at a price range of composition programs, including Microsoft Publisher, PFS Publish, Aldus PageMaker, and QuarkXPress for Windows.

Word processors have one distinct advantage over dedicated page composition software: they manage the creation of words better than just about anything else. While programs like PageMaker and QuarkXPress offer search and replace, and spell

mar and thesaurus functions of high-powered word processors. Likewise, developing the text for long documents, a difficult task at best, is often faster with a good word processor. A word processor's weak suit is its lack of easy integration of text and graphics.

That's where a page composition program, like PageMaker, shines. Windows has made all software easier to use—word processors have undoubtedly benefitted the most from Windows' graphical user interface. What seemed clumsy and awkward with a DOS word processor seems easy and natural using the Windows version of the same product. Adding any level of graphics with a DOS word processor was shooting in the dark; it was pure chance if you got what you wanted. With Windows word processors you work with a realistic, accurate image of the page.

In computer years, WordPerfect has been

Word processors have one distinct advantage over dedicated page composition software: they manage the creation of words better than just about anything

There are any number of ways to dress up a pull quote. The easiest (and most mundane) is to box it. I personally like adding one or more lines above and below, and putting quotation marks (try exaggerated dingbat-type quotation marks) around the pull quote. Some examples of dressing a pull quote are shown below.

uments right now and you may not realize it. Perhaps you use your Windows word processor for merely office correspondence, your spreadsheet just for simple financial calculations, or a Windows

> You can begin
> publishing your
> own documents
> right now!

database to store names and addresses. However, any of those programs, and most other applications contain a powerful variety of tools that let you turn mere words and numbers into dynamic documents that sell, communication, train, persuade (and make you look good!).

Scratch almost any Windows application and you'll find desktop publishing capabilities. Most allow you the freedom of selecting a size and style of font (even the lowly Cardfile lets you create custom headers and footers). Most

with their own commands, or by cutting and pasting a graphic from another pro-

> You can begin
> publishing your own
> documents right
> now!

gram, or linking the graphic using Object Linking and Embedding). And, since Windows controls the printer, you

> **"You can begin
> publishing your own
> documents right
> now!"**

can print almost any document to a PostScript laser printer and get realistic

print fonts in virtually any size to just about any printer). So, before you rush out and buy a specialized page composition program, let's first look at what you probably already have running in

> You can begin
> publishing your
> own documents
> right now!

Windows—word processors, like WordPerfect for Windows or Microsoft Word for Windows, spreadsheets like Microsoft Excel, and drawing programs like Microsoft PaintBrush and Micrografx Draw. Then we'll look at a price range of composition programs, including Microsoft Publisher, PFS Publish, Aldus PageMaker, and QuarkXPress for Windows.

Word processors have one distinct advantage over dedicated page com-

IMPROVING THE LOOK OF YOUR PAGES

English, and much of the world's languages, is read from left to right, from the top of the page to the bottom. It is little wonder that we tend to observe a page diagonally from the upper left-hand corner down to the lower right-hand corner. And we tend to reserve the upper left quadrant for information of higher importance. Since our eyes are accustomed to starting on the left side of the page, it is generally accepted that headlines should begin flush left, rather than centered or flush right. The left alignment of heads, just as with text, is a natural part of reading. The left side of the page will carry slightly more importance in the matter of stories and graphics than the right side. As you decide where stories and pictures will be placed on the page, keep in mind our subjective affinity for the left side.

Have you ever glanced at a publication and immediately noticed a professional touch that makes it stand out? Have you seen newsletters or brochures that for some reason you just can't put your finger on, seemed slightly amateurish? The difference between an impressive publication and one that turns readers off is a fine, but significant line. It is often not the words, not the graphics, not the design that looks unappealing, but some combination of all three. Let's look at easy ways of dressing up any document, and adding that professional touch that is instantly recognizable.

Select and Use Attractive Fonts

The fonts (or typefaces) you select to use in your document have a direct bearing on how professional your will page look. The typography of the page is the mortar that holds the page together. Up close, the words themselves must be legible and attractive, but even at arms length the fonts contribute to the overall contrast of black and white—text and paper. Too much contrast (type that is too heavy for a given size, or is too tightly spaced) gives a stark, slightly ominous look to the page. The IRS 1040 instruction booklet is the best example I can think of for a high-contrast page, and who wants to read that! We address the subject of fonts and typography in the next chapter, but let's take a brief look at some ways of dressing up your pages with the typefaces you choose.

Learn more about...

Getting the most out of your fonts	See Chapter 5, "Different Strokes for Different Folks."

- **Don't borrow your neighbor's fonts.** Use only professional-quality fonts—either Adobe Type 1 fonts or TrueType fonts—from a reputable vendor. Don't be attracted to the ads that offer 2,500 fonts for $49. In all likelihood you don't need a lot of fonts, just a few beauties. Fonts from Agfa, Monotype, Microsoft, Adobe, and other high-end type suppliers insure that you are using type that will reproduce with grace and style.

- **Choose a typeface for body and heads and stick with them.** You will often see documents with an inordinate number of fonts—each story is set in a different font; heads for each story are different as well. This is confusing to readers who subconsciously note that body text is in a certain font, heads in another, and expect to see those same fonts on all the pages of the publication. We are used to seeing this consistency and we naturally segregate editorial words from advertising words by the typeface. It would be as if each chapter of this book were set in a different typeface; readers would find it most confusing. Look through any nationally-sold magazine and you see they have one family of typefaces for all editorial words (and those typefaces probably aren't allowed to be used by advertisers so that ads are well-defined and separated from editorial copy).

- **Choose a thin, delicate serif typeface for text.** If you are producing the final pages on a 300 dpi laser printer, this is important. Lower-resolution laser printers tend to add more beef to all typeface characters in smaller sizes (to help make up for their lower-resolution image of the typeface), so start with the most delicate typeface you can find. If you are producing your final pages on a high-resolution imagesetter, the significantly higher resolution brings out the true, delicate beauty of the typeface. Palatino, which is a resident font on most PostScript laser printers, is a lovely, delicate design—a much better choice than using Times Roman, which is downright fat in comparison:

> This is 12-point Times Roman: the most commonly used font since the invention of the PostScript laser printer. There's nothing wrong with Times other than the fact that it is seen so frequently in laser-printed
>
> This is 12-point Palatino, a font with similar serifs to Times, yet a more attractive typeface for body copy in relatively small sizes. Palatino is also resident on most PostScript laser print-

- **Typefaces with serifs are preferred for body copy.** The serifs, the added strokes at the tops and bottoms of the letterforms, actually help lead the eye from word to word. An example of the difference between serif and sans serif body copy is shown below.

> An excellent example of a serif text is Adobe Garamond. Note the fine finishing strokes, which help lead the eye from one letter to the next.
>
> Adobe's Gill Sans is a classic example of a sans serif face. Very modern looking, it is generally used in headings, captions or callouts in illustrations.

- **Speaking of Times Roman, stay away from it.** Because it is resident on virtually all PostScript laser printers, it is by far the most used font in the world. Times Roman is all right for memos and business letters if you must use it, but keep it out of more important publications.

♦ **Choose an extra bold, condensed sans serif font for headings.** The rich compressed boldness of the letters means that you can get away with a smaller size for heads and subheads; and that means you can get more words on a line. The condensed or compressed font keeps more of your headings from going to a second line, giving you more room for body text and graphics. Sans serif (meaning literally *without serifs*) typefaces for headings are a natural counterpoint to serif-style body copy. The larger, bolder styles of headings and subheadings are easily read and visually exciting from a distance. The difference between simply bolding a serif font and using a bold, compressed sans serif font is clearly evident in Figure 4.12.

Figure 4.12   *The font on the left is not nearly as readable (nor attractive) as the font on the right.*

Headings should grab your attention

The heading above is Adobe Garamond set in 18 points and bolded. While it is an attractive typeface to admire, it doesn't hit you over the head they way a headline should (why do you think they're called *heads*...just kidding).

Headings should grab your attention

Now this headline tells you it's coming! While it is smaller than the Garamond example (only 14 points), it is Gill Sans Ultra Bold Condensed, designed specifically for use in headings and subheadings. This particular typeface is so heavy you could probably get away with the 12-point size in a subheading.

The Right Way to Use Captions, Bylines, and Photo Credits

Captions, bylines, and *photo credits* are small, insignificant items compared with the monumental task of putting together a brochure, newsletter, proposal, or magazine, but when done right they can add a professional aura to the page. Captions are any explanation offered to a graphic, photo, or other illustration. In technical books, text books, and proposals, captions are usually numbered; in newsletters and magazines they normally aren't. Captions should offer a complete explanation of the illustration it is describing without needing the body copy to support the description. Captions should also be attention-getters since they are describing illustrations that hopefully will draw the reader's interest. Write them in the active voice, using action verbs and exciting adjectives.

A byline is the name of the story's author; the photo credit is the name of the photographer who took the picture used in your publication, or the name of the person or company granting permission to use the photograph. Often bylines begin with the words "Story by..." and photo credits say something like "Photo by..." or "Photo courtesy of...." Regardless of the wording you add to bylines and photo credits, keep the wording consistent throughout your publication. Here are some more suggestions for sprucing up captions, bylines, and photo credits.

- **Don't use a period following the figure number in a numbered caption.** Despite what many style manuals say, I believe you should not use a period after the figure number and before the figure caption. The period interrupts the flow of reading the caption. If you must add punctuation, use an em-dash or a colon following the number.

- **For numbered captions, differentiate between number and caption text.** Bold the figure number, show it in a different color, italicize the number or italicize the caption, but not both.

- **For side captions flush the side abutting the illustration.** If the caption is on the left side, make the caption either flush right or justified alignment. If the caption is on the right side of the illustration, the caption can be flush left or justified, like the example shown below:

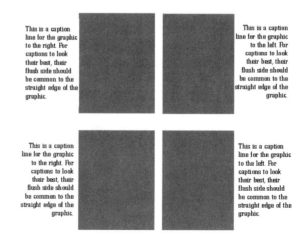

- **In magazines and newsletters, group the captions together.** Use arrows to orient each caption to its illustration. Grouping the captions lets you design a photo layout without having to leave an area next to each photo for its captions. Center the grouped captions and let the arrows show the reader which caption goes with which photo.

Left: Caption for the photo begins first since we naturally look at these photos in clockwise order.
Right: Caption for the right photo is next in order. If the Left, Right, Bottom titles are bolded, you needn't space between them.
Bottom: Is the last caption in order.

- **Format captions in a typeface and style different from the body copy.** For example, if the body copy is set in a serif typeface, set the captions in a sans serif face. If you want captions to also be serif, then make them italic, so that there is a distinct demarcation between caption text and body text.

- **Format captions in a slightly smaller type size than body copy.** For instance, if the body copy is set in 11 point type, choose 9 or 10 point type for the captions. The smaller size gives you more words in a given space, which you may need to create well thought-out captions.

- **Tables don't have captions, only photos and illustrations.** If you have a table in your publication, add the table number and the table title to the top of the table. Make the title descriptive enough to serve as a caption.

- **Be consistent in positioning bylines and photo credits.** Once readers see the first instance of either, they expect it in the same style and position from then on.

- **Some bylines are added after the end of the story.** I'm not crazy about this idea as I often find myself flipping to the end of the story to find out who wrote it. A better position for bylines is following the headline.

- **Set bylines in a complementary but different typeface than body copy.** Changing the font here is permissible because of the signature quality of the byline.

- **Set bylines in a type size smaller than the body copy that follows.** Keep the byline legible but unobtrusive.

- **Set photo credits very small.** Perhaps 6 or 7 point type in a bolded sans serif typeface is a good place to start. Sans serif type is easier to read than serif type in small sizes; bolding the type makes it even more readable.

- **Consider turning the photo credit on end.** Try running the credit up the left side of the photo or down the right side. I don't know the origin of this idea, but I like it.

Be Consistent

It's sometimes difficult to be consistent when putting together a publication. Readers (probably more than you) expect consistency and turn their inconsistency radar on your pages to try and catch a mistake. Readers are demanding masters we all serve. They expect a consistent look to all the pages of a publication: page numbering exactly the same, rules marking margins or column gutters to be the same, ads to be separated from editorial copy in a consistent manner. Worse yet, they expect that subsequent issues of magazines, newsletters, and newspapers have the same look. It means that you, the designer, must make up your mind and stick to the decisions you reach. Here are some areas to be particularly careful:

- **For issue-oriented publications, don't change the format.** If you are publishing a newsletter, magazine, or newspaper, leave the format alone. If you must change it, give fair warning (why not do a story on the upcoming format change). A newsletter that changes format tells me they don't know what to do (and maybe they're not the authority they declare themselves to be). So save your credibility and leave the format alone.

- **Don't change the front cover design.** For periodicals, the front cover is a publication's unique signature. Change it very often and you risk losing your readership.

- **Keep sections of periodicals and chapters of publications and books consistent.** If you bolded certain words in one chapter, you better be darn sure you bold them in the next chapter. Everything should carry over from one section to the next, from one chapter to the next. To be successful, a publication needs to build a feeling of confidence with readers. Readers must be comfortable and know where they are in a publication.

- **Keep ads visually separate from editorial.** Readers should always know whether what they're reading is editorial copy written by the publication's staff or ad copy written by someone trying to sell something. If there are crossover areas, such as ads sharing the same graphic designs as editorial pages, or shared typefaces in both an ad and on an editorial page, chances are you lose your readers' attention, if not their subscriptions.

- **In marketing literature, stick with a family approach to design.** If you develop a theme in an ad, carry that same theme forward to brochures, fact sheets, cover letters, reply cards, trade show exhibits, sales seminars, overhead sales presentations, and anything else that represents your products. Hit the customer from all sides with not only the same sales message, but the same logos, color schemes, photographs, typography, and packaging and you have the best chance of making an impression (and a sale).

- **For your company stationery, create a design that can be consistently applied.** You want to apply the design to every piece of paper with the company's name on it, from letterhead, to envelopes, business cards, mailing labels, invoices, business forms, product packaging, and even the sign out front. Try designing and producing the business card first. It's usually the hardest because of its size, and if the design works on a business card it will work on anything larger.

I could go on and on with examples, but I hope you have gotten the point: that consistency is of paramount importance to communication, corporate and professional image, and the accurate comprehension of your message.

Tease Readers to Get Them Inside

It's relatively easy to get readers to scrutinize the front page of a newsletter, the front cover of a magazine, or the first few pages of a technical manual. But it's a universal truth that it takes the imagination of the designer and the curiosity of the readers for them to keep on reading. Often we can pull readers inside with an exciting front cover photograph, or a particularly good lead story. Here are some other ideas to whet interest:

- **Fill your front page with headlines and lead paragraphs to all your stories.** Then jump them all to inside pages. Add photos or graphics to the jump page and other inside pages to keep things interesting.

- **Create a front page column of story catchlines (or teaser lines) to pull readers inside.** Title it *Inside This Issue*, *Come Inside*, or some similar title, and spice up the catchlines to perk the reader's curiosity. Your front page might look like the examples shown below:

- **Use photos to pull the reader into your publication.** Position unusual photos (a la *National Enquirer*) and add page numbers to get the full story…Inquiring minds want to know.

- **For books, proposals, and more formal publications, use the Preface to explain what can be found inside.** Proposals can include an executive summary that cross references the larger proposal document. Technical manuals and books should have a formal table of contents showing at least first and second order headings. If you make the headings descriptive and interesting the table of contents pulls the reader in for a closer look. See "Making Heads and Subheads Pop" later in this chapter.

Using Alternative Text Alignments

There really is no right way to design a page as much as there are interesting and visually exciting ideas that attract and hold attention. Being different is certainly one way to grab the reader's interest. Certainly with newsletters (where you find so many bland lookalike issues), a design that departs from the norm can be a refreshing change. That difference can be as simple as using a sans serif typeface for body copy (very popular in Europe, but the idea never quite caught on in the U.S.) to changing the alignment of columns of body copy. For example, instead of the "normal" justified alignment of copy that we see all the time, arrange the copy flush left. Changing the alignment to flush left means that the spacing between words will be more even (since the spacing doesn't have to be adjusted to make each line justified on the right edge of the column). I think left-aligned columns look more natural and are easier to read, as shown in Figure 4.13.

Figure 4.13   *Left-aligned text in a column compared to justified text (notice the difference in word spacing).*

You can begin publishing your own documents right now and you may not realize it. Perhaps you use your Windows word processor for merely office correspondence, your spreadsheet just for simple financial calculations, or a Windows database to store names and addresses. However, any of those programs, and most other applications contain a powerful variety of tools that let you turn mere words and numbers into dynamic documents that sell, communication, train, persuade (and make you look good!).

Scratch almost any Windows application and you'll find desktop publishing capabilities. Most allow you the freedom of selecting a size and style of font (even the lowly Cardfile lets you create custom headers and footers). Most have the ability to add graphics (either with their own commands, or by cutting and pasting a graphic from another program, or linking the graphic using Object Linking and Embedding). And, since Windows controls the printer, you can print almost any

You can begin publishing your own documents right now and you may not realize it. Perhaps you use your Windows word processor for merely office correspondence, your spreadsheet just for simple financial calculations, or a Windows database to store names and addresses. However, any of those programs, and most other applications contain a powerful variety of tools that let you turn mere words and numbers into dynamic documents that sell, communication, train, persuade (and make you look good!).

Scratch almost any Windows application and you'll find desktop publishing capabilities. Most allow you the freedom of selecting a size and style of font (even the lowly Cardfile lets you create custom headers and footers). Most have the ability to add graphics (either with their own commands, or by cutting and pasting a graphic from another program, or linking the graphic using Object Linking and Embedding). And, since Windows controls

Using a mix of the two alignments is perfectly acceptable as long as there is some reason shown to the reader. For example, you might have all your columns left-aligned, but choose justified alignment for sidebars that are highlighted in a shaded box. Or, if you have a regular feature, like a new products feature or celebrity interview, you might change the text alignment to make it stand out.

Since text in most books is in a one-column format, the opened, two-page spread of the pages is more symmetrical if text is justified. However, you can add a refreshing touch by making numbered or bulleted lists in the columns left-aligned. It helps the list stand out from the body copy and adds a nice finishing touch to the page, like the example shown in Figure 4.14.

Figure 4.14   *The book's body text is justified, but the numbered list is indented and made flush left to visually separate it from the surrounding paragraphs.*

Properly adjusted standing rigging has the highest impact on the sailboat's balance and speed. Yet tuning the rig is probably the most overlooked maintenance item on your boat. Contrary to popular belief wire shrouds do stretch and need to be checked regularly. Here are some techniques to use:

1. Check the vertical alignment using a measuring tape from the center of the mast.
2. Adjust the main shrouds while sailing.
3. The leeward shroud should not be slack.
4. Sight the mast while underway and check for mast tip bend.

It may take a number of tuning sessions before you achieve the balance of rigging tautness to sailing performance that you want. Remember that over-tight rigging is not only hard on the mast, but strains the chainplates, swagged or mechanical fittings and in extreme cases can bend the hull.

Other areas in books that can handle an alignment change might be:

- *Chapter introductions.* Falling on the first page of a chapter, there is no matching left-hand page to interfere with the balance of the two-page spread.

- *Chapter summaries,* since they are on the last page of a chapter.

- *Notes, cautions, warnings, or tips* that are boxed or otherwise separated on the page.

Tricks to Help Readability

Help the reader's ability to comfortably absorb the page and you gain a loyal, interested audience. When readers struggle with the mechanics of the page (such as the line measure being too long or short, difficult-to-read typefaces, too little or too much letter or word spacing) it's hard for them to enjoy the words and pictures. Let's look at some ways to help the reader.

- **Use unequal width columns.** You can create an exciting page design and get the proper line measure you need for a narrow page. Position lead stories in the wide column if you're designing a newsletter or magazine, and use the narrow column for graphics that relate to the story, photos, or sidebars. On the front page of a newsletter, the narrow column can hold an insider table of contents (or a "What's Inside" graphic), a calendar of coming events, a notice of the next meeting place, or a list of club officers and titles.

- **Use margin notes in the narrow column.** You can add at-a-glance information that summarizes the longer paragraph in the text column. Margin notes are a great way to give the reader a quick overview of the page, but you really need more room than just the left or right margin. Create two unequal width columns and put the notes in the narrow column.

- **Be careful of tombstones, ladders, and other obstacles.** They will compete for visual attention on the page. When two or more photos or graphics are aligned across from one another in a multi-column page, the photos are *tombstoned,* like the example on the next page.

♦ **Be careful using heads that are tombstoned.** When you have headings or headlines that are the same size adjacent to each other, the heads are tombstoned like this:

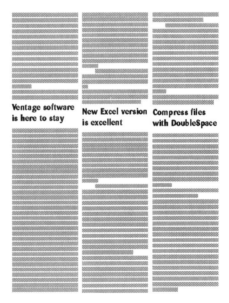

+ **Watch out for ladders.** A *ladder* is two or more lines of text containing a stack of one or more words in exactly the same place in a column of text. Some ladders aren't noticeable, while others stand out like a sore thumb. If a ladder is noticeable to you, the designer, you can be sure the reader will notice it. Ladders are eliminated by editing a word preceding the stack which then changes the order of words in the column. There are also ladders of hyphens created when two or more words in a row are hyphenated at the end of the line. Opinions differ as to whether two hyphens are considered a ladder or whether three or more become offensive. Many page composition programs allow you to control the number of acceptable hyphens in a row.

+ **Use jump pages to concentrate more stories on your front page.** A jump page contains continuations of stories from previous pages in the publication. Jumping a story means you don't have to fit the whole thing on a single page, giving you room to add other stories to the page. More stories mean a variety of headlines and graphics that make the page more interesting and inviting. Sometimes all stories are jumped to a single page, which is handy for the reader who always knows where to look for the continuation of stories. However, jumping stories to inside pages wherever they fit is a nice way of closing up small gaps in your page layout where nothing else seems to fit.

Remember White Space

White space (the lack of anything but the color of the paper) is a design element, the same as color, text, graphics, or anything else you can have on the page. White space is probably the single most important element. It is relief from the dark masses of ink that crowd the page and vie for your attention. White space is the balance that every line of type needs to rest comfortably and attractively on the page. White space visually tells the reader this is a restful place to be, that's easy on the eyes. White space is the counter-balance to powerful graphics and an imposing visual force if used correctly.

Learn more about...

Handling typographic spacing   See Chapter 5, "Understanding Horizontal and Vertical Spacing."

White space is absolutely essential for clean, clear typography. As you'll learn in the next chapter, there are a number of ways to add typographic space—between the letters in words, between the words in lines of text, and between the lines of text on the page. Yet, it is just as important to consider other types of space:

- The space between paragraphs.
- The space between columns (gutters).
- The space between text and the edges of the page (margins).
- The space between the edges of graphics and the edges of columns of text (text standoff).

Make any of these spaces too tight and the page can become overly concentrated. While each of these spaces takes up little room, together they can do much to open up the page and significantly improve the overall look of your document. Let's look at some ways of adding space.

- **Gutters** should be wide enough to show a clear break between columns of text. Gutters that are too narrow fail to notify readers of the normal end to the line; the eye tends to skip across the narrow gutter and continue reading. Narrow gutters are a sure sign of squeezing more words on the page (and a sign to readers that this is a tough page to wade through). The example shows the marked difference between narrow and wide gutters.

own documents right now and you may not realize it. Perhaps you use your Windows word processor for merely office correspondence, your spreadsheet just for simple financial calculations, or a Windows database to store names and addresses. However, any of those programs, and most other applications contain a powerful variety of tools that let you turn mere words and numbers into dynamic documents that sell, communication, train, persuade (and make you look good!).

Scratch almost any Windows application and you'll find desktop publishing capabilities. Most allow you the freedom of selecting a size and style of font (even the lowly Cardfile lets you create custom headers and footers). Most have the ability to add

lowly Cardfile lets you create custom headers and footers). Most have the ability to add graphics (either with their own commands, or by cutting and pasting a graphic from another program, or linking the graphic using Object Linking and Embedding). And, since Windows controls the printer, you can print almost any document to a PostScript laser printer and get realistic looking fonts (Chapter 5 explains how to print fonts in virtually any size to just about any printer). So, before you rush out and buy a specialized page composition program, let's first look at what you probably already have running in Windows—word processors, like WordPerfect for Windows or Microsoft

how to use it. WordPerfect is the best selling word processor of all time, and the single most popular application in the world. There are versions of WordPerfect that run on PC's, DEC and Data Generala nd IBM minicomputers; there's even an IBM mainframe version. The non-windows versions all look alike, all operate the same way (version 5.1 for DOS is shown in Figure 2.1 below). It's little wonder that WordPerfect can be found just about everywhere, used as a business tool to generate office correspondence. And, until the Windows version of WordPerfect, office correspondence, reports and other text documents were what WordPerfect was best at.

Although the DOS version of WordPerfect touted some cryptic desktop publishing features, to actually use them in a document, with any kind of precise formatting, was as act of extreme patience and faith. If you tried to add more than one or twofonts to a document, for example, you were flying blind, with no real idea of what the finished piece would look like until it was printed. Similarly, while you were supposed to be able to add graphic boxes on a page, WordPerfect wouldn't actually show you what were in the boxes—again, you were

too narrow   *much better*

You can get away with narrower gutters if you add a vertical rule down the center of the gutter. If you use a rule, make it as thin a hairline as possible. Hairlines in page composition software are generally one quarter of a point wide, which is about the thinnest line a 300 dpi laser printer can reproduce. You can also reduce the effect of a thin, ruled gutter by increasing the leading of the paragraphs on each side of the gutter, like these before and after examples.

own documents right now and you may not realize it. Perhaps you use your Windows word processor for merely office correspondence, your spreadsheet just for simple financial calculations, or a Windows database to store names and addresses. However, any of those programs, and most other applications contain a powerful variety of tools that let you turn mere words and numbers into dynamic documents that sell, communication, train, persuade (and make you look good!). Scratch almost any Windows application and you'll find desktop publishing capabilities. Most allow you the freedom of selecting a size and style of font (even the lowly Cardfile lets you create custom headers and footers). Most have the ability to add

lowly Cardfile lets you create custom headers and footers). Most have the ability to add graphics (either with their own commands, or by cutting and pasting a graphic from another program, or linking the graphic using Object Linking and Embedding). And, since Windows controls the printer, you can print almost any document to a PostScript laser printer and get realistic looking fonts (Chapter 5 explains how to print fonts in virtually any size to just about any printer). So, before you rush out and buy a specialized page composition program, let's first look at what you probably already have running in Windows—word processors, like WordPerfect for Windows or Microsoft

own documents right now and you may not realize it. Perhaps you use your Windows word processor for merely office correspondence, your spreadsheet just for simple financial calculations, or a Windows database to store names and addresses. However, any of those programs, and most other applications contain a powerful variety of tools that let you turn mere words and numbers into dynamic documents that sell, communication, train, persuade (and make you look good!). Scratch almost any Windows application and you'll find desktop publishing capabilities. Most allow you the freedom

lowly Cardfile lets you create custom headers and footers). Most have the ability to add graphics (either with their own commands, or by cutting and pasting a graphic from another program, or linking the graphic using Object Linking and Embedding). And, since Windows controls the printer, you can print almost any document to a PostScript laser printer and get realistic looking fonts (Chapter 5 explains how to print fonts in virtually any size to just about any printer). So, before you rush out and buy a specialized page composition program, let's first look at what

- ◆ **Margins** can be skimpy if you are generous with white space elsewhere on the page. However, the combination of narrow margins, tight typographic space, and heavy graphics screams *TOO MUCH* for most readers. Adding wider margins is an easy way of introducing white space without necessarily affecting space elsewhere. It is also not necessary for top, bottom, and side margins to be the same dimensions. Offset margins are one of those little touches that can separate your design from the typewriter pages of bland newsletters. In magazines and book production, you must take into account the inside bend of opened pages. The thicker the document, the wider the inside margin should be to accommodate the binding.

- ◆ **Text standoff** should be ample to comfortably separate the graphics from the text column. Again, there is no reason to squeeze text right up against graphics and photos, it just adds a level of clutter and interference to the overall look of the page. An example of this appears on the next page.

base to store names and addresses. However, any of those programs, and most other applications contain a powerful variety of tools that let you turn mere words and numbers into dynamic documents that sell, communication, train, persuade (and make you look good!).

Scratch almost any Windows application and you'll find desktop publishing capabilities. Most allow you the freedom of selecting a size and style of font (even the lowly Cardfile lets you create custom headers and footers). Most have the ability to add graphics (either with their own commands, or by cutting and pasting a graphic from another program, or linking the graphic using Object

they lag behind the spelling, grammar and thesaurus functions of high-powered word processors. Likewise, developing the text for long documents, a difficult task at best, is often faster with a good word processor. A word processor's weak suit is its lack of easy integration of text and graphics.

That's where a page composition program, like PageMaker, shines. Windows has made all software easier to use—word processors have undoubtedly benefitted the most from Windows' graphical user interface. What seemed clumsy and awkward with a DOS wordprocessor seems easy and natural using the Windows version of the same product. Adding any level of graphics with a DOS word processor was shooting in the dark; it was pure chance if you got what you wanted. With Windows word processors you work with a realistic, accurate image of the page.

In computer years, WordPerfect has been around forever. It has been my principal word processor for the

too narrow   *much better*

- **Allow white space for photos** of people to look into. If you use a photo of someone looking to one side, offset white space to the side that they're looking. By the same token, a photo of a car driving needs space to drive into, or a boat needs room to sail into.

- **Headlines and headings** need room at the top. Strong, bold headlines and heads need some breathing space. The space is more important visually above the head than below. Allow for one-third space below, give the head two-thirds space above.

You can begin publishing your own documents right now and you may not realize it. Perhaps you use your Windows word processor for merely office correspondence, your spreadsheet just for simple financial calculations, or a Windows database to store names and addresses. However, any of those programs, and most other applications contain a powerful variety of tools that let you turn mere words and numbers into dynamic documents that sell, communication, train, persuade (and make you look good!).

This Head is too tight

Scratch almost any Windows application and you'll find desktop publishing capabilities. Most allow you the freedom of selecting a size and style of font (even the lowly Cardfile lets you create custom headers and footers). Most have the ability to add graphics (either with their own commands, or by cutting and pasting a graphic from another program, or linking the graphic using Object Linking and Embedding). And, since Windows controls the printer, you can print almost any document to a PostScript laser printer and get realistic looking fonts (Chapter 5 explains how to print fonts in virtually any size to just about any printer). So, before you rush out and buy a specialized page composition program, let's first look at what you probably already have running in Windows—word processors, like

Word processors have one distinct advantage over dedicated page composition software: they manage the creation of words better than just about anything else.

This head is too loose

While programs like PageMaker and QuarkXPress offer search and replace, and spell checking features, they lag behind the spelling, grammar and thesaurus functions of high-powered word processors. Likewise, developing the text for long documents, a difficult task at best, is often faster with a good word processor. A word processor's weak suit is its lack of easy integration of text and graphics.

This head is just right

That's where a page composition program, like PageMaker, shines. Windows has made all software easier to use—word processors have undoubtedly benefitted the most from Windows' graphical user

Making Heads and Subheads Pop

Headings in a book, manual or proposal act as the readers' road map. They establish the hierarchial structure of the text, letting the reader know the importance of what is being read in relation to what has been read and what is going to be read. Headings, when handled properly, always answer the reader's question, "Where am I, and where are these words leading?" Headings and subheadings may seem small and unimportant, but they are a vital guide through the chapters. Here are a few ideas to keep in mind:

- Where is this subhead taking me? Have you ever been reading along only to come across a heading that seemed out of place, not part of the rhythm of the chapter? It's likely the head or subhead is out of synch with the hierarchy of the other headings in the chapter. Headings are simply an abbreviated outline and should stick to the same rules as any good outline.

- Who does this subhead belong to? Glance at a page of text and headings. You should instantly discern which heads and subheads belong to which paragraphs. If you can't tell where the heads belong it's because there's not enough space above the head and maybe too much space below. As noted earlier in this chapter, devote two-thirds of the space above the head and one-third below. Rather than pressing the Return key to add space above and below the head, most page composition programs (and some word processors) allow you to automatically add a designated amount of space above and below headings. (Chapter 7 explains how to create a headline style to do all the formatting of heads and subheads automatically.)

- Establish an obvious pattern of formatting to display the heading hierarchy. If you are working with three levels of heads, the first-level heads should be larger or bolder than the second-level subheads that follow. The second-level subheads should be larger and bolder than the third-level heads, and so forth. If the division between the ranks of heads is obvious, readers absorb the hierarchy without realizing they're doing so.

- Create interesting, descriptive headings. These literally advertise the paragraphs that follow, so make them interesting. Use action verbs and the active voice. Keep them simple and descriptive of what follows, don't make the reader dig into the paragraph to figure it out.

- Avoid cute headings. They may get a chuckle from you but publishing stays around for a long time and what's cute or hip today (are things still hip?) may not be so in a few years.

CHAPTER SUMMARY

There is an ageless Zen story that goes something like this:

A Zen master was sitting with a student one day, talking about Zen things, when the student (an unsui, *or priest-trainee) asks the master (called the* roshi) *how he acquired his incredibly deep understanding of Zen. The* roshi *answers that after studying Zen for a lifetime, he was walking through the garden one night when he banged his shin on a rock, and at the same moment attained complete enlightenment. The* unsui *is in awe of the master's reply, and that night heads for the garden in search of a rock...*

I love telling that story, but there is also much in it that applies to this chapter. For one thing, don't wait for the perfect design to fall out of the sky (or knock you on the shin). Designs happen mostly through gray-matter percolation and desktop experimentation, spiced with a good dose of "we need it yesterday." Also, simply copying a design you've seen and liked doesn't necessarily do anything for you or your document. Like the *unsui* searching for the 'rock of knowledge,' you too will miss the point if you don't see the why of designs—why they work (and don't work), why you are drawn to them, why certain fonts and colors are used, and so forth. Studying graphic design, like studying Zen, is a lifetime of exploration. Finally, it's easy with today's powerful computer hardware and software to take for granted the simple act of design, while thinking if you could just get faster equipment, or more fonts, or a better laser printer your designs would somehow improve. Don't be like the *unsui* who looks for instant enlightenment in a banged shin—don't look to PageMaker for the inspiration that comes only from experience and trial and error.

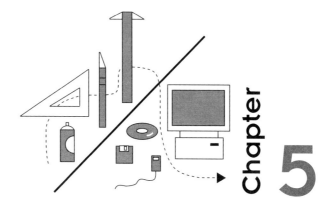

Chapter 5

Typography: Working with Fonts

Long ago, our prehistoric ancestors used charred sticks to draw symbolic stories on the walls of their caves. Though they lacked an alphabet and a written language, depictions of geese, deer, and rabbits told of good hunting; fire and family symbols revealed the tranquility of the home cave. While archaeologists may not bear me out, I suspect some cave artists were more skillful than others, creating images that exactly captured the mood of a story. Other cave dwellers would copy the work of these artists to draw similar symbols on their own cave walls. After a while, Nagoo the cave artist became known for his exacting hand at rendering forest animals. Others called the drawings *Nagoo Fine*, because they were fine drawings. Thus was born the first prehistoric type developed by the very first type designer. While it may be a stretch to construct the history of type before the invention of the alphabet, some of our most admired typefaces came from similar, humble beginnings.

Even if you know nothing about typography (you will by the end of this chapter), the business of type is so embedded in our lives that the names of some earlier pioneers of type design may still be familiar. Claude Garamond, Christphe Plantin, William Caslon, and John Baskerville, were all printers who developed uniquely designed typefaces bearing their names hundreds of years ago. (The Garamond typeface was created more than 450 years ago and is still considered one of the most beautiful text fonts.) I have Adobe Garamond, Monotype Plantin, Adobe Caslon Expert, and Berthold Baskerville fonts in my Windows computer and use them daily—as they've been used in one form or another for the last several centuries!

What is Typography?

Typography is the art of dressing up the words we read in ways that add to the communicative power of the message. Typography is an extra dimension that can significantly improve printed material. Typography is the chief ingredient in any successful page design. With it, you can create depth, color, texture, proportion, and scale. Yet, typography is so fundamentally important to printed language that you can elicit emotions and memories from your words; or endow them with movement, energy, and creative force.

Types of Type

There are thousands of different typeface designs that are available for use in your Windows computer. Regardless of which typefaces you use, they break down into two major formats: Type 1-compatible or TrueType-compatible. *Type 1* is the worldwide standard for printing type on PostScript printers and imagesetters. The standard was developed by Adobe Systems, the inventors of PostScript. The standard means typeface used in your computer and printed with your laser printer is exactly the same as an identically-named font used in any other system (regardless of whether it is a Macintosh, Windows, or OS/2 computer). *TrueType* is a standard developed jointly by Apple Computer and Microsoft. It works the same in Windows and Macintosh computers, and can be printed on both PostScript printers and TrueImage-compatible printers. Many type manufacturers (called *foundries*) offer the exact same typefaces in either Type 1 or TrueType formats, meaning you can get the best of both worlds.

Many Type 1 and TrueType fonts are newly designed originals; many are variations of old, established originals—like Garamond—produced by a number of different type foundries, like Adobe, Agfa, Berthold, International Typeface Corporation, Linotype-Hell, Monotype, Morisawa, and others. So you might see Adobe Garamond, or Berthold Garamond, or even ITC Garamond. Each is a slightly different font, and each can be used in documents you design and produce. Fonts or typefaces (the two terms are used synonymously in this book) are roughly categorized as headline styles, body text styles, script styles, and ornamental styles. Let's look at some stunning examples (although the examples are all Adobe Type 1 fonts, there are equally beautiful TrueType fonts as well).

Headline and Decorative Fonts

Headline typefaces are designed to be used in larger sizes, grab attention, and set a particular mood for the reader. They tend to be heavier in weight than comparably-sized fonts for body text. Decorative fonts are for those occasions when a more conservative typeface simply won't do. First let's look at some fonts heavy enough for rigorous headline work:

Figure 5.1   *Berthold's AG Old Face Outline (Adobe font 249).*

Figure 5.2   *Berthold's Barmeno Extra Bold (Adobe font 286).*

Figure 5.3 *Berthold's Colossalis Bold (Adobe font 259).*

Type ABCDEF efghijklm

Figure 5.4 *Berthold's Imago Extra Bold (Adobe font 217).*

Type ABCDEF efghijklm

Sometimes you may need a more compressed typeface. *Compressed*, or *condensed* fonts are squeezed together, allowing you to add more words to a given line measure at a given size. Here are some examples that work well in larger sizes:

Figure 5.5 *Linotype-Hell's Bodoni 2 Poster Compressed (Adobe font 118).*

Type ABCDEF efghijklm

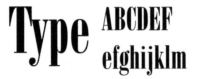

Figure 5.6 *Monotype's Runic Condensed (Adobe font 258).*

Type ABCDEF efghijklm

Figure 5.7 *Linotype-Hell's Helvetica Condensed Black (Adobe font 14).*

Type ABCDEF efghijklm

Figure 5.8 *Adobe's Mesquite (font 122) gives an Old West flare.*

TYPE ABCDEF EFGHIJKLM

Decorative fonts make a definitive statement, often recalling a special era or lifestyle (for example, many fonts can cast a strong 1940's or 50's look to your page , which may be a look you want for a particular publication). On the following page are some other decorative fonts that work well for the right circumstances:

Figure 5.9 *For a very formal, all-caps, chiselled look, try Monotype's Castellar (Adobe font 246).*

Figure 5.10 *Try Monotype's Goudy Text Lombardic (Adobe font 242) for an old English, or old European look.*

Figure 5.11 *For a hint of the Greek Isles (you can almost taste the feta cheese with this one), use Adobe's Lithos (font 121).*

Body Text Fonts

The only requirement for a successful body text font is that it should promote comfortable reading in relatively small sizes. In the U.S., we reserve *serif* styles for text (remember, serifs are the small, finishing strokes to the letters of the typeface). In Europe and elsewhere in the world, *sans serif* styles (fonts without serifs) are used often for body text with equally good results. Depending on the look you want to achieve, use your judgement as to serifs:

Figure 5.12 *A classic style found in many publications, Adobe's Garamond (font 100) is hard to beat for body text.*

Figure 5.13 *Compare Adobe Garamond with this: ITC's Garamond (Adobe font 9).*

Figure 5.14 *A slightly heavier typeface is Linotype-Hell's New Century Schoolbook (Adobe font 5).*

Figure 5.15 *A beautiful sans serif face, particularly adaptive for body text, is Linotype-Hell's Helvetica Light (Adobe font 13).*

Figure 5.16 *Probably the most classic compromise between serif and sans serif is Lino-type-Hell's Optima (Adobe font 6), which offers thick and thin letterforms to make up for a lack of serifs.*

Script Fonts

Script fonts can be very formal or very informal. Script fonts bring to mind the typeface of traditional wedding invitations, but an informal font can be used to add a personal touch to your message. Informal script fonts give a hand-written appearance to your words.

Figure 5.17 *The most classic script font is ITC's Zapf Chancery Medium Italic (Adobe font 3).*

There are many imitations, but Chancery is literally the original italic font. It was invented by an Italian printer named Aldus Mantius in the 16th century. He named his new script-like typeface Chancery, but it became commonly known as italic. Aldus published small, pocket-sized books and needed to make the books as thin as possible. Chancery was popular because it was compressed, adding more words to a given line measure, and making printing more economical.

Figure 5.18   *Linotype-Hell's Nuptial Script (Adobe font 110) is another classic typeface for invitations.*

Figure 5.19   *Some script fonts, like Monotype's Biffo (Adobe font 289) are as casual as the previous example is elegant.*

Ornamental and Symbol Fonts

Ornamental fonts contain icons or black and white drawings that have come to be known as *dingbats*. A dingbat in desktop publishing is just about anything other than a character, symbol, or number. Here are some examples:

Figure 5.20   *Adobe's Carta (font 35) gives you a number of useful symbols.*

Figure 5.21 *Adobe's Minion Expert Ornaments collection (font 144) has beautiful flourishes for you to use.*

Figure 5.22 *Adobe's Wood Type Ornaments (font 160) offers ornamental, old-time woodcuts.*

Figure 5.23 *ITC's Zapf Dingbats (Adobe font 3) is the original dingbat font, and is resident in most PostScript laser printers.*

There are many ornament and symbol fonts. A look through Adobe's catalog shows fonts for:

- Musical notes—Adobe's Sonata, font 21

- Greek and math symbols—Linotype-Hell's Universal Greek and Math Pi, font 78

- Playing cards and chess pieces—Linotype-Hell's Game Pi, font 240
- Recreation symbols—Linotype-Hell's Holiday Pi, font 237
- Fractions—Helvetica Fractions, font 234
- Astronomy symbols—Linotype-Hell's Astrology Pi, font 253.

Anatomy of Type

Regardless of the style and shape of a particular typeface, we can describe any type character by certain common characteristics. Let's look at the parts of a typeset character.

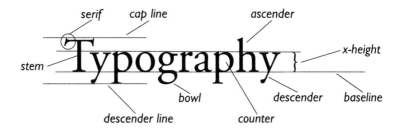

- **Baseline.** The all-important, invisible horizontal line on which type rests. If there were no baseline, the type would not line up across the page. The baseline helps the lines of type characters to align, just as the lines of a writing tablet help us write across the page.

- **X-height.** The height of the letters of a font less the height of ascenders and the depth of descenders. Different fonts have different x-heights, as shown in Figure 5.24 on the next page. The x-height determines the readability of the type in a given size. Fonts with a large x-height appear larger, are easier to read but require more space between the lines than fonts with a smaller x-height.

Figure 5.24 *ITC's Benguiat (Adobe font 11) on the left has a larger x-height (but is also heavier) than Monotype's Joanna (Adobe font 236).*

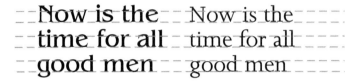

- By using the x-height of a particular font to your advantage you can achieve a specialized look. For instance, by using Benguiat (and adding more space between the lines to compensate for the larger x-height) you open up the type more than with a smaller x-height font, like Joanna:

Now is the time for all good men to come to the aid of their country. Now is the time for all good men to come to the aid of their country.

Now is the time for all good men to come to the aid of their country. Now is the time for all good men to come to the aid of their country.

- The larger x-height on the left makes the font appear larger than the font on the right. The x-height also affects the line length: the larger the x-height, the less characters fit in a given measure. As you can see in the example, the larger x-height of the left font creates a longer line length as well.

Now is the time for all good men to come to the aid of their country. Now is the time for all good men to come to the aid of their country.

Now is the time for all good men to come to the aid of their country. Now is the time for all good men to come to the aid of their country.

12.7 picas

10.6 picas

♦ So, you can see that the x-height of a given font, while a seemingly small detail, is actually very important to the overall effect the font presents in your document. It is one of the basic design questions you should address when you first consider the concept for a publication.

♦ **Ascenders.** Anything that sticks up above the x-height is an ascender (the stems of the *b, d, f, h, k, l, t*). In some fonts, the ascenders of some lowercase letters rise above the height of uppercase letters.

♦ **Descenders.** Anything that drops below the baseline is a descender (the legs of the *g, j, p, q, z*). The depth of the descenders varies with different fonts.

♦ **Cap line.** An invisible horizontal line (like the baseline) that marks the tops of capital letters in a given font. The cap line can indicate the extreme height of the characters in a line; however, in some fonts, lowercase ascenders rise above the cap line.

♦ **Descender line.** An invisible horizontal line that marks the extreme depth of all descenders in a given font.

♦ **Serif.** The finishing strokes of the letters. Serifs were originally created as chisel marks by Roman stone cutters (hence, the use of the term *roman*, as in Times Roman, to indicate one of a broad category of fonts with serifs). Serif type is considered more stately and traditional than sans serif type.

♦ **Stem.** The up-and-down vertical strokes of letters.

♦ **Bowl.** The round circles of letters (like *b, e, g, o, p, q*).

♦ **Counter.** The inside of the bowl. If you specify type too small (or too low a resolution), you risk filling up too much of the counter with ink, which makes the letters look like blobs.

Styles of Type

The word *style* is used a lot in this book to indicate many different things. There is the overall style of a page and there is high-class style that a certain design can have. There are styles that you can set up in page composition software that speed up the process of specifying type on the page. But here, the term style refers to different typestyles that you can use with just about any font. For example, the type you're reading now is the normal style for this font. It is how the designer intended it to be used. But with this font, and most fonts, you can choose the bold style instead of normal. You can also choose the italic style, or an underline style. The actual variations are shown below. In addition to these styles, many desktop publishing programs give you more style choices, such as outlines, or shadows dropped behind the letters.

Normal, **Bold**, *Italic*, ***Bold Italic***

Often, bold, italic, and bold/italic versions come with the basic font that you purchase; however, you may have to purchase these styles separately. If you only have the basic normal font you can still create the varying styles shown above, but it is only a computer interpretation of the bold or italic style, not the actual style itself.

Basic Typographic Rules

There are none. Oh, there are some do's and don'ts that I'll cover in a moment, but for the most part there really aren't any rules. It matters only what you, the designer, envision for the printed page. If the typography works (if the page attracts attention and promotes the responses you want) then whatever you did was the right thing. This is not a book that teaches typography and I have tried to keep from overly complicating the subject. For the purposes of this book, I'll cover what you need to know to use the fonts in your Windows computer effectively.

- ♦ **Make use of size and weight.** There is nothing worse than a dinky little headline, trying to be noticed but afraid to state fact or opinion. Headlines are like road signs, they've got to be noticed quickly and attract your attention. For instance, which looks better to you:

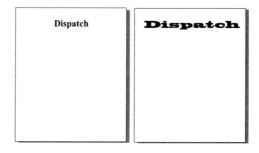

◆ **Give adequate space for your type to rest in.** The white space around type (the space between letters, words, lines, text, graphics, and the space between text and the edges of the page) acts to define the typography and give your eyes much-needed rest. Just as a musical composition must have pauses without sound, so should type have areas of white space to counterbalance the page.

◆ **Be careful mixing typefaces.** Two different sans serif fonts, both used for body text, or both used for heads, can fight for your attention. You can mix and match, but there needs to be some significant difference. In Figure 5.25 the two sans serif fonts, Gill Sans Condensed and Optima, are too similar to work together. However, change the weight of one typeface from Gill Sans Condensed to Gill Sans Ultra Bold Condensed and they look perfectly natural together.

Figure 5.25   *The two subheads in the left example are too alike and vie for attention. On the right a bold version of the same font makes a visually-pleasing difference.*

Housing starts up 25%
-brings building boom

Housing starts up 25%
-brings building boom

◆ **Don't overdo white type on a black background.** Reversing type out of a black background is a nice effect, but do so with care. For one thing, it's harder to read text-weight type (you need to increase the size and weight if you have reversed more than a few words). Also, it is difficult for your commercial printer to print large masses of solid black. If the printer is not careful, you wind up with small pinholes of white which can look pretty ugly. If the printer over compensates by laying down extra black ink, the still-wet ink can rub off (or *offset*) onto other pages of your document, making a real mess.

◆ **Don't be afraid to expand or contract type for effect.** Many desktop publishing programs have tools to stretch or squeeze characters. The effects, as shown in Figure 5.26, can be impressive, if not overused.

Figure 5.26 *Aldus FreeHand squeezed and stretched 24-point ITC's Fritz Quadrata (Adobe font 11) by changing horizontal spacing. Reflection was done with a click of the Reflect tool.*

Squeeze

Stretch

Reflection

- **Don't get too complicated.** The reader probably won't pay as much attention to your pages as you do, and complicated typography may be lost, or even distracting. Keep it simple; the reader will appreciate your efforts.

- **Don't forget to use dingbats and flourishes.** As seen earlier in this chapter, there are some beautiful little doodads in the dingbat fonts from Adobe and other foundries. Some, when enlarged, look like originally-created art.

Kona Isle
Resort

❋

Island Living
as Close as the Bahamas

Walker's Cay
800-980-7000

- **Don't forget: A little goes a long way.** That is possibly the most important rule of typography and design. Remember not to overdo italics, or bolding; they lose their effect if seen too often on the page. The same goes for size changes and font changes. Decide on a size for text and a size for heads and stick to them. If you follow this rule, when you do something different on the page, it will pop out and be noticed. Just remember, if it looks overdone to you it will clearly seem overdone to your readers.

UNDERSTANDING HORIZONTAL AND VERTICAL SPACING

If the term *space* keeps popping up in this book it is because space is the counterpoint to the ink that represents type and graphics. Space gives the ink room to be seen, words room to be digested, and graphics and pictures room to be admired. Space, or the lack of space, is most visible in typography. The effect of inadequate space is most evident when:

- Readers struggle through your words with little appreciation of the effort that went into designing the page.

- The document is just put aside.

When type is spaced properly, there is a visual proportion of white to black—paper to ink—that is maintained. Simply put, the darker the text, the more space you need for balance.

Adjusting the Space Between Characters

The idea of horizontal space between characters and words has changed. You used to just press the space bar between each word. The characters that were printed on your dot matrix printer were all the same width, called *monospacing*. Though the page was indifferent looking, very little was expected of dot matrix or daisy-wheel printers. The best example of monospacing is the font Courier. Each of the characters in the font takes up the same amount of horizontal space. As a matter of fact, the space for each letter is the width of the capital M, which is the widest letter in the alphabet. Typeset characters are proportionally spaced, meaning the space that each character takes up is scaled proportionally to its own width. Since narrow characters like owercase *l*'s take up less room than wide characters like *M*,

B, or W, less space is allotted on either side of the narrower characters. The difference between monospacing and proportional spacing is shown in Figure 5.27. Notice the difference between the space of the letters *i, t,* and *l.* It is not possible to adjust the fixed letter spacing of a monospaced font like Courier. Luckily, Type-1 fonts are mostly proportionally spaced, meaning you can adjust the horizontal spacing of lines of type by changing *kerning* and *tracking* values.

Figure 5.27   *Courier, set in 18 points in the top example, takes up much more space than 18-point Times Roman below it.*

```
Character spacing isn't trivial
```
Character spacing isn't trivial

The term *kerning* refers to the space between pairs of letters in a given font. Some pairs of letters naturally need to be closer together than other pairs. For example, the space between the characters *A* and *V* should be closed up a bit to make the pair of letters look better. Another pair that needs some spacing help is the letters *T* and *i.* Each Type-1 font has a built-in kerning table that contains the ideal amount of space for these pairs of letters and many other pairs. If the pairs are not adjusted—kerned—they will look unwieldy, but by kerning (tightening up the space between the letters) they will look more natural.

spaces kerned

Kerning becomes more critical as the type size is increased—generally you do not notice kerning in body text sizes, but the need for kerning is very obvious in headlines and headings. Most page composition programs have an option to automatically kern all the letter-pair combinations, at your request, above a specified point size. So, to kern headings 30 points and larger, but not the 12-point body text, you simply tell the software to kern above 29 points.

If you're thinking why not simply turn automatic kerning on for all size type in your document, there are several important reasons not to kern body text. First of all body text needs some white space around the individual letters, so that:

- ◆ The type is more readable in smaller sizes.

- ◆ There is some space to use in adjusting justified lines of text (the more letter space available, the less need for exaggerated space between words to make the justified line fit).

- ◆ When printing your document on a 300 dpi laser printer, you will get the best reproduction of the typeface possible (the printer is not able to exactly duplicate the fine details of most typefaces in small sizes, so extra toner is added to the letters to make them more distinctive—but fatter). Since the letters are slightly thicker from the extra toner, closing up the space between letters only makes matters worse. If you are doing your final printing to a high-resolution imagesetter, all typefaces appear slightly more delicate in body text sizes, so you can afford to trim away a little bit of letter space.

To change the spacing of more than a pair of letters at one time, you will change the tracking of the letters. Tracking is similar to kerning. To change tracking for a group of letters, highlight the letters and use the Tracking (or letter spacing) command in your page composition program.

Adjusting the Space Between Words

The space between words is naturally changed in justified text. In order for the text to end evenly along the right margin, the software makes small adjustments to the space between letters and words—either adding space or reducing space to make the lines come out even. Without the space adjustments, a relatively narrow column of justified text might have obviously large spaces between some of the words, as shown in the example on the next page.

> Justified lines of text
> create columns of text
> with even left and
> right margins, at the
> cost of different space
> values between
> different words.

However, by adjusting the space between words in minute increments, the excess space can be evened out among the words in the column, like this:

> Justified lines of text
> create columns of text
> with even left and right
> margins, at the cost of
> different space values
> between words.

Each program adjusts word spacing differently. PageMaker, QuarkXPress, and Adobe Illustrator allow minimum, optimum, and maximum percentage values for the internal word spacing of justified lines of text. Each of the values is a percentage of 100 (100 percent being the perfect spacing according to the designer of the typeface). If you need tighter word spacing, you might set the optimum spacing at 90 percent (which would be 10 percent tighter spacing than intended by the typeface designer). Minimum spacing might be set at 65 percent (meaning that word spacing is squeezed 35 percent tighter than recommended), and maximum spacing at 135 percent (or 35 percent wider spacing than normal). Aldus FreeHand lets you set up a minimum space value, which the program observes in attempting to properly adjust the word spacing of justified lines.

Adjusting the Space Between Lines of Type

The vertical space between lines of type is called *leading* (pronounced ledding). Leading is specified in points just as type size is specified. Generally speaking, normal leading is about 120 percent of the size of the type. So, if you have a line of 10-point type, acceptable leading is in the neighborhood of 12 points. Since the leading value for a given line includes the size of the type plus the space between the line and the next line, shown in Figure 5.28. The 12 points of leading would include the 10 points of type plus the 2 points of space. Most page composition programs call this 120 percent rule *auto leading*. If you choose the auto feature, the program will automatically assign a leading value of 120 percent of the type size. Leading can also be specified as *solid*, meaning the leading is the same size as the type (12 points of type would have only 12 points of leading). As you increase the amount of leading between lines, you add more space between the lines.

Figure 5.28 *As leading is increased from none (solid) to 24 points, space is added between lines of 18-point type.*

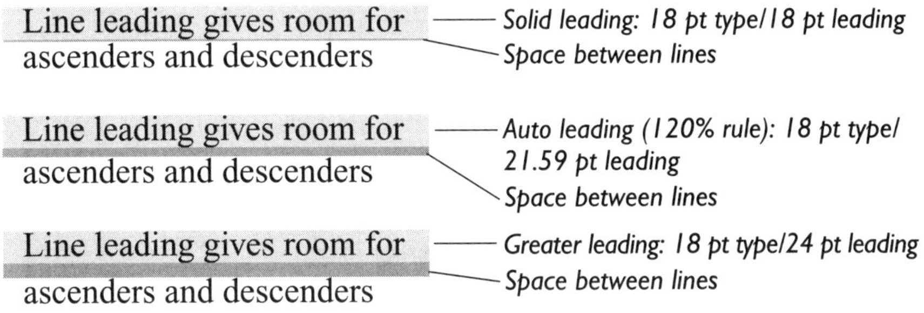

Line leading gives room for
ascenders and descenders
—— *Solid leading: 18 pt type/18 pt leading*
Space between lines

Line leading gives room for
ascenders and descenders
—— *Auto leading (120% rule): 18 pt type/*
21.59 pt leading
Space between lines

Line leading gives room for
ascenders and descenders
—— *Greater leading: 18 pt type/24 pt leading*
Space between lines

DIFFERENT STROKES FOR DIFFERENT FOLKS

The shape of a particular font has a lot to do with its presence on the page: Strong statements should be made by strong-looking typefaces. Add a look of informality with a script typeface. Add impact with size, or by using a typestyle like the outline or shadow effects to cinch your message. Choosing a slab serif font can add an official quality to your words, as shown below.

Personnel Policy Handbook

While the opposite sort of font, Ransom (from the Microsoft Font Pack 2 collection), for example, can be most expressive with the right message:

C☺me ☜ the W*in*ter ʃark ℿall (☺r e*l*se)

Sometimes Being Different is the Best Idea

Opposites attract and adding typography that's off the beaten track can turn heads and get the attention you're looking for. For example, use size and space to your best advantage. Play around with exaggerated letter, word, and line spacing. Adding space between the letters of a word can change the whole complexion of your page, like the top of this ad:

P   R   E   S   E   N   T   I   N   G

Better Banking Hours
(all 24 of them)

Adding a dingbat to the space between each letter might be just what you're looking for to dress up your page.

P ✦ R ✦ E ✦ S ✦ E ✦ N ✦ T ✦ I ✦ N ✦ G

Use an exaggerated letter to catch the eye. Proportionally space text in relation to the letter, and you might have an interesting visual effect.

Use flush left and flush right text alignment in an unusual way to attract attention (you must be careful to separate the two columns, as in the example).

Decisions | *Decisions*

Our Orlando	Our Winter
store has the	Park store has
latest fashions,	the latest
accessaries and	fashions,
and a roving	accessaries
violinist to	and a sidewalk
serenade you	ice cream cafe

Creating Large Initial Caps

Beginning a paragraph of text with a large initial capital letter (called an *initial cap*) is a traditional way of adding typographic hot sauce to the page. The initial cap indicates the starting point for your eye, and is an attractive way to begin a story, article, or chapter. There are two kinds of initial caps:

- *Initial drop caps* that are even with the top of the first line of text and drop down several lines.

- *Initial raised caps* that are even with the bottom of the first line of text and are raised the equivalent of several lines above the first line.

I nitial caps are an attractive way of sprucing up pages full of boring columns of text and few illustrations. If initial caps are used, they should indicate the beginning of a story, article or chapter and not be used at the beginning of every paragraph.

I nitial caps are an attractive way of sprucing up pages full of boring columns of text and few illustrations. If initial caps are used, they should indicate the beginning of a story, article or chapter and not be used at

Once you decide on the style of initial cap, either raised or dropped, you can spruce up the initial cap in any number of ways. For example, you can use a different, but complimentary font for the initial cap, or an italic, outline, or shadow type style. Several ideas for initial caps are shown below.

▌nitial caps are an attractive way of sprucing up pages full of boring columns of text and few illustrations. If initial caps are used, they should indicate the beginning of a story, article or chapter and not be used at the beginning of every paragraph.

*I*nitial caps are an attractive way of sprucing up pages full of boring columns of text and few illustrations. If initial caps are used they should indicate the beginning of a story, article or chapter and not used as the beginning of every paragraph.

▌nitial caps are an attractive way of sprucing up pages full of boring columns of text and few illustrations. If initial caps are used, they should indicate the beginning of a story, article or chapter and not be used at the beginning of every paragraph.

T nitial caps are an attractive way of sprucing up pages full of boring columns of text and few illustrations. If initial caps are used they should indicate the beginning of a story, article or chapter and not used as the beginning of every paragraph.

I nitial caps are an attractive way of sprucing up pages full of boring columns of text and few illustrations. If initial caps are used, they should indicate the beginning of a story, article or chapter and not be used at the beginning of every paragraph.

I nitial caps are an attractive way of sprucing up pages full of boring columns of text and few illustrations. If initial caps are used, they should indicate the beginning of a story, article or chapter and not be used at the beginning of every paragraph.

How Fonts Work in Your Computer and Printer

There is little that's more impressive than the ability to play with typography on your computer. Fonts are shown realistically, and as you apply styles or size changes, are transformed before your eyes. Typography in a page composition system running on your Windows computer is a long way from the good 'ole days of dealing with typesetting shops. Having realistic-looking fonts on your system also gives you the ability to play "What if?" You can make changes, experiment, print the results, and try something else.

What is a Font?

Believe it or not, there are still ostriches, with their heads stuck in the sand, who tell you that Adobe Type 1 fonts are not real. They think that the

PostScript version of ITC's Lubalin Graph is not the same font as the Lubalin Graph produced by a dedicated photo-typesetter (does anyone even use dedicated photo-typesetters anymore?). Don't believe them—the fonts running in a Windows (or Macintosh) system are as real as they can be—humor these people and they'll go away. But if you wonder what exactly these things called fonts are, read on, and I'll tell you all you need to know.

A *font* is a collection of all the characters, numbers, punctuation marks, and all other symbols that comprise a single typeface in a single size. Since the rage of desktop publishing, the term *font* has pretty much become synonymous with the term *typeface*—although traditional typographers and designers will probably grimace. A font in your Windows computer, either Type I or TrueType, has two parts: a *screen font* and a *printer font* (also called a *soft font*).

The screen font is what you see when you specify Lubalin Graph 36 point, and begin typing. It is actually a rather crude, bitmapped representation of Lubalin because the computer's monitor lacks a high-enough resolution to display the shape of the characters accurately (as shown below). The printer font, or soft font, is sent to the printer whenever you decide to print the Lubalin type that is displayed. The printer font file contains all the characters in the font. Once it is received by your laser printer, the Lubalin characters are sent as a part of the document to be printed. The laser printer then picks and chooses from among the characters in the printer font to find the characters you've used, and those are printed.

What is a Font Rasterizer?

A *font rasterizer*, sometimes called a font manager, smooths out the edges of the font, making it appear almost as perfect as the printed version. Without a rasterizer, type in larger size is just plain ugly, the edges become so jagged you can't align the font accurately on the page.

Not very pretty

Adobe Type Manager (ATM) was the original type manager and does a great job of displaying and managing Type I fonts. ATM allows you to make as many of your fonts active as you want; it's easy to install or de-install the fonts you want in your application. ATM is very inexpensive and comes free with a number of applications, including PageMaker, QuarkXPress, and Adobe Illustrator. The ATM control panel is shown in Figure 5.29. All the currently active fonts in your system are displayed in the font list. To add or remove fonts from the list, click on the appropriate button.

Figure 5.29 *ATM Control Panel.*

With ATM at the helm, you no longer suffer the jaggies; nor do you have to worry about printer fonts having to be sent to your laser printer. As a matter of fact, with ATM turned on, you can print the actual Type 1 fonts not only to any PostScript printer, but virtually any printer, including HP LaserJets, color inkjet printers, and even dot matrix printers. That's because ATM takes a snapshot of the page and sends the file as a graphic image to your printer; any printer that is capable of printing graphics can print your composed page, fonts and all.

If you opt for TrueType instead of Type 1 fonts, don't despair; you too have a font rasterizer built right into Windows 3.1. The TrueType manager does the same job as ATM; smoothing out the jagged edges of screen fonts, and sending the necessary printer font information down to the printer. TrueType fonts live happily along with Type 1 fonts, and you can have both Adobe Type Manager and the TrueType manager working side-by-side without squabbling. While TrueType fonts print effortlessly to HP LaserJet printers, You can also print TrueType fonts on a PostScript printer. Just follow these easy steps:

1. Open the Windows Control Panel (in the Main work group) and double-click on the **Printers** icon.

2. In the Printers dialog box, click on the PostScript printer driver and choose the **Setup** button.

3. You will see a dialog box named for the PostScript printer you have (or it might say Apple LaserWriter II). Click the **Options** button.

4. In the Options dialog box, click the **Advanced** button (are you still with me?).

5. Finally, at the top of the Advanced Options dialog box, in the TrueType Fonts area, you will see the Send to Printer as list box. Click the list box arrow and choose **Adobe Type 1**. Then select **OK** in each dialog box to close them and return to your application.

Now, the TrueType fonts that you specify in your publication will be converted to Type 1 fonts when they're sent to the PostScript printer, and print just as nicely as your real Type 1 fonts.

One more item about TrueType: If you purchase the TrueType Font Pack 2 from Microsoft (which is a great deal, by the way—44 fonts, including headline, decorative, text, and script fonts, for about $40) you will get Microsoft's Font Assistant. The Font Assistant is a very handy tool for organizing large numbers of fonts into work groups. Let's say, for example that your work includes a lot of business correspondence, a bit of brochure designing, and a whole bunch of proposal writing. With the Font Assistant, instead of having all of the 44 TrueType fonts listed in the font dialog boxes of all your Windows applications, you can put selected fonts in specialized groups and then just pick the group you want to work with. You could have a Correspondence Group with fonts for letters; a Brochures Group with headline, dingbat, and text fonts; and a Proposal Group with just the fonts you want to use in proposals. The Font Assistant dialog box is shown in Figure 5.30.

Figure 5.30 *Microsoft Font Assistant organizes your TrueType fonts into work groups.*

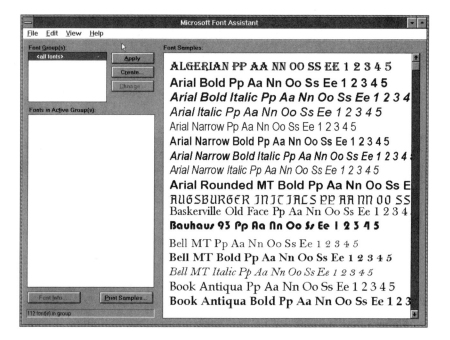

To create a new work group for that brochure work, click the Create button. You will see the Create Group dialog box, as shown at the top on the righthand page. Choose the font in the Available Fonts list that you want to add to the group and click Add to Group button. The font names move to the Fonts in Group list. When you have added all the fonts you want, click OK to save the group.

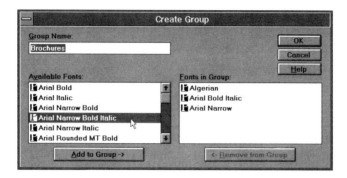

Once you have created the groups that you want, simply double-click the group name in the Font Groups list box (see Figure 5.30) to add a checkmark to the group. The checkmark means only those fonts will be active in your applications. Click Apply to apply the fonts in the group to all your Windows applications and close the Font Assistant. When you open PageMaker, Microsoft Publisher, or WordPerfect, you'll see only the fonts listed in the Brochures group. That's all there is to it.

Downloading, Uploading, and Off-Loading Fonts

Some printer fonts, namely Helvetica, Times Roman, Courier, Palatino, and some others are permanently installed in your laser printer. These fonts are said to be *resident* because they live in your PostScript laser printer. As I mentioned earlier, printer fonts that are not resident must be sent to your laser printer when you print your document. These fonts are said to be *downloaded* to your printer. Actually, it all happens automatically in the background: As your document is printed the fonts needed for each page are downloaded into your laser printer, the page is composed in the printer, and finally printed. If you use a particular font on a number of different pages, the same printer font must be downloaded a number of times which can slow down the printing process. In these cases you may want to manually download all the fonts in your document first, then print the document.

You must use a font downloader to manually download fonts, and one of the best is provided free by Adobe, if you own any of their fonts. The Adobe downloader is displayed in Figure 5.31 on the next page. With it, you can click on the fonts you want to download (the fonts contained in the document you want to print) and choose the Download button to send them to the printer. You can also set up groups of fonts to download simultaneously (much like the font groups you create in Microsoft Font Assistant). Click the Create Font Group button, and add all the fonts you want in the group. Notice in Figure 5.31, the font Garamond is in parentheses. It is a font group consisting of all the Adobe Garamond fonts— AGaramond-Regular, AGaramond-Italic, AGaramond-Semibold, and AGaramond-Semibolditalic.

Figure 5.31   *Adobe PostScript Font Downloader handles manually downloading fonts to your laser printer.*

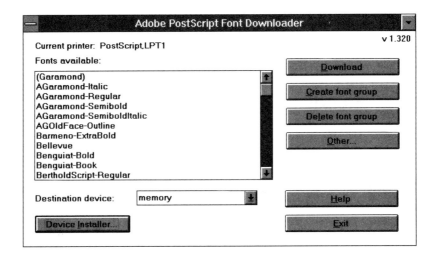

Adobe's downloader has a few other tricks as well. If you have a hard disk connected to your laser printer, the downloader can format the hard disk and load all (or most of) the fonts in your system into the printer's hard disk. Adding printer fonts to a hard disk connected to your laser printer is the next best thing to having all your fonts resident in the printer's memory; they work much faster than when they are in your computer and must be sent to the printer before each print job. It can also print a status page showing exactly which fonts have been downloaded, and how much of the printer's memory is still free. Altogether a very worthwhile tool, especially considering Adobe gives it away. To receive your copy, you must be a registered owner of an Adobe font. Just give Adobe a call (800-833-6687), ask, and you shall receive.

CHAPTER SUMMARY

Typography builds the substance of your document. Like the walls of a building, typography supports the weight of the document's design, and provides the fabric that holds the design elements together. Typography can be solid brick, delicate lattice work, or simple concrete block. It can be adobe mud, or New England clapboard. In short, typography—the style, format, look, and allure of type that hold our thoughts—is the very essence of the printed page.

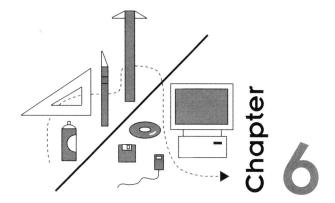

Graphics: Adding Lines, Boxes, Photos, and More

▼**T**his chapter covers all the goodies of desktop publishing: adding graphics, photos, and color to your pages. Graphics can be as simple as a line or two, perhaps in a different color; or as complex as full-color photographs. Until a few years ago graphics, especially photos, were the domain of hard-working graphic artists, who used expensive color separation companies to prepare photos for color printing. No more! Your Windows system and some specialized software handle all the chores of adding color photos, simply and inexpensively.

ADDING LINES AND BOXES FOR EMPHASIS

Lines emphasize, point, and direct. Lines are an easy way of dressing up your pages, and add a professional touch. If done correctly, adding lines and boxes will enhance your pages; but loading up the page with lines and boxes only adds a level of noise to your message. Lines add to the level of ink (from type, lines, boxes, graphics, photos, and anything else printed on the page) and thus contribute to the overall blackness of the page. If text is heavy and leading tight, adding lines can overly darken the page. So keep in mind that for a line to be effective, there must be space set aside for it.

If this chapter finds you gleefully adding lines and boxes with a page composition program, take note: your pages will look like you just discovered the line drawing tools. Lines and boxes are certainly tempting: they are the easiest graphics to add to the page. And, if you've ever had to draw lines in India ink using a Rapidograph pen and a tee square, the ease of doing so in Windows can be intoxicating. However, a word of caution. Lines and boxes (which are really just lines connected to each other) have distinct purposes. All too often, lines are added just for the sake of adding them, giving an unkept, amateurish look to the page. Like all design elements, a little

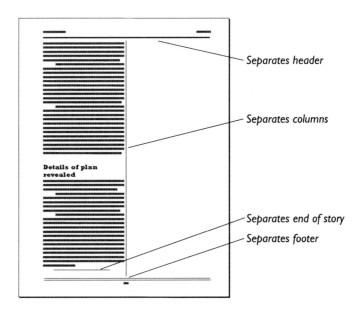

Separates header

Separates columns

Separates end of story

Separates footer

Details of plan revealed

goes a long way with lines and boxes; and while you might chortle about how easy they are to add, your readers may find them distracting and unnecessary. Let's look at some ground rules for adding lines and boxes:

- **Use lines to direct the reader's attention.** Probably the best example of lines to direct attention are lines between columns of text, header and footer lines at the top and bottom of the page, and left or right (or both) margin lines. All of the lines serve to help the reader focus on the text of the page, and distinctly segregate peripheral information like headers and footers.

- **Keep the lines from boxing the page.** Unless it is a conscious design decision, boxing the page should be discouraged. Decide which of the lines you need most to keep your readers on track. For example, if you have a lot of header information, you may need a header line, but if you only have a page number at the bottom of the page, you almost certainly won't need a footer line.

Figure 6.1   *Too many lines spoil the white space, creating a box effect.*

◆ **The weight of lines can burden the page.** Lines should generally be light to keep from competing with text and headlines on the page. Overly-heavy lines can spoil an otherwise attractive page.

Jones' math class? Can you honestly say you paid attention with him pacing back and forth across the room, hands behind his back, bent over like Grocho Marx? Yes, Mr. Jones was a trip; especially

Did Tim Nelson always have big ears, or was Mr. Jones the culprit? Read on.

when he'd send Bill Bowman to the office for talking in class. Bill should have gotten a C in Office Sitting instead of Algebra!

◆ **The heavier the line the greater its impact.** Heavy lines needn't be as long as thin lines. As shown in the example below, shortening the pull quotes lines serves the same purpose but doesn't intrude.

back and forth across the room, hands behind his back, bent over like Grocho Marx? Yes, Mr. Jones was a trip; especially

Did Tim Nelson always have big ears, or was Mr. Jones the culprit? Read on.

when he'd send Bill Bowman to the office for talking in class. Bill should have gotten a C in Office Sitting instead of Algebra!
But for all his weirdness, none of us who had Mr. Jones for math will

COLOR PLATE 1 Examples of Photo CD images; resolution is very close to professional quality. These photos are printed with a scanning resolution of 200 dots per inch, and a 150-line screen. Images courtesy Eastman Kodak Company.

Original

Flip

Mirror

Rotate Left

Rotate Right

COLOR PLATE 2 Some ot the ways to manipulate images in Kodak PhotoEdge photo enhancement software. The attitude you select is saved with the file. You can also adjust the attitude of an image in most page composition programs. The images are printed with a scanning resolution of 150 dots per inch and a 133-line screen. Image courtesy Eastman Kodak Company.

 **COLOR PLATE 3** Using Kodak's Photo CD Access soft-ware, the tower was isolated with the cropping dialog box, and and the cropped area enlarged. To ensure the best resolution, try to start with a photo scanned at the image size as close as possible to the size you will use in your document. The enlargement shown above was made from a much larger scan of the photo. Both of these images are printed with a scanning resolution of 150 dots per inch, and a 150-line screen. Image courtesy Eastman Kodak Company.

300-ppi resolution creates a 2.06 megabyte file

200-ppi resolution creates a 940 kilobyte file

150-ppi resolution creates a 528 kilobyte file

115-ppi resolution creates a 310 kilobyte file

100-ppi resolution creates a 235 kilobyte file

72-ppi resolution creates a 122 kilobyte file

COLOR PLATE 4 Decreasing resolutions for the same image size creates different results. All of these images are printed with a 133-line screen, meaning that the 150-ppi image is marginally at the lower end of the resolution-to-line-screen ratio of 1.2. The three lower resolutions fall far below—judge the results for yourself. Also notice the significant differences in image file size. Image courtesy Eastman Kodak Company.

Cyan separation

Magenta separation

Yellow separation

Black separation

Finished, printed photo

COLOR PLATE 5   Once the image is saved in the CMYK color mode, it can be placed on a page in PageMaker or QuarkXPress. The page composition software can then print the actual separations, shown above. When each sep is printed precisely on top of one another the colors combine to form the finished photo, shown bottom right. Image courtesy Eastman Kodak Company.

Original

Using the Smudge tool

Using the Text tool

Using the Magic Wand

COLOR PLATE 6 You may not be fooling Mother Nature, but using some of the special tools in image enhancement software sure comes close. If you look closely at the examples above, you will see a number of modifications to the original photo. Using Photoshop, the Smudge tool **(upper right)** wipes out the wind vane and the two small steeples on the roof of the barn. Smudging works like dragging your finger through the wet paint of the foreground color. The Text tool **(lower left)** adds text in the font of your choice to the photo. The color you select for the text will be separated as a part of the image. Photoshop's Magic Wand lets you isolate shapes by judging differences in color. Notice that the roof **(lower right)** has been painted (painting a real barn roof should be so easy) and foliage has been added to the right side of the pond. Image courtesy Eastman Kodak Company.

Original

Crystallize filter

Diffuse filter

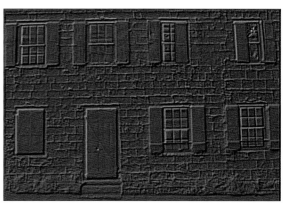

Emboss filter

Trace Contour filter

Wind filter

COLOR PLATE 7   A number of specialized Photoshop filters are applied to the original photo. Most filters allow you to vary the special effects by adjusting values in dialog boxes. Image courtesy Eastman Kodak Company.

Original

Graphic Pen Effect

Charcoal Effect

Watercolor Effect

COLOR PLATE 8 Aldus Gallery Effects can give your photos a variety of looks. Image courtesy Eastman Kodak Company.

♦ **Use boxes to assign importance.** Boxes are an excellent way of separating groups of body copy. Sidebars are often boxed to indicate their distinction from a main story. Graphics, photos, maps, charts, and other visual aids are often boxed with a shaded or colored background.

Reunions

10th—Class of '83
June 21 on Campus

20th—Class of '73
August 2 in Gym

30th—Class of '63
July 2 at Hilton Hotel

Your newsletter staff:

Cynthia Smith—Editor
Jerry Winslow—Writer
Martha Davis—Sales
Len Scott—layout

room, hands behind his back, bent over like Grocho Marx? Yes, Mr. Jones was a trip; especially

Did Tim Nelson always have big ears, or was Mr. Jones the culprit? Read on.

when he'd send Bill Bowman to the office for talking in class. Bill should have gotten a C in Office Sitting instead of Algebra! But for all his weirdness, none of us who

♦ **Use lines to help the eye.** A line leading to an indented first line of a paragraph can act much like an initial large cap to signify the beginning of a story. A line preceding or following a writer's byline is a nice touch, as shown in the examples below. Lines above and below figures quickly show readers what is the figure and what's not, shown in the example on the next page.

Alum Assoc. reaches record high members

————We didn't believe we could top last year's record-setting membership drive, but by golly we did it—157 new members,

Alum Assoc. reaches record high members

We top last year's member pledge!

by Jerry Winslow

We didn't believe we could top last year's record-setting

yet it is the apparent wind that we must be concerned with in judging the best angle of attach for the sails—closer than a broad reach we must keep the sails from stalling; farther off the wind stalling the mainsail becomes more important.

70 degrees	5.4 knots	
90 degrees	5.8 knots	
130 degrees		6.2 knots
150 degrees		6.7 knots
160 degrees		6.9 knots
170 degrees		7.1 knots
180 degrees		6.6 knots

Figure 3 How boat speed is determined by apparent wind angle

As you can see from Figure 3, as the boat heads off the wind from close-hauled to a broad reach, boat speed increases dramatically. If you assume the use of a spinnaker will be used from a broad reach to an angle off the wind, speed will continue to increase. Without the larger sail, as the boat moves farther off the wind than a broad reach, speed will begin to decrease. Apparent wind angle is not the only source of information about sail trim, but it is the most important. Remember, as boat speed increases, apparent wind angle shifts

Figure 2 Boats on a downwind leg

♦ **Use lines to make tables and charts easier to understand.** Use horizontal lines or shaded bars if the important facts are across from each other in the table or chart; vertical lines if the data is presented on the vertical axis. Lines or shaded bars can make the difference between just presenting the data and directing the reader to the proper conclusions.

70 degrees	5.4 knots	
90 degrees	5.8 knots	
130 degrees		6.2 knots
150 degrees		6.7 knots
160 degrees		6.9 knots
170 degrees		7.1 knots
180 degrees		6.6 knots

Figure 3 How boat speed is determined by apparent wind angle

◆ **Lined boxes intrude, unlined, shaded boxes are more inviting.** Lined boxes are just boxes, but an unlined, shaded box is visually more striking, and less combative with other lines added to the page. By varying the shading or colors, you can get away with a number of unlined boxes—do the same thing with lined boxes and your page starts to look like a city map.

◆ **Use lines to balance the page, not to add clutter.** Think of lines as graphics and not as typographic underlines. Use them as you would any other graphic—frugally—and they will reward you with beauty and balance. Adding a line opposite heavy text or graphics brings symmetry to your page. Be daring and create a diagonal line to draw interest to your design. Diagonal lines tend to be more noticeable than vertical or horizontal lines.

◆ **Delicate lines tend to look better than heavy lines.** Resist the temptation to increase the weight of lines. Thin, delicate lines are generally more useful than heavier lines. Thin lines require less white space and seem less pushy than heavier lines. Since high-resolution imagesetters can reproduce just about any thickness of hairline, take advantage of the resolution and work with thin lines.

+ **If you add a heavy line, consider reversing type out of it.** When is a heavy line not a heavy line? When type is reversed out of it. The reversed type adds some of the white space the heavier line would ordinarily need and can be a nice addition to the page. Carefully though, reversed type is more difficult to read so don't overdo it.

Line and type same height; line is too heavy, space is too tight

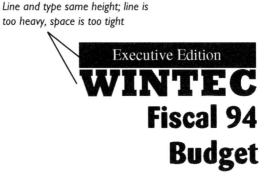

+ **If you use a heavy line, match the size to another element on the page.** For example, make the line the same thickness as a font, or even the heavy serifs of a font. The match between line and element can invisibly link the two, integrating the line as a part of the element or typography.

Line and serif same height; but space is too tight

- **Give lines enough space to comfortably occupy.** Space, space, space. I can't stress the importance enough. For the line to be seen, it obviously needs white space around it. The more space, the more noticeable the line becomes.

Line, space, and serif all the same height

- **Keep square-cornered boxes and round-cornered boxes separate.** As a rule you probably shouldn't have one box inside another box, but if you do, keep the corners the same. For that matter, I wouldn't mix the two types of corners on the same page.

ADDING CLIP ART IMAGES

Computer clip art has come to mean a huge variety of graphic images and drawings that you can use in any of your documents. Need an arrow for a particular purpose? Just open your clip art file and sort through a collection of arrows. Need a drawing of a policeman or fireman? Just choose the one you want from your clip art collection. So where do I get clip art, you might ask? You probably have clip art collections and may not realize it. For example, both WordPerfect for Windows and Word for Windows come with large clip art collections. As we mentioned earlier, Microsoft Publisher and PFS Publisher also come with large libraries of clip art.

Clip art derives its name from the fact that, before desktop publishing, graphic artists used to buy books of small drawings—faces, arrows, signs, household items, almost anything you could think of—and the artist would cut out (or clip out) the drawing needed for a particular design. Thus the name *clip art*. While it's not clipped out of your computer, clip art comes with just about every art/drawing/painting program, and is legally available for you to use for any purpose. Micrografx Draw, for example, comes with a huge library of clip art images, and a dialog box (Figure 6.2) that let's you preview the images before you add them to your page. Just choose the Clipart command from the File menu to see the Clipart Catalog dialog box. Use the dialog box to scroll through the list of topics to find the clip art image you want. In Figure 6.2, you see that the general category is MONEY01.DRW, which contains a number of different drawings, including images of the Dollar, Franc, Pound, Yen, and more. While the actual graphic file contains all these images, you can pick just the image you want by clicking the ClipArt Symbol check box in the lower list box.

Figure 6.2 *ClipArt Catalog dialog box in Micrografx Windows Draw.*

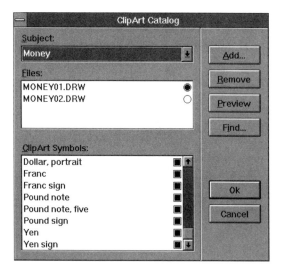

To see just the British Pound image, for instance, click its check box and choose OK. The clip art image is added to the Windows Draw page, as shown in the following example.

Micrografx Draw clip art images end in the extension .DRW (as do most Micrografx files) and import easily into page composition programs like

PageMaker and QuarkXPress. Most Windows art software includes clip art files—some of which is pretty impressive. For example, Aldus FreeHand comes with beautifully-detailed maps, including maps of the British Isles (shown in Figure 6.3), Europe, Africa, North America, and many others. The maps can be scaled to any size you need, or cropped to show only part of a country. The maps and other FreeHand clip art are named with the extension .FT3 (indicating a FreeHand template). You can export the template as an encapsulated PostScript file (use the Export command on the File menu) and then add the .EPS file to a document in any other page composition program.

Figure 6.3 *An Aldus FreeHand clip art map of the British Isles.*

Most clip art images consist of a multitude of parts. Depending on the program that created it, you can disassemble (called *ungrouping*) the image and use only the part you need. For instance, a sports image in FreeHand includes the soccer ball shown on the left. By clicking the image to select it, and choosing the **Ungroup** command on FreeHand's Element menu, the individual components that comprise the image are made available for your use. Choose just the soccer ball, copy it to a new page, and you have the beginning of a new piece of art work.

If the clip art that comes with Windows applications isn't enough for you, there are clip art software services (the modern-day equivalent of clip art books) that can provide you with thousands of clip art images, much of it sold on CD-ROM. There are maps of just about anything you can map—Cartesia Software (800-334-4291) provides county maps of every county in the U.S. Other clip art software houses include:

- ProArt (800-447-1950)
- TechPool (800-925-6998)
- Creative Media Services (800-358-2278)
- PolyType (800-998-9934)
- Metro ImageBase (800-525-1552).

There are clip art houses that specialize in background, such as ArtBeats (800-444-9392); U.S. government emblems and seals are available from Federal Clip Art (800-258-5280); and Illustrated parts of the human body from MediClip (800-998-8705).

In fact, if you look carefully, there is almost certainly any kind of clip art you can dream up.

UNDERSTANDING GRAPHIC FORMATS

Regardless of the clip art subject, these images, as do all computer-generated graphics, fall into two major types: *bitmapped* or *raster formats*, such as TIF files and vector formats, like EPS (encapsulated PostScript) files. The difference between the two types is the way in which the graphic image is described, so your computer can display and print it.

You may remember that by definition, a bitmapped image is a representation of the image built out of tiny square dots. If you enlarge the image, bitmapped graphic files may become slightly rough, or ragged, along any curved edge—while vector-type graphics have smooth, uninterrupted curves. When an image is enlarged above its original size, the difference is striking. When bitmapped images are enlarged, the stair-stepped edges of curves become exaggerated; the results can be less than complimentary. Figure 6.4 shows an example of a dialog box, saved as a bitmapped image, and a portion of the dialog box enlarged. The larger the right-hand example is scaled, the more exaggerated the bitmapping becomes. By the same token, to improve the look of a bitmapped graphic, reduce its size to less than its original size.

Figure 6.4   *A bitmapped TIF image reduced from its original size (left) and a portion enlarged (right).*

By comparison, let's enlarge a portion of the FreeHand map shown in Figure 6.3, which is a vector graphics image. Figure 6.5 on the next page shows that despite the increased size, curved lines remain nicely curved, not stair-stepped. Vector graphics remain smooth regardless of their enlargement because the shapes are defined mathematically, rather than mapping the image as a series of bits. Vector graphics, like PostScript fonts, are infinitely scalable and print with equally high quality to both low-resolution laser printers and high-resolution imagesetters.

Figure 6.5   *County Kerry, Ireland, from the map in Figure 6.3, enlarged 600 percent.*

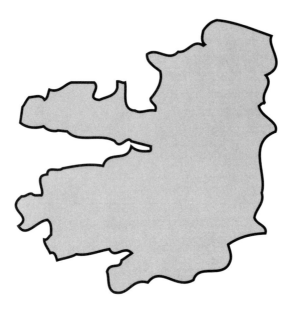

Graphics software can save files in a number of different formats; some formats are bitmapped and others are vector graphics. The most popular bitmapped format is the *tagged-image file format* (TIF). All the reproductions of dialog boxes in this book were captured in TIF format, as were a number of photographs. If you scan photos with your scanner (or order scans from a photo scanning service), you will probably save the resulting files in TIF format.

Encapsulated PostScript (EPS) files are the most universally popular format for vector graphics files. While you generally cannot alter the image of an EPS file in any program other than the one that created it, EPS files are very stable among most Windows and Macintosh applications. If you add text in a font to a file you are saving in EPS format, in most cases you must include the font with the graphic file if you move the file to another computer. In other words, if you used Optima text in a graphic saved as an

EPS file and sent the file to another computer, that computer must also have Optima installed in order to print the text in Optima. If Optima isn't present, the font Courier will be substituted. Some programs, like Aldus FreeHand, allow you the option of including the actual Type 1 fonts used in the graphic that you are saving in EPS format. If you include the fonts, they will print on any computer, regardless of whether the font is installed on the computer or not. (However, this applies only to Type 1, not TrueType fonts.)

Table 6.1 *Graphic format abbreviations.*

Graphic Format	File Name Extension
Adobe Illustrator	.AI
Amiga	.IFF, .HAM
Computer Graphics Metafile	.CGM
Encapsulated PostScript File	.EPS
Encapsulated PostScript file (Desktop Color Separation)	.DCS
Hewlett-Packard Graphics Language	.PLT
JPEG (photo compression format)	.JPG
Kodak Photo CD	.PCD
Lotus	.PIC
MacPaint	.PNT
Micrografx	.DRW
PC Paintbrush	.PCX
Pixar	.PXR
Tagged-Image File Format	.TIF
Targa	.TGA, .VDA, .ICB, .VST
Windows Bitmap	.BMP
Windows Metafile	.WMF

Table 6.2 *Different graphic application formats.*

Graphic Program	File Formats
Adobe Illustrator	.AI, .BMP, .CGM, .DRW, .TIF, .WMF, .WPG
Adobe Photoshop	.IFF, .HAM, .JPG, .PXR, .RAW, .TGA, .EPS
Adobe Streamline	.AI, .DRW, .CGM, .WMF
Adobe TypeAlign	.AI, .EPS, .TAL, .WMF
Aldus FreeHand	.AI, .EPS, .TIF, .WMF
Aldus Gallery Effects	.TIF, .BMP, .TGA
Aldus IntelliDraw	.EPS, .WMF
Aldus PhotoStyler	.TIF, .BMP, .EPS, .PCX
Arts & Letters	.CGM, .AI, .EPS, .TIF, .WMF
AutoCAD	.EPS, .PLT
Excel Chart	.XLC
Harvard Graphics	.CGM, .EPS, .PLT
Kodak Photo CD Viewer	.TIF, .BMP, .PCX, .EPS, .RAW
Kodak PhotoEdge	.TIF, .BMP, .PCX, .EPS, .RAW
Lotus Freelance	.CGM, .EPS, .PLT, .TIF
Macintosh MacPaint	.PNT
Micrografx products	.CGM, .DRW, .PCX, .TIF, .EPS, .DCS
PC Paintbrush	.PCX, .TIF,
Publisher's Paintbrush	.BMP, .EPS, .PCX, .TIF
Textronix Plot 10	.PLT
Windows PaintBrush	.BMP, .PCX
WordPerfect	.WPG, .WMF

While Table 6.1 and Table 6.2 may tend to confuse you with all the different graphic formats, I wouldn't worry too much. As you can see, every graphics program can export files in more than one format, so chances are you'll find a common format between the application that created the graphic and the page composition program. Clearly, .EPS, .TIF, and .WMF files are supported by just about all applications.

WORKING WITH PHOTOS

Using clip art for illustrations in your documents certainly has its place, but for my money nothing beats a good photo for dressing up the page. Color photos are even better. Until recently, photos were the last justification for producing documents on a drawing board instead of a computer. Now, however, there are a number of ways to get the photo into your computer (getting the photo into your computer is called *digitizing* the photograph, which we'll get to in a moment). Once there, you can do anything you want with it: add it to the pages of your documents, blow it up and print it by itself, even use it as part of a slide or overhead presentation. You can even change the color balance of the photograph—something that until recently was reserved for only the most expensive, custom color separation and imaging systems (costing upwards of $750,000)—and you can add special effects to give a unique look to your photos. I think the real beauty of using photos in your documents, instead of clip art, is that you can visually reinforce exactly what you're talking about. If you're proposing a change to a street intersection you can go out and take a picture, digitize it, and add it to your description of the present street corner. With Windows, page composition software, and a photo scanner it's simple and it works.

Currently there are several ways to digitize your photos: First of all you can hook up your Camcorder or video cassette recorder to a special video board and copy still frames from the video tape onto your hard disk. This system is straightforward to hook up, but the video board is a bit pricey. You can also use one of a number of digital cameras on the market to take the photos. Instead of recording the images on film, they are recorded digitally onto a floppy disk inside the camera. Insert the floppy disk into the computer and your photos are instantly available—again, this is a straightforward arrangement, but the cameras are expensive and the photos don't yet have the quality of film-based cameras. So let's limit ourselves to digitizing photos from normal still cameras. Currently there are two ways: using a photo scanner (or a photo scanning service bureau), or using Kodak's new Photo CD technology.

Photographic scanners have been around for a long time, yet were mainly too expensive for the average computer user to afford. Several years ago Hewlett-Packard, Microtek, Logitech, and some other manufacturers began selling low-priced, low-resolution scanners. Now you can select from a number of reasonably priced (less than $2,000) 600 dpi color scanners. All do a fairly good job of scanning color photos; none provide scanning resolutions high enough to make the photos in your document really stand out. While you can spend the money for a scanner, or mess around with a hand scanner that only scans a four-inch width of the photograph. Kodak Photo CDs do away with all that, providing you with a beautiful, high-resolution scan of your photograph for about the same cost as getting the photo printed at the drug store. There are a number of excellent books on using scanners (some are listed in the appendix) but for those of you new to desktop publishing, let's let Kodak worry about scanning. Here's how.

Using Kodak Photo CDs

Does anyone not know what a compact disc is? If you don't, you haven't visited a record store in the last eight years. There is a computer equivalent of the CD called CD-ROM (the ROM part means *read-only memory*, which is an obscure way of saying that you can only play what is on a CD-ROM, not record onto it). Computer CD-ROM is a new development that has blossomed overnight. Now, many computers can be purchased with CD-ROM drives (looking slightly like floppy drive units), and many mail order catalogs sport inexpensive CD-ROM kits that are easy to install.

There is also a wealth of information available on CD-ROM—everything from whole encyclopedias, dictionaries, atlases, fonts, and games. Some software applications are available on CD-ROM, including CorelDRAW and Windows NT. As more and more CD-ROM players are installed, you'll see more software on CD-ROM and less on floppy disks. The reason is simple: a CD-ROM holds about 600 megabytes of information.

You can do a lot in 600 megs of space, and one of the best uses is to store the images of scanned photographs—which is exactly what the folks from Kodak figured out—and along came Kodak Photo CD. It works like this: Instead of you mucking around with a scanner, simply take the pictures you want with your own camera. Send the roll of exposed film to any of several thousand Kodak Photo CD processing centers around the country (eventually the local drug store will do this for you just like they process your film now). Your photos are scanned and recorded onto a CD-ROM disc and mailed back to you. It comes in the same jewel case as audio CDs come in, and shows thumbnail prints of your photos on the front cover. Drop the CD in your CD-ROM player and your photos are available to applications like PageMaker 5.0 and Microsoft Publisher 2.0. Color Plate 1 shows the resolution and detail provided by the scanned images.

NOTE   Kodak Photo CDs work with most, and I stress most, CD-ROM drives. To access the photographs, the drive must be *single-session* or *multi-session enabled.* A session means the process of adding scanned images to your CD-ROM disc. If the drive is single-session enabled it means you can only add scanned photos once to the disc. Multi-session means you can send the disc back to have more photos scanned onto it. A disc can hold about one hundred 35mm photos. If you are shopping for a CD-ROM drive, be sure that it is CD-ROM XA compatible, which means it can read and understand Kodak Photo CDs. By the way, the XA designation also means that your CD-ROM drive can play your audio compact discs. All you need is a sound card, which comes with many CD-ROM kits. So, when you finish adding the photos you need from your Photo CD, drop in Telare's recording of Maazel and the Cleveland Orchestra performing *Moussorgsky's Pictures at an Exhibition.* (If *Night on Bald Mountain* doesn't inspire you, you're deaf!)

To get started using Kodak Photo CDs, take your exposed print or slide film, or existing negatives, or 35mm slides to a Photo CD processing center. (To find a center close to you call Kodak at 800-242-2424, extension 36 within the U.S; or 716-724-1021, extension 36 outside the U.S.) The charge for scanning a photo can range anywhere from about 80 cents to a few dollars depending on who is doing the work—professional photo labs that can handle Photo CD generally charge a bit more but offer faster turnaround.

Previewing Photo CD Images

Although some page composition software can directly access the images on your Photo CD—they can import images with the Photo CD file name extension PCD—unless there is some method of previewing the photos, you probably won't know what you're getting. That's because of the obscure file name Kodak assigns to each image. Actually Kodak doesn't know what you want to call an image anyhow, but I'm sure a computer assigns the image names on the disc automatically. For example, opening the Place Document dialog box in PageMaker—which you use to import a Photo CD image—isn't very helpful, as shown in Figure 6.6 below.

Figure 6.6 *PageMaker's Place Document dialog box lists the cryptic Photo CD image file names, but offers no preview.*

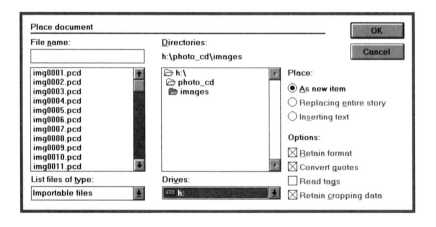

A better method for viewing the images is to use Kodak Photo CD Access, a $35 program that lets you open and view images on your Photo CD disc. Photo Access is a Windows application. Start it from the Kodak group that's created during installation. Photo Access automatically loads a contact sheet, shown in Figure 6.7, showing you thumbnail images of your photographs.

Figure 6.7   *Kodak's Photo CD Access Software lets you preview your images before you select them.*

Now, you can click on the photo you want to use, and load it into Photo Access using the Load Selected Photo command on the File menu, as shown on the next page.

Once the photo is loaded, Photo Access gives you a number of features to modify the photo:

◆ Change the photo's orientation or attitude. You can rotate the photo clockwise or counter clockwise. You can also flip the photo (turning it upside down) or mirror the photo, which reverses it (like looking at it through a mirror). See Color Plate 2.

- Change the number of colors displayed in the photo. You can choose among 16 colors, 256 colors, 24-bit color (16.7 million colors), as well as 16 or 256 shades of gray. The more colors you can display, the more realistic your photographs look on your computer monitor. Use the 256-color option, which offers fine color for viewing the images.

- Trim away part of the photo you don't want and enlarge the part you do want. See Color Plate 3.

- Change the size of the image. Each scan of your photos includes several different-sized images, shown in Table 6.3. Photo CD image sizes can be a bit confusing because Kodak shows them in wide and tall pixels, instead of inches. Think of a pixel as a dot on your computer's monitor. The normal resolution for a monitor is 72 pixels per inch (ppi), and each size image has a certain number of pixels in it.

Table 6.3   *Kodak Photo CD image sizes.*

Image	Size in Pixels	Size in Inches 72 ppi	106 ppi	150 ppi	200 ppi	Memory Needed to Open
Wallet	128 × 192	1.7 × 2.6	1.2 × 1.8	0.8 × 1.2	0.6 × 0.9	2.5 MB
Snapshot	256 × 384	3.5 × 5.3	2.4 × 3.6	1.7 × 2.5	1.2 × 1.9	3.0 MB
Standard	512 × 768	7.1 × 10.6	4.8 × 7.2	3.4 × 5.1	2.5 × 3.8	7.5 MB
Large	1024 × 1536	14.2 × 21.3	9.6 × 14.4	6.8 × 10.2	5.1 × 7.6	15 MB
Poster	2048 × 3072	28.4 × 42.6	19.2 × 28.9	13.6 × 20.48	10.2 × 15.3	30 MB

Clearly, as the pixel-per-inch resolution goes up, the overall size of the image goes down. For instance, a wallet size at 72 ppi resolution is a respectable size (about 1-3/4 × 2-1/5 inches), but at 200 ppi resolution the image size is only about a half-inch by an inch. The reason for this is the resolution needed to print the photo.

Understanding Photo Resolution

The resolution shown in Table 6.3 refers to the resolution of the printed photograph. The finer and more life-like you want the photo, the higher its resolution needs to be. Without going into a lot of technical details, let me explain basically how photos are printed. Photos that you take with your camera are called continuous tone prints or slides. If you look at them with a magnifying glass you see colors—tones—that blend seemlessly from one to another, comprising the image. Well, you can't reproduce those tones with a printing press. Instead, you must first break up the continuous tones with a lined screen. The screen forces the image into dots of ink. The darker the ink, the closer the dots are to each other. The lighter the ink, the more white space is around each dot. Look at any printed picture under a glass and you'll see what I mean. The lines of the screened photo determine how clearly it is printed. An example of different screens is shown in Figure 6.8 and Figure 6.9 on the next page.

Figure 6.8 *A 15 lines-per-inch version of a photo.*

Figure 6.9 *A 60 lines-per-inch version of the photo in Figure 6.8.*

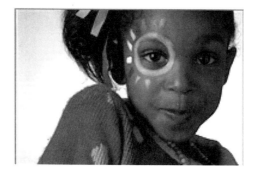

Once you have decided on the number of lines per inch (the finer and smoother the paper, the higher number of lines per inch you can use), you must decide the resolution (pixels or dots per inch). The higher the number of dots per inch resolution, the smaller and closer the dots are and the finer the lines can be. When combined in the correct ratio, the right number of lines per inch and the right number of dots per inch make a printed photo look like its original, continuous-tone brother.

The ratio of dots per inch and lines per inch should be somewhere between 1.2:1 and 2:1 for the best printed results. Since normal, high-quality color printing requires at least a 133 lines-per-inch screen, the resolution for the photo should be somewhere between 159.6 (which is 1.2 times the lines-per-inch) to 266 dots per inch (twice line screen). How low a ratio can you get away with in color printing? See Color Plate 4 for some examples.

Using the Correct Sized Photo CD for the Correct Resolution

Now that you have a grasp of the line screen resolution needed for a quality reproduction of a photo, let's go back to that table of sizes and see what we need to add a photo to the page. Keep in mind two rules in determining the right size photo for the right resolution:

1. Keep the file size of the scanned photo as small as you can.

2. Try not to increase the size of a photo, rather choose an image size close to, or a little larger than what you need, and reduce the image by either scaling or cropping to the size you need. When you enlarge a photo over its image size (based on the resolution you'll be using) you add imaginary pixels, which reduce the clarity of the printed photo. When you reduce the size of a photo, you simply don't use some of the pixels available (which has no effect on the quality of the printed photo).

GLOSSARY

Scaling and ***cropping*** are both ways of resizing a photo. When you scale a photo, you enlarge or reduce its size by a percentage of the original size. For example, if you have a space for a photo that's two inches wide, but your photo is four inches wide, scaling the photo by 50 percent would make it fit the opening— while the size is proportionally smaller, the whole image is still visible. Cropping, on the other hand, trims away that portion of the photo that you don't need. Think of a cropping tool as electronic scissors.

Here's how you go about picking the right size image from your Photo CD:

You need a photo to fit in a 3-by-5 inch space on a page. If you refer to Table 6.3, you can see that the snapshot-sized image fits the bill at 72 ppi, but that resolution is too low for the type of printing you want. The standard size, however, is a little larger than what is needed at 150 ppi resolution (which is adequate resolution for the 133-line screen you plan to use). You could use it and reduce as necessary, or you could also go with a higher resolution of the large size image and reduce both the size and the needed resolution. The difference between the two would be file size—the large image, even reduced in size and resolution, would be considerably larger than the standard size image.

Saving your Photo CD Image

Now, let's save the image in a recognized graphic format. Choose the Export command from the Photo Access File menu to display the Export Photo to File dialog box, shown in Figure 6.10, and give the image a more descriptive name than what Kodak gives it. Open the Format list box and choose TIF as the format to save the photo in. Open the Size list box and choose the size you want to work with (it should be the same size that you want to use in your document, or slightly larger, not smaller). Open the Colors list box and choose 24-bit as the color resolution if the photo will be printed as a color photo, or 256 shades of gray if the photo will be printed as a black and white photo. Finally, locate the directory in which you want to store the photo in the Directories list box. Choose OK to save the photo.

Figure 6.10   *Kodak Photo CD Access Export File dialog box.*

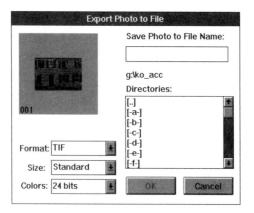

If you are printing your document on a laser printer, or as a black and white document with no color, that's all you have to do. Just import the photo you just saved into your document, position it where you want it, and print the pages. If you are printing the document in color to a color printer, like the QMS ColorScript 100, the color photo (if you saved it in color) prints adequately.

However, if you want your document color printed professionally by a commercial printer, you must go through one more step with the photograph in order for it to be printed. You must open the photo in a photo enhancement program, like Adobe Photoshop, or Aldus PhotoStyler, and save color separations of the photograph. Regardless of the format you saved your image in, it represents color values specified as variations of red, green, and blue. Called *RGB*, these colors represent the primary colors of transmitted light. That's fine for the color monitor on your computer (or your color television) but we need to convert the RGB colors to colors that can be printed. While you can't print RGB-based colors—mainly because printed colors are *reflected*, not transmitted—you can print a reflective version of the colors called *CMYK*, which stands for cyan, magenta, yellow and black. CMYK are your commercial printer's primary color equivalents of RGB. You'll learn more about printing color photos in a moment. First let's see how we can convert your RGB photo to a CMYK photo.

Saving Images as CMYK Photos for Commercial Printing

The three most popular photo enhancing programs are Adobe Photoshop, Aldus PhotoStyler, and Micrografx Picture Publisher (in probably that order). Any of them can take the RGB TIF file that you saved in Kodak Photo CD Access and convert it to an equivalent CMYK file. All three do a lot more than just convert file formats, including minute color correction, image manipulation, special effects, and much, much more. For the purposes of this book, we'll look at Photoshop; however, the other two programs work equally well.

Start Photoshop (which takes quite a while to get rolling as it checks and loads a variety of tools), and open your TIF image you just saved in Photo Access. The Photoshop main window is displayed, shown on the next page.

Notice that the title bar of your photo indicates RGB. Click the Mode menu and choose CMYK Color as the color model for this photo. Photoshop will take a few moments to convert the RGB colors to CMYK colors. Then choose the Save command on the File menu to save the photo in its new color model. That's all there is to it. You have created a CMYK TIF file that can be separated in either PageMaker and QuarkXPress. If you're wondering what I mean when I say separated, and why that's important, let's look briefly at how color photos are actually printed on a commercial printing press. This is a very involved subject and I'm only going to scratch the surface, but you'll have enough information to prepare your own photos for color printing.

How Color Photos are Commercially Printed

The CMYK photo that you just created is separated into the primary colors cyan, magenta, yellow, and black. Together, in different combinations and in differing degrees of intensity, these colors can simulate just about any visible color. That color gets printed onto paper by first creating a printing plate for each of the primary colors (the intensity of the color is created by a closer dot pattern—bright reds would be shown by lots of dots on the magenta plate and the yellow plate; a deeper red might have some black dots as well—the more dots, the more color; fewer dots with more white space around them makes a lighter tint of the color). To create the printing plates of each primary color, you must have film negatives, which are printed by a high-resolution imagesetter. Both PageMaker and QuarkXPress can print the individual primary color separations (also called *seps* or *printers*) directly to the imagesetter. Paper that the photo is printed on is then run across each of the plates: the cyan plate is printed, then the magenta plate is printed precisely over the cyan plate, then the yellow plate is printed precisely over the magenta plate, and finally the black plate is printed over the yellow plate. Combined together in precise alignment, the dot patterns of the four plates blend together to create the colors and images you want in your photograph. See Color Plate 5.

The key to all this is to remember that you must get from an RGB image—which is the normal color model created when the image is scanned—to a CMYK image. RGB may be nice to look at, but you can't separate it and you can't print it commercially.

There are a number of ways to help your commercial printer print your color photos, and save yourself some money. The simplest and most cost effective method is to follow the procedures I've already described:

1. Digitize your own photos.
2. Convert them to CMYK color.
3. Place them on your PageMaker or Quark pages.
4. Separate the whole document.

Have your service bureau create film for your printer, which will be used to create process printing plates. Appendix B gives you more information about preparing color photographs for printing.

Creating Photographic Special Effects

There are any number of creative ideas you can apply to your photos with photo enhancement software, including altering the colors, removing parts of a photo, adding type over the photo, and assigning special effect filters to the photo. Adobe Photoshop, Aldus PhotoStyler, and Micrografx Picture Publisher can each handle these and many other alternations to your original photography. Color Plate 6 shows some of the image editing tools that you can apply; Color Plate 7 shows some of the many special effects. Another interesting way of altering your photos is by using Aldus Gallery Effects software (about $200). Gallery Effects changes your photographs to art work, applying different artistic styles to emulate watercolors, charcoal, pen and ink, and fresco drawings; and other unique effects (see Color Plate 8).

CHAPTER SUMMARY

Graphics can add a touch of magic to your documents that words alone can't hold a candle to. Lines, when used correctly, can help define your page and lead readers where you want them. Photographs and expertly-done clip art can add enormous momentum to your documents. And color photos can set a document apart from its competition. You've seen how easy high-quality color photos are to use with Photo CDs. Now grab that camera, and go take some pictures.

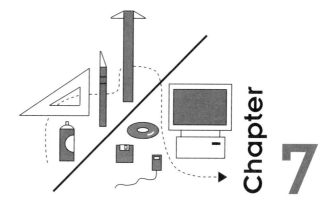

Making Your Work Easier with Templates and Styles

I t was during a summer job before college I first heard the term *template*. I spent the summer working in a boat factory making fiberglass runabouts. After the bare hulls were cured, several of us were ready to screw down all the hardware, like cleats, seats, and windshields. Instead of measuring where to drill each of the holes for the hardware, we laid templates onto the hulls and marked the holes for drilling. The templates fit the appropriate sections of the boats and had holes already punched out where we were to drill. The templates saved us hours of measuring and prevented mistakes, which is exactly what templates can do for your desktop publishing efforts.

235

WHAT ARE TEMPLATES AND STYLES?

Templates and styles are time-savers, nothing more. They save hours of measuring and prevent mistakes. Templates use some essential parts of one document to create other similar documents. If none of the documents you design and produce are ever the same, you'll have little use for templates. But for a lot of users, many of the documents you develop can have remarkable similarity: an eight-page brochure, regardless of the design and message, still has eight pages and usually the same overall page size. Page headers may be different but the pages probably have headers and footers. Columns will later be filled with unique text, yet the columns themselves may well be a standard size. By combining like attributes of a *standard* brochure into a brochure template, you save the need for these formatting steps each time you go to create a new eight-page brochure.

Group similarities of text and paragraphs under common style names. Once a style is assigned to specific text, you can change the specifications of the style to automatically assign the same changes to all text in the document assigned with the style. For instance: let's say you have set up styles for an eight-page brochure. You've created a headline style that formats all heads in 22 point Helvetica bold with 25.2 points of leading, an additional 18 points of space above the head, and 12 points of space below the head. The text for the heads is formatted in small caps, with loose tracking in the color process blue. Finally the first line of the head is indented 12 points and the full headline is set flush left. Now, let's say that you want to change from Helvetica to Gill Sans Extra Bold, set in 18 points, with 22 points of leading, set flush right in process red. If you have assigned the heads to the headline style, the only changes you need to make are to the specifications of the style itself. If you haven't used a style, you must change the headline specification for each headline. If you have 18 heads in your brochure, that means you must:

- Change the font from Helvetica to Gill Sans Extra Bold, 18 times.
- Change the type size from 22 to 18 points, 18 times.
- Change the leading from 25.2 to 22 points, 18 times.
- Change the text alignment from flush left to flush right, 18 times.
- Change the color of the headlines from process blue to process red, 18 times.

In other words, you would make 90 specification changes without styles, versus five specification changes by altering the headline style. That's how styles can save you time. Styles can save you from mistakes by making all the specification changes for you (what happens if you made only 87 of those changes instead of all 90?).

CREATING TEMPLATES AS PLACEHOLDERS

Templates can be simple or complicated:

- Elaborate—such as templates assigned to Microsoft Word for Windows documents.
- Basic—such as a PageMaker template.
- Non-existent—such as WordPerfect 5.2 for Windows, which has no template capability.

While you can get as fancy as you want (and the application allows) remember that the goal is to save time. Make the template as detailed as it needs to be to save you work; if the details of the template aren't applicable to all the documents of the type the template represents, then reduce the complexity of the template.

A Look at PageMaker's Templates

PageMaker has three different kinds of templates: those that you create from scratch—let's call them modifiable templates; those that come already designed and ready to use—we'll call these programmed templates; and those programmed templates that you can modify and save as your own templates.

For example, you can start with a new document page and begin building a template for floppy disk labels; you can open a programmed template called *Diskette Labels* and choose *Avery 7163*, which are labels for 5.25-inch diskettes. Or, you could modify the programmed template to fit your specialized needs and save it as a separate template.

Creating Modifiable Templates

PageMaker creates templates from scratch by saving an existing document as a template. Use the Save as command on the File menu to open the Save publication dialog box, shown in Figure 7.1. You can save any document as a template—doing so doesn't in any way affect the original document, but creates a second document that PageMaker recognizes as a template. Once you have designated a document as a template, PageMaker tries to protect the template from inadvertent changes by prompting you to re-save the template as a new document to apply the changes to.

Figure 7.1 *PageMaker's Save publication dialog box lets you save documents as templates.*

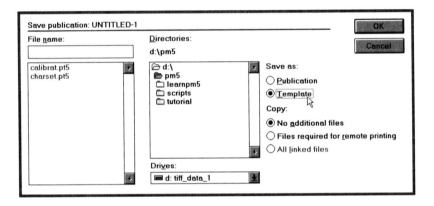

To save a document as a template, click the Save as: Template option button. Type a name for the template in the File name text box. PageMaker differentiates between documents and templates by changing the file name extension. Documents are assigned the extension .PM5; templates are given the .PT5 extension. By clicking on the Save as: Template option, PageMaker automatically adds the template extension for you.

Now is a good time to take a moment and think about what you will be doing with this template. For instance, if you share the template with other PageMaker users on other computers, and the template contains graphics, click the Copy Files for remote printing option button. PageMaker will include all files necessary to duplicate the template on another system. To internally link graphic files to your PageMaker template (meaning the files are incorporated in the file structure of the template file) click the Copy: All linked files option.

Once your file is saved as a template, add whatever recurring material you will need for your documents. For example, if the template is for a weekly newsletter, add the nameplate, the masthead, sectional or department titles, and lines used in the overall design. Define the page size, margins, the number of pages, the number of columns, and any headers or footers. Add page numbers for all interior pages, apply colors (if used) to recurring items on the pages.

If you are using recurring clip art or photos, add them. Even if you don't use the same graphics in each issue, add *placeholder graphics* to show where the issue-specific graphics will be located. (Placeholders mean that they will eventually be replaced by real graphics or stories.) When it comes time to create an issue of the newsletter, you can automatically replace the placeholders with actual graphics and stories by following these steps:

1. Select the graphic or story placeholder you want to replace with a real graphic or story by clicking it with the Pointer tool.

2. Choose the **Place** command on the File menu to open the Place Document dialog box (shown below).

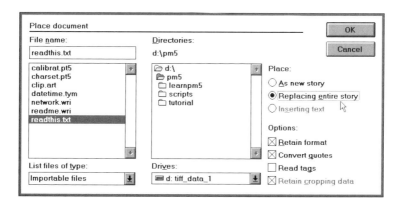

3. Click the graphic or story you want to import, and choose the Replacing entire story option button. When you click the OK button, the placeholder will be replaced with the graphic or story you want.

Opening Programmed Templates

You won't find PageMaker's programmed templates in the Open Publication dialog box. Instead, you must look to the Open Template addition. Additions are activated by choosing the Additions submenu on the Utilities menu. Choose Open Template to see the Open template dialog box, shown in Figure 7.2.

Figure 7.2 *PageMaker's Open template addition shows you a preview of its many professionally-designed templates.*

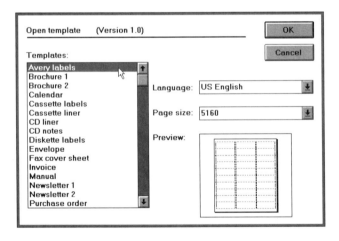

To open a template listed in the list box, click the template name. Check the Size list box to see if there is more than one size offered. For instance, the Avery Labels template provides a number of different sizes to suit specific Avery label sizes. Also, if you have more than the U.S. English dictionary installed, you can choose templates created in British English or foreign languages. Choose OK to open the template. You'll notice that the template opens automatically as a new, unnamed document.

Modifying Programmed Templates

While PageMaker doesn't allow you to modify its programmed templates, once the template is opened, it becomes a normal PageMaker document. You can change it any way you want, and re-save the document as a modifiable template. To do so, simply make whatever changes you want to the new document, choose the Save As command from the File menu, and in the Save Publication As dialog box, click the Save As Template option button. Give the template a new file name, and click OK. Now you can open the modified template whenever you want, save it as a new document, or continue refining it to service your specialized needs.

A Look at Microsoft Word Templates

Word for Windows lets you create powerful, customized templates that include text and graphics, glossaries, and even macro functions. (Glossaries can be either text or graphics that you use on a regular basis, such as the closing of a business letter.) To create a template, start with a normal document and add the common elements that you want included in the template. Then choose the Save As command from the File menu to open the Save As dialog box, shown in Figure 7.3.

Figure 7.3 *Word for Windows Save As dialog box lets you save documents as templates.*

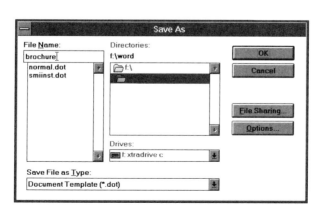

Give the template a file name and choose Document Template in the Save File as Type list box. Word will add the extension .DOT to the file name, indicating the file is a Word template. Choose OK and Word will display a Summary Info dialog box, shown below. Use this dialog box to add vital information about the template—the information may seem obvious to you but will certainly help someone else understand the purpose of this template.

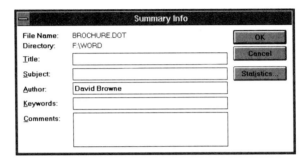

To later open the template and save it as a document, choose the Open command from the File menu. In the Open dialog box select Document Templates in the List Files of Type list box. Choose the drive and directory containing your template that is displayed in the list of file names. Choose OK to open the template. Then select the Save As command from the File menu, and save the template as a normal Word for Windows file.

To include a Word glossary with the template, type the text specified the way you want, or create the graphic you want. Select the text or graphic with the mouse and choose the Glossary command on the Edit menu. You will see the Glossary dialog box, shown in Figure 7.4. Type a name for the glossary and choose the Define button to save it and add it to the list. Then, whenever you want to insert the contents of a glossary in a template (or document, for that matter), position the insertion point where you want the glossary, choose the Glossary command, and double-click the glossary you want.

Figure 7.4   *Word for Windows' Glossary dialog box saves often-used phrases or graphics.*

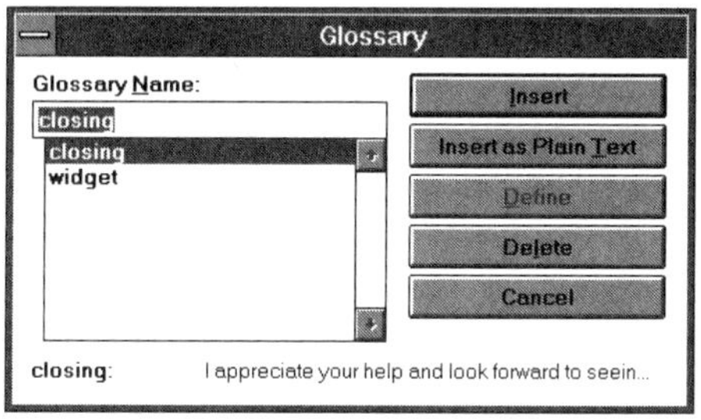

Faking Templates in WordPerfect

WordPerfect has no template feature, but that's not to say you can't fake one—here's how. One of the benefits to the way WordPerfect stores file names is that it doesn't care, nor require, what the extension is. Normally, I save WordPerfect documents with the extension .WP5, because that's what PageMaker looks for to import WordPerfect documents; but could use any valid three-character extension. Consequently, there's nothing to stop you from creating your own WordPerfect templates with a special template extension. A good template extension might be .TEM or .WPT, but don't use .TMP since programs often store their own temporary files with this extension.

So now that we've decided on a template extension, let's create a template. First open a new document, sized the way you want, with margins set according to the needs of the future documents this template will represent. Add whatever text and graphics you want to include. Now choose the Save command on the File menu to open the Save As dialog box, shown in Figure 7.5 on the next page. Enter the name you want for this template, with the template extension you've decided to use. Choose Save to save the new document as a template.

Figure 7.5 *WordPerfect for Windows' Save As dialog box saving a document as a fake template.*

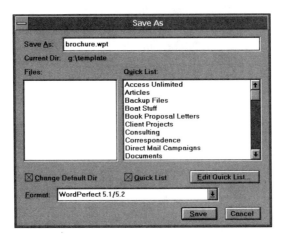

If you decide to save an existing document as a template, open the document and choose the Save As command from the file menu. In the Save As dialog box, give the existing document a new template name and choose the Save button. Another interesting thing you can do with WordPerfect's Save As dialog box is to create a Quick List entry for templates and store all your templates in the Quick List category. Just click the Edit Quick List

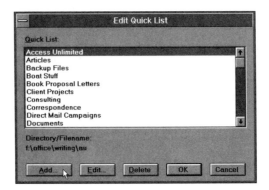

button to see the Edit Quick List dialog box, shown on the lower left page. Choose the Add button to enter a directory name and Quick List name for the category. Choose Save to save the entry. Now all your templates are easily filed together in the same directory.

CREATING STYLES FOR EVERY OCCASION

As I said earlier in this chapter, styles can save you the tiresome chore of manually changing dozens, if not hundreds of individual type and paragraph specifications. Just think about a sizeable document for a moment, use this book as an example. Think about the time necessary if someone decided that the first order heads should really be set with two points more leading. Then some poor soul (probably you) has to spend half the night scrolling through each of the chapters, highlighting each of the heads with the mouse, opening the leading menu and choosing the new leading specification. Scroll, swish, click, click, click. Now, let's say you have to change three or four other aspects of the head at the same time. Night will turn to a gray, dreary dawn before you're through. My vision blurs just thinking about it. If, on the other hand, you've tied all the type and paragraph specifications to styles, a few clicks of the mouse and you're done.

Saving Time and Money with Styles

The important thing to remember about styles is not so much what goes in a style, but that you assigned a style to each paragraph in your document. You needn't do any formatting, simply open up a new document, go directly to the styles setup dialog box, and start creating styles for all the different types of text you think you may need. After the style names are created, go about the business of writing or importing the text, and assign style names throughout the document. Now, here's the secret to getting the most out of styles: do all your formatting in the create (or define) styles dialog box. As you make a type or paragraph change you can save the style and return to your document to see the instant results of your formatting. To make more adjustments: back to the styles. When you use styles in an interactive way, they become a powerful efficiency tool that saves you enormous amounts of time and creative energy.

Styles for Brochures

A basic set of styles for a brochure might look like this:

Table 7.1   *Styles for brochures.*

Style	Font	Size	Attributes
First order heads	Gill Sans Condensed	18pt	Bold, Initial caps
Second order heads	Gill Sans Condensed	14pt	Bold, All caps
Third order heads	Gill Sans Extra Bold	11pt	Bold, Initial Caps
Body text	Times Roman	12/14	

There's nothing spectacular about the styles shown above. But they are basic styles and a good place to start for any brochure, flyer, fact sheet, or marketing piece. In general, heads can be smaller and more compact with marketing brochures because you generally have pictures and other graphics on the page to offer visual relief. Notice that the text for this brochure is set in 12 point type. Brochures can again get away with slightly large body text; you're often working with longer, irregular line measures, and frankly brochures need to shout a little bit to be read. To dress up the words, you might offer an indent to the first line of each paragraph, but keep the heads all flush left (we expect heads to begin flush left, probably because we are trained by daily newspapers which have always tended to use flush left heads).

Styles for Books and Manuals

Basic styles for proposals, manuals, documentation, and books offer a slightly different look, in the following table.

Table 7.2   *Styles for manuals and books.*

Style	Font	Size	Attributes
First order heads	Friz Quadrata	24pt	Bold, Initial caps
Second order heads	Friz Quadrata	16pt	Bold, Initial caps, 119% horizontal scaling
Third order heads	Friz Quadrata	14pt	Bold, Initial caps
Body text	Benguiat	10.5/14	

Longer, text-dominant publications like books, manuals, and wordy proposals must rely on typography as their only form of visual relief. You must start with type for both heads and body copy that is appealing to see and easy to read. Friz Quadrata, for example, has a nice balance of thick and thin strokes, with very slight finishing serifs. When bolded, it's heavy enough to stand out in a headline, yet still light enough to keep from adding to the darkness of type on the page. The sizes for heads are a good balance, large enough to stand out and act as signposts for the reader, but not overwhelming. The second order head style was stretched a bit horizontally to add a little more weight to the size (without increasing its height).

Body text is set in Benguiat, an attractive face with medium serifs that won't break up when printed in small sizes. You may have noticed that even though Benguiat is set in 10.5 points, it appears as large or larger than the 12 point Times Roman. That's because Benguiat has a very tall x-height, which makes it appear larger than it is. The larger x-height gives the font high marks in reading-ease, but you must treat it like it was a larger size and give it more leading than normal. Here, the 13 points of leading offers a nice amount of space for the lines.

CHAPTER SUMMARY

If you haven't used templates and styles, I hope this chapter has whetted your interest to do so. Templates and styles bring organization to projects that are often chaotic by nature. In the rush to get your documents to the printers, or during those last-minute efforts to find and correct the last of the typos, there isn't much time to think about creating templates or adding styles. So think about them now: where can templates of special documents help you? Where would styles save the persistent need to make minor typographic changes throughout documents? And where can both templates and styles be combined to help you with the important stuff: saving you time and making you money.

Be Your Own Printer

You simply must buy a laser printer, if you don't own one already. A laser printer is fundamental to desktop publishing. Without it, you can't accurately proof your work, nor print final, camera-ready pages. Luckily, prices are most attractive, competition fierce, and features abundant. A modern PostScript laser printer does just about everything for you except fix coffee. Fonts come out crisp and clean, their position on the page is exact. Graphics are perfect. Crop marks are entirely accurate. The PostScript laser printer is the unsung hero of desktop publishing and a powerful force in the general acceptance and popularity of desktop publishing systems. It wasn't always so.

Perhaps you remember back before the days of PostScript laser printers, back to the old days, when holiday banners would appear in the computer room spelling out *Merry Christmas and Happy New Year*? The giant letters of the banner were made up of individual printer characters drawn to represent the larger letters, as shown on the next page.

Boy, did we think we were cool getting a dot matrix printer, or a mainframe line printer, to print out those huge banners. Almost like typesetting, wasn't it? *Wrong.* It was the farthest thing from typesetting. At the time, making letters a foot tall out of pica or elite characters on a dot matrix printer was all we had. A far cry from what the least expensive PostScript laser printer can do with the same letter:

A lot of technological ground has been covered since then. PostScript laser printers, like the Apple LaserWriter, became the workhorses of early desktop publishing, but were so expensive that many designers were forced back to dot matrix printers to proof their work. I rushed to buy the very first Texas Instruments PostScript printer in 1986, which sported plug-in ports for font cartridges, carried an unheard of 1.5 megabytes of memory, printed a whooping eight pages per minute, and set me back close to $6,000. Over seven years it printed more than 100,000 pages for me, and when its power supply finally died, I replaced it with a faster, quieter, smaller PostScript printer for less than $900! Today, for the cost of my first laser printer, you can buy a 1200 dpi laser printer that rivals PostScript imagesetters in high-resolution text and graphics.

Laser printers, high-resolution imagesetters, even fonts, have dropped in price, and the cost of a PostScript printer is hardly more than a non-PostScript printer, such as the HP LaserJet. The LaserJet, instead of being controlled by PostScript, has its own control language called *PCL* (for *Printer Control Language*). LaserJet 4s come with PCL version 5, a remarkable system that allows for scalable fonts and some graphic printing. Yet, PCL printers cannot print Type 1 fonts (without some help, which I'll explain in a moment). PCL printers can't print color separations, nor do they understand how to print halftone screens at specified angles (something any PostScript printer can do). Depending on what you want to create with your desktop publishing system, a PCL-type laser printer may serve you well. However, for the majority of users (and for a few dollars more), I strongly recommend buying a PostScript laser printer, almost all of which can emulate a LaserJet anyway. Some specific suggestions for PostScript printers are offered in Appendix A.

THE BEAUTY OF POSTSCRIPT COMPATIBILITY

The PostScript printer is the heart of desktop publishing—without it you'd have the desktop but no publishing. PostScript is a term that crops up throughout this book (you can hardly find a book about Windows or the Macintosh without repeated references to PostScript), it's what makes desktop publishing possible. You have the folks at Adobe Systems to thank for PostScript; in particular, John Warnock and Martin Newell did much preliminary work on PostScript in the late '70s. Chuck Geschke and John later started Adobe and finalized PostScript—a page description language that describes graphic shapes. The brilliance of PostScript is that it is not tied to any one type of printer (as are page description languages such as PCL). Each printer carries its own PostScript interpreter that interprets the graphic descriptions in light of the printer's own capabilities. So fonts look absolutely great on inexpensive 300 dpi laser printers, and even more gorgeous on 3000 dpi imagesetters. It would be an understatement to say that PostScript has singlehandedly revolutionized publishing as much as, if not more than, the Gutenberg press.

The fact that PostScript printers decide how to best print PostScript files is fundamentally important to the design and development of documents. It means that by simply changing the Windows printer driver we can choose which printer we want to print our document. For example, in a large production facility you might have several different laser printers for proofing different-sized pages; a QMS ColorScript 200 for proofing color pages; a Linotronic L-260 for high-resolution output of black and white pages; and an Agfa SelectSet 5000 for high-resolution output of color work. All can be connected to your Windows computer system and you can send the same file to any printer by simply choosing the appropriate Windows printer driver. The file remains the same regardless of which printer the file is sent to for printing.

PostScript compatibility also means the assurance that your files print, first time, every time to any PostScript printer. In shopping for a PostScript printer make sure it is a true PostScript-compatible device: there are PostScript clones that purport to be fully compatible (which I would question) and there are always ads for PCL clones that make dubious claims about supporting desktop publishing. Be careful—sticking with PostScript means you know exactly what you're getting.

THE BEAUTY OF WINDOWS PRINTER COMPATIBILITY

Just as PostScript files print on any PostScript printer, files from Windows applications print on any printer defined with a Windows printer driver. Think about the significance of this for a moment. Windows applications don't really care which printers you have defined. If it's available in the Windows Control Panel, the printer can print the application's files. That's because Windows uses a centralized printing facility in the Control Panel to control printers. And I'll tell you a secret: You *don't* have to have a printer connected to your computer to print to it (which means you can theoretically print to any printer). For instance, I print lots of documents to a $60,000 Linotype-Hell L-330 imagesetter, and I certainly don't own one. (I'll explain how to print to non-existent printers in a moment.) All you need is the Windows printer driver for the printer you want, regardless of whether the printer is physically attached to your system. Windows printer compatibility means that you have access to hundreds of printers—several dozen laser printers, color printers, and a number of high-resolution imagesetters from Agfa, Linotype-Hell, and Varityper—without spending a penny to own them.

Understanding Printer Drivers in Windows

Unlike applications in DOS, Windows applications share one common set of printer drivers. Only one driver needs to be loaded and selected in order to print in any application, be it a database, spreadsheet, word processor, personal information manager, or desktop publisher. You can review the list of installed printers by opening the Control Panel. Here's how:

Control Panel

1. Double-click the Control Panel icon in the Main group, as shown on the left.

2. The Control Panel icon opens to show the following window:

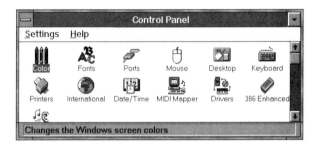

3. Double-click the Printers icon to open the Printers dialog box:

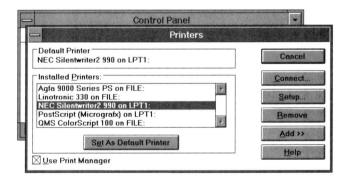

The printers currently installed in your system are shown in the dialog box list. Double-click the printer you want to select for your print job. If you want that printer to always be the standard printer for printing your work, click the Set as Default Printer button. To install more printers in your system, click the Add button. The bottom of the dialog box drops down to show the following list of available printers:

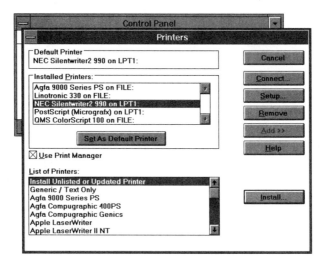

Scroll through the list to find the printer you want to add to your Windows system. Double-click the printer and it will be added to the list. (Windows may ask you to insert one of the original Windows installation diskettes in the A: drive to find the printer driver you selected.)

Changing Printer Drivers at Any Time

You can change the selected printer at any time, either by going through the Control Panel as we just explained, or by using the application you're working in. For instance, in PageMaker, open the Print dialog box and click on the Print to box arrow to see the same list of printers as in the Control Panel:

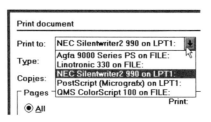

In Microsoft Publisher, open the Print Setup dialog box, and click on the Printer list box arrow, to see the same list of printers as in the Control Panel:

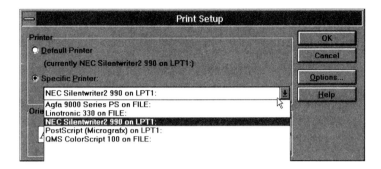

In all cases, if you go back to the Control Panel and install another printer, that printer will be part of the available printers list in all your Windows applications.

USING PRINT MANAGER TO SPEED UP PRINTING

Print Manager is one of the many Windows 3.1 programs installed on your system—you may or may not be using it. Print Manager is a *print spooler*, meaning it accepts the print job from the application you're printing in, stores the job temporarily, and resends the job automatically at a rate the printer can accept. Without Print Manager, since the printer can't print as quickly as the application can send the job to the printer, the application must wait as each document page is processed and printed. Unfortunately, while the application waits, you wait. If you use Print Manager, it does the waiting, returning the application back to you and your work. Print Manager runs entirely automatically, in the background. You need not click on its icon (as you must other applications) to start it running, it starts by itself whenever you print a page.

To use Print Manager, look at the bottom of the Printers dialog box in the Control Panel for the Print Manager check box. If there is an X in the box, Print Manager is operational; if there is no X, click the box to add an X.

With Print Manager activated, printing one or more documents from any Windows applications stacks the print jobs in the Print Manager's queue, as shown in Figure 8.1. You can move to the Print Manager by holding down the Alt key and repeatedly pressing the Tab key until you see the Print Manager window. The status of each print job is clearly shown, along with the file name, and in some cases the application that created the print job.

Figure 8.1   *The Windows Print Manager handles all your printing tasks, while you continue to work.*

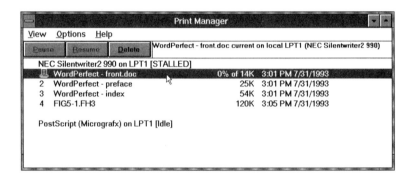

Managing Print Queues

With several documents stacked in the queue, like in Figure 8.1, you may find that you need a document printed immediately that is waiting behind other documents to be printed. It's a simple matter to change the order of the print job. Click the job whose order you want to change, and drag it to a new position in the queue. For example, if you want the FreeHand drawing to be printed immediately, click the file name and drag it over the file in the second position. You'll see a double line over the file where the file you're moving will be inserted, as shown below:

🖳	WordPerfect - front.doc	0% of 14K	3:01 PM 7/31/1993
2	WordPerfect - preface	25K	3:01 PM 7/31/1993
3	WordPerfect - index ⇧	54K	3:01 PM 7/31/1993
4	FIG5-1.FH3	120K	3:05 PM 7/31/1993

When you release the mouse button, the FreeHand file is inserted above what was the second file and the new priority list is displayed:

🖳	WordPerfect - front.doc	0% of 14K	3:01 PM 7/31/1993
2	FIG5-1.FH3	120K	3:05 PM 7/31/1993
3	WordPerfect - preface	25K	3:01 PM 7/31/1993
4	WordPerfect - index	54K	3:01 PM 7/31/1993

Changing Printing Priorities

Windows is often called *multitasking* (able to do two things at once), but in fact it isn't. What it can do is fool you into thinking it is running both your application and Print Manager simultaneously by dividing its time into very quick segments and jumping between Print Manager and your application. If it jumps fast enough, you won't notice the small interruptions while Print Manager goes about the business of printing your documents. You may find at times that it's more important to get the jobs printed in Print Manager at the expense of suffering some minor interruptions. Another time you might find it beneficial to have Printer Manager suffer the interruptions while you concentrate on your application. Either way you simply change Print Manager's priority. Open Print Manager (if it's not running already) by clicking on the Print Manager icon in the Main group. Then open the Options menu to see your choices, listed in detail on the following page.

Figure 8.2 *Print Manager's Options menu lets you adjust its priority in relation to other Windows applications.*

Options Help
Low Priority
Medium Priority
√ **H**igh Priority
Alert Always
Flash if Inactive
√ **I**gnore if Inactive
Network Settings...
Network **C**onnections...
Printer Setup...

- Choose Low Priority if you want to devote the most priority to the application you're using, and the least attention to Print Manager. Your printing probably takes a little longer with this setting.

- Select Medium Priority if you want an equitable balance between both the application you're using and Print Manager.

- Choose High Priority if you want to get your documents printed at the expense of minor interruptions in your application.

CONTROLLING YOUR LASER PRINTER

For a device as intelligent and versatile as a modern PostScript laser printer, it actually has few controls. Generally speaking, it handles the business of printing your pages without fuss or bother. By comparison, configuring and controlling a little dot matrix printer that costs a tenth as much can be a real headache. But there are a few features that need to be included in this chapter. First a few words about resolution and memory. The resolution of a PostScript laser printer is a very subjective thing. It's kind of like the horsepower of your car's engine—most of the time you need very little of it, but when you have to pass a truck on a two-lane road you want all you can get. Printer resolution is like that: most of the time 300 dpi is perfectly acceptable; but on rare occasions you may need more. Printer memory is similar in that more is usually considered better. Let's set things straight. Unless you are printing camera-ready pages that include photos (and you need a higher line screen than 106 lines-per-inch), 300 dots per inch from a modern PostScript laser printer is in most cases absolutely fine. While your pages look better coming from a 600 dpi printer (which costs about twice what a 300 dpi PostScript printer costs), the improvement isn't noticeable in most instances. The same advice applies to printer memory. You really need 2 megabytes to adequately handle PostScript files. However, 2 megabytes of memory is more than enough in most instances. Printer memory is expensive and you may be better off spending the same amount of money on more RAM for your computer. In those rare instances when you need higher resolution than 300 dpi, consider using a serivce bureau.

Changing Page Orientation

Page orientation refers to whether the page is printed in portrait mode or landscape mode. When the top of the page is one of the narrow sides of the paper it is in *portrait mode. Landscape mode* is when the long side of the page is at the top. There are two page orientations you must specify in the process of developing and printing documents. The first orientation is the *composition orientation*—how the page is oriented for layout and composition. You specify the composition orientation when you create and set up a new page—some applications call the two modes of orientation *tall* or *wide*. The result is that the page is oriented on the pasteboard in the manner you select when you set up the new page. However, in order for it to print in that same orientation, you must select a second page orientation each time the page is printed.

Changing the page orientation for printing is done through the Control Panel (or the individual application's print setup). Open the Printer dialog box, as previously described, and choose the Setup button to open the Setup dialog box:

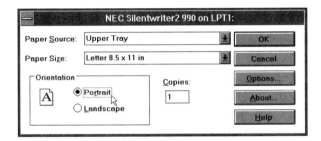

Click the Orientation option button you want for the document that will be printed (it should match the composition orientation you have already specified). While we're looking at this dialog box, let's see what you can do with it:

- **Set the source for paper.** Based on the type of laser printer you have, you can specify where the paper comes from: the upper or lower trays (you can have different sized paper in each), a manual feed slot, or an envelope tray.

- **Choose the size of paper.** Different laser printers can handle a variety of different-sized paper. Even though you may have specified a paper tray that contains 8.5-by-14 inch paper, you must still tell Windows the size of the paper in this list box.

- **Specify the number of copies.** If you want more than one copy of each page, enter the number of copies in the Copies text box.

Scaling the Size of the Printed Page

One of the many advantages of PostScript printers is the ability to reduce or enlarge the printed page, called *scaling the page*. Scaling can be set in the Control Panel. Some applications, such as PageMaker and QuarkXPress, can set a scaling value in their Print dialog boxes. If you have the choice between the application and the Control Panel, always use the application. For now, let's see how to set scaling in the Control Panel.

Open the Control Panel, click the Printers icon, and click the PostScript printer in your list of installed printers. Choose the Setup button, and in the Setup dialog box, choose the Options button. You see an Options dialog box for your PostScript printer, as shown below:

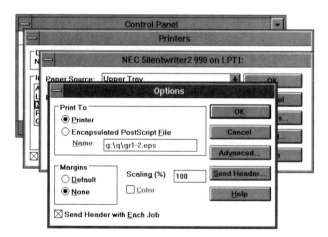

You can specify any scaling value as a percentage of the page's original size, which is always 100 percent. So, if you want to print a page that is half the original size, you would enter 50 in the Scaling text box. Similarly, if you want to print the page twice as large as the original, you would enter 200 in the Scaling box. By the way, in order to print crop marks on an 8.5-by-11 inch page (if that's the widest size paper your laser printer holds) enter a scaling value of 75 percent in the scaling text box. Your pages will print at about three-quarters their original size and you'll see the crop marks in place.

Controlling Memory

If you click the Advanced button in the Options dialog box, you will open the Advanced dialog box. In the dialog box you can specify the amount of virtual memory contained in your printer.

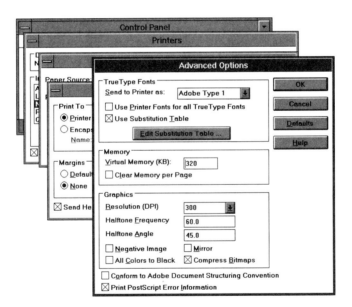

The amount of memory entered in the Virtual Memory text box is not the total memory contained in your printer, but that portion devoted to keeping downloaded fonts in memory. No, this doesn't mean that you can set up more memory than your printer actually has—entering an amount larger than what is physically in your printer makes absolutely no difference. However, if you are trying to print a document with a larger number of fonts on each page, and your printer is experiencing difficulty, try entering a lower figure than the actual memory. Your printer is forced to clear its memory more often and will have less difficulty handling the fonts.

To find out how much memory your printer sets aside for fonts, download a test file included with Windows 3.1 called TESTPS.TXT. To download the file, double-click the MS-DOS icon in the Main group. Once you are in DOS, type the following command:

```
copy C:\WINDOWS\SYSTEM\TESTPS.TXT LPT1
```

Where c:\WINDOWS\SYSTEM is the actual directory for Windows (it might be on another drive) and LPT1 is the actual printer port your printer is connected to (if it's cabled to LPT2, than enter that port instead). Be sure to leave one space between *Copy* and *C:* and one space between the name of the file and the printer port.

When you have typed the command, press the Enter key. DOS reports [1 file(s) copied]. In a moment, your printer will eject a sheet of paper with information similar to the example:

Max Printer VM (KB):	317.0
Max Suggested VM (KB):	269.0
Baud Rate:	9600
Data Bits:	8
Parity:	None
Stop Bits:	1
Flow Control:	Xon/Xoff

To get back to Windows, type **EXIT** at the DOS prompt. Now reopen the Advanced Options dialog box in the Control Panel and compare the amount of virtual memory with what is on your report. By the way, the rest of the information on the report shows the current communication settings for your laser printer if you need to connect it to a COM port, instead of an LPT port.

N O T E

Which is the fastest port to connect a laser printer to? PostScript printers carry a variety of printer ports, usually including Appletalk, serial (COM ports), parallel (LPT ports), and sometimes Ethernet ports. If your printer has an Ethernet port, it is by far the fastest, but requires installing an Ethernet card in your computer, running Ethernet cable between the two machines, and some intricate adjustments in Windows. Ethernet is usually reserved for either network printers or for high-resolution imagesetters that print huge graphic files. The next fastest port is the parallel port; significantly slower is the Appletalk port and the slowest of all is the serial port.

Printing Proofs

As I said at the beginning of this chapter, the best use of a PostScript laser printer is to proof your work. Proofing is an integral part of document composition and production, and the only way you can actually see the results of your efforts. As good as WYSIWYG desktop publishing systems are, they are really WYPIWYG—What You Print is What You Get—for it's the printed results that are the proof of this pudding. Proofing doesn't necessarily take any time away from your design efforts: use Print Manager to reduce the time your application is distracted, and, since graphics slow down printing the most, reduce their resolution (or eliminate them altogether) from printed proofs.

Both PageMaker and QuarkXPress allow you to print pages without printing graphics. PageMaker's Print dialog box, using the Options command (Figure 8.3) allows you to eliminate the printing of TIFFs altogether. Choose it or the Low resolution option to greatly increase the speed at which TIFFs print. QuarkXPress uses a Suppress Printout option in the specifications for graphic boxes. Click on the option to add an X and the picture box prints, but whatever graphic is contained in the box won't print.

Figure 8.3 *PageMaker's Options dialog box (inside the Print dialog box).*

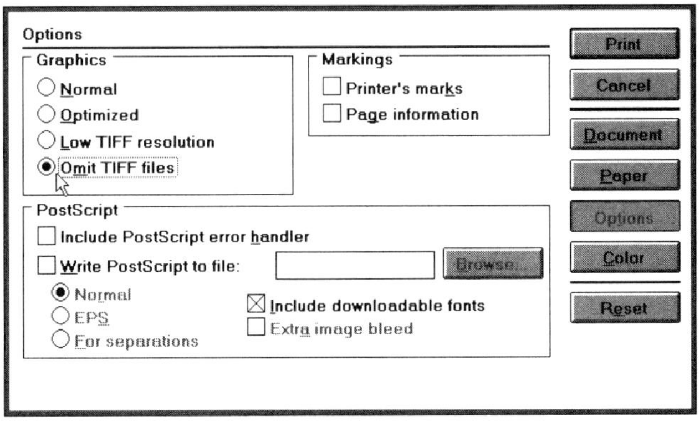

If the application you're using lacks a provision to specifically eliminate graphics from a printout of the document, here are a couple of tricks.

Ways to speed up proof printing:

- **WordPerfect.** In the Print dialog box, click the Graphics Quality list box and set to Do Not Print.

- **Word for Windows.** In the Print dialog box, move to the Options dialog box and click the Draft Output check box to add an X.

- **Excel.** In the Print dialog box click Fast, but No Graphics check box to add an X.

- **FreeHand.** In the Print dialog box, move to the Options dialog box and enter a flatness value of 5 or more, which simplifies draft printing.

- **Microsoft Publisher.** Open the Tools menu and choose the Hide Pictures command to remove the checkmark and disable the command. Your graphics will disappear. Print the file as you normally would; graphics will be missing and your proof will print much faster.

Printing Your Final Pages

Once you have gone through printing proofs to check the layout, type, and graphics, you're ready to print the final version of your document. Before doing so, you must decide what you will do with the final pages, and how they will be reproduced. If you simply need one copy to send to a client, by all means print that copy on your laser printer, if possible. If you need 20 copies, depending on the number of pages in each copy, you might be better off using your laser printer to print the copies. If you need a larger printing run, you can print the final master of the document on your laser printer and deliver it to your commercial printer, or send the job to a service bureau.

Using Your Laser Printer

If you choose to print the final copies of your document on your laser printer, remember to turn off whatever options you may have used to disable the printing of graphics. If you are running 8.5-by-11 inch paper through your printer, and the final page size is 8.5-by-11 inch, you needn't make use of crop marks (nor would you see them). If you are printing a document that is smaller than 8.5-by-11 inch, crop marks will help you trim the document (take the pages to your commercial printer—they'll do a better job than you can do with a pair of scissors).

Adjusting the toner can make a significant difference in the quality of the printed image. If your laser printer has controls for lightening or darkening the toner make the following adjustments: for pages with lots of text, especially in small sizes, or for pages containing lots of hairlines or very thin lines, set the toner adjustment as light as you can so that the edges of characters don't appear fuzzy under a magnifying glass. For pages with lots of graphic halftones, lots of black, or for pages with very large, heavy type, increase the toner adjustment until the black prints without streaks. By taking the time to make minute adjustments and test the results, you can get pages that are very close in quality to what an imagesetter can give you.

Finally, load your laser printer with the smoothest paper you can find—the smoother the finish the crisper the toner appears. Hammermill, Xerox, and other manufacturers make paper specifically treated with an extra smooth finish for laser printers. For instance, Hammermill Laser Print 32-lb. is an extra smooth finish, as is Weyerhaeuser First Choice.

Using a Printer Not Connected to Your Computer

For larger printing runs, generally higher than 150 *impressions*, it is probably more economical to use a commercial printer than your laser printer (an impression is one sheet of paper run once through a printing press—150 copies of one page equals 150 impressions, as do 10 copies of a 15-page document). If you will be coughing up the expense of commercial printing, you might as well have your camera-ready pages produced by a high-resolution imagesetter. Unless you happen to have an imagesetter in your office, you need to send your document on disk to a service bureau for processing. Now, if the document was created in PageMaker or QuarkXPress, chances are you could send the .PM5 or the .QXD file to the service bureau and they would print it. However, giving the service bureau application files means that you must also give them all the fonts used in your document (which probably violates the font license agreement). It also means that someone at the service bureau could mistakenly change something in the file.

A better, safer way of supplying documents on disk is as PostScript files (also called *print-to-disk files*, or PRN files because of the .PRN extension).

PostScript files are files that are printed to the hard disk instead of the printer. Because they're prepared to print, all the necessary font information, and all of the graphics are already included in the file. Everything is included in PostScript files; all the service bureau does is resend the file—this time to the printer instead of the hard drive—and the file prints as it should. The key to creating PostScript files is to choose the Windows print driver for the printer or imagesetter the service bureau will use when they process the file. This necessitates a call to the service bureau to ask three questions:

1. What is the model imagesetter you will be using to print the file I'm going to send you? It will most likely be a Linotype-Hell, Agfa-Compugraphic, or Varityper model.

2. What version or type of RIP are you using for that model? The RIP (*raster image processor*) is a computer in the printer that translates the PostScript file into dots that the printer can understand. There are different versions of RIPs depending on how old the equipment is.

3. Based on the paper size of my job, what size paper (or film), and what orientation will you be using to run my job? The service bureau may run your job on larger paper, or may turn the pages by specifying a different orientation.

Now go to the Control Panel, open the Printers dialog box, click Add and look down the list of printers until you find the one that corresponds to the service bureau's imagesetter. Install the printer. Click the Connect button to open the Connect dialog box, shown below, to choose the printer port for this printer.

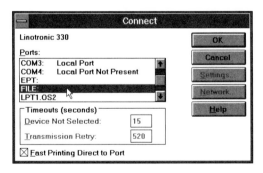

The Connect dialog box specifies the physical connection for each printer. In this case you're not connecting to a real printer, so scroll down the Ports list and click on File. Choose OK to return to the Printers dialog box, and select Close to go back to the Control Panel.

The final step is to open the application that created the document, move to the Print dialog box, and print the document with the imagesetter printer driver. If the service bureau wants a specific-sized paper, open the Paper Size list box and choose the correct size. When you choose OK to print, you see a small dialog box asking for the name of the file. Enter a path, filename, and extension of .PRN, like this:

`A:NEWSLTR.PRN`

Which means the file is created on a floppy drive in the A: drive, and its name is NEWSLTR.PRN.

Send the .PRN file to your service bureau. If they have PCs, they use the Copy command to send the file to the imagesetter. If they have Macintoshes, they'll need to change the name of the extension to .PS and download it to the imagesetter with a file downloading utility.

CHAPTER SUMMARY

The PostScript laser printer is an intelligent device, with as much processing power and memory as many computers. Designing and producing documents without a PostScript laser printer is like trying to get through college without ever buying your textbooks. Designing and producing documents with a PostScript laser printer is a natural extension of the power and versatility you have in your Windows computer. Or, as we say in the South, they're like chicken and dumplins, they just go together.

PART III

Publishing Companion for the Desktop

ffice projects, ah yes...all those little projects that stack up on the desks of freelance artists. The simple little projects that always seem to come back wrong. And late. And way, way over the initial estimate. Literature with the wrong color scheme, a sales staff without business cards, forms that need correcting, product literature that still isn't finished. From the desk of memo pads, parking signs for the new executive lot, a new menu for the cafeteria, a dwendling supply of stationery—design and print jobs subcontracted to outsiders who don't know your priorities and don't care.

If you've felt helpless and frustrated you're certainly not alone. "If I could just do these little things myself," you think, "and get them done." Well here's your chance. Those little projects that raise your blood pressure into the danger zone are going to be little once again. With your Windows computer and the chapters in Part III, you take control of your communication projects, begin saving time and money, and get on with more important aspects of your work and your life.

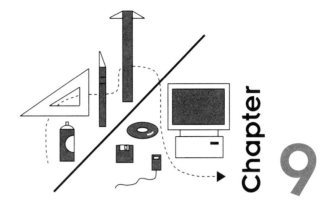

Designer's Cookbook of Office Projects

This chapter explains how to design and create a wide variety of business communication tools: fact sheets, stationery, forms, business cards, corporate logos, advertisements, and more. I call this chapter a cookbook because it contains exact instructions for creating a number of everyday business documents. Use as much of the ideas as you like; discard or change what you don't like. These ideas are just starting points—follow them and then head off in your own creative direction.

Each project is divided into four tasks of production: planning, layout, refining, and printing.

At the end of most of the projects you will find a table summarizing the document, layout, and typographic specifications. If you're starting a similar project and need only a pinch of help, just turn to the appropriate specification table and use the values I show as a starting point for your work. If you need more help or inspiration, turn to the appropriate project, get out the mixing bowls, and start reading.

271

CREATING BUSINESS COMMUNICATIONS

Trust me on this one, as soon as you create a few documents of your own, the word will get out and you'll be flooded with requests for everything from business cards for new employees, name badges for the next trade show, or banners for the grand opening of the new branch office. You'll find yourself producing the company newsletter one week and dreaming up an overhead slide presentation the next. In the middle of all this you'll probably be dealing with the normal documents any business uses to communicate: memos, stationery, fax transmittal sheets, mailing labels, forms, maybe even developing a new company logo.

Memos

Memos, like stationery, have always been somewhat proprietary in corporate offices; possibly less so where e-Mail has replaced the memorandum as the most common form of interoffice communication. Your company may have a standard memo design that can be altered, or you might design a better memo form and test its effectiveness. At the very least, you can almost certainly duplicate the existing memo design on your Windows computer and create an electronic mechanical that can be used for future printings.

Memos are pretty ordinary pieces of paper. They begin with headings like these, and do little more than offer blank space where you can write:

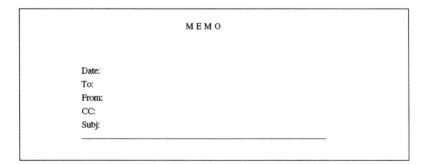

Planning

What is a memo exactly? The *Random House Dictionary* offers five definitions; all stress the word informal, and all imply a short, direct message of action. Okay, memos should be short and sweet. They should be informal, invoke action, or record events. It sounds like memos should be designed to be short and to the point; yet memos seem to ramble on, beating around the bush, leaving the reader in the dark. So let's make the memo physically smaller, demanding brevity. And to force the memo's author to reveal the message, lets expand the idea of the subject line into an Action line. Let's make the memo direct, if not downright blunt, and summarize the whole thing at the top as well by adding a Summary line. To make sure the reader understands the priorities and requirements expressed in the memo, let's add a *Time for Action Needed By* line at the top.

So, to review, we've now got a short form, with information at the top about the author, the addressee, the subject, the action requested, a summary of what's included in the memo, and a deadline spelled out for the requested action. Sounds good—so good you might not have to bother reading the body of the memo!

Layout

For this project, you can use any page composition program, a Windows word processor, or even a spreadsheet, like Excel—basically you're setting some type on the page and possibly adding some simple graphics. Here are the steps:

1. Open a new document. Set the page size at 11 inches high, but only 4.25 inches wide.

   Remember, we're going to limit those prolific writers with a smaller memo form. The narrower form accomplishes the same thing as if we used an 8.5-inch width but only a 5.5-inch height. The advantage of the tall, narrow memo is that, when shuffled together with all the other letter-size paper in an in-box, the 11-inch height keeps the memo from being lost in the crowd. Another reason for a tall, narrow memo is that, since memos are often paper clipped to other documents, the narrower memo lets half the document underneath show.

2. Set left and right page margins fairly narrow, to make the most of the narrow page, but increase white space with larger top and bottom margins. Try .5-inch on the sides, 1.75-inch at the top and 1.25-inch at the bottom of the page.

3. Add text to the page indicating the information we chose for the new memo. Add the word MEMO boldly to the page—make sure everyone knows at a glance what this thing is. The top portion of the memo should look like Figure 9.1. Notice how much information this memo will provide.

4. Add a line below the information area to designate the narrative area. You might also add a footer line at the bottom.

Finally, if you are using a program capable of rotating type, give the word memo a little bump to jazz it up.

Figure 9.1 *Example of the new, improved memo.*

Refining

The only thing this design lacks is the corporate logo. There's enough room at the top to accommodate corporate identity without making the memo top heavy. Another improvement might be to add lines to the information areas at the top, which might look like this:

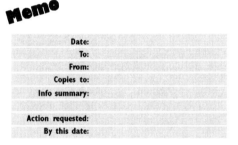

Looks a little too much like a form doesn't it? To reduce the forms effect, try shaded, unlined boxes:

Memo

Date:
To:
From:
Copies to:
Info summary:

Action requested:
By this date:

Finally, you might want to add routing information to the memo, in the form of department names, or manager's names.

Printing

You can print this form on your 300 dpi laser printer without fuss or bother. Before printing, let's get the most economy, by laying out a second memo form next to the first one on the same page. Print the forms *two-up on the page* and trim them apart. To add the second memo to the page, choose the Select All command from the Edit menu, and choose Copy to copy the form to the Clipboard. Now, open a new document, set up as a normal 8.5-by-11 inch page. Copy the form to the page using the Paste command. Then paste a second copy precisely beside it. Print the mechanical on 8.5-by-11 inch paper and carry the stack down to your local quick print shop, who, for a couple of dollars will trim the memo forms with a professional paper cutting machine.

Specifications at a Glance

Page Size	Margins	Orientation	# of Pages	Guide Settings	Columns
4.25" by 11"	sides .5", top 1.75", bot 1.25"	portrait	1	none	1

Font	Size	Leading	Indents	Space above/below	Align	Hyph
Gill Sans Extra Bold	10pt	15pt	none	none	Left and right	n/a

Fax Transmittal Sheets

A fax transmittal sheet is simply the cover page that precedes the actual faxed document. The cover page must indicate who the fax is addressed to, the date, and possibly the subject of the fax. If you use dedicated fax equipment, you need an additional printed cover sheet for each transmission. If you use fax modems in your computers, the fax software can provide a customized fax cover sheet. Let's put together a basic cover that works with either type of fax. You can customize and improve the design to your own particular needs.

Planning

I fail to understand why, it seems, the majority of fax cover sheets use type three inches tall to spell out the pertinent details of the fax. Are we suddenly all nearsighted? The tendency toward huge block-type cover sheets stems from our lack of faith in what the fax looks like at the receiving end of the phone line; so we make the cover sheet as large as possible. Funny we don't do that with the letters or documents that follow the cover sheets. So, let's design an attractive cover sheet that projects the same professional image as your company's letterhead.

Layout

I expect you may want to design this form using a page composition program, so you can take advantage of guidelines, proper typographic spacing, and easy graphic tools. The one advantage to using your Windows word processor is that the cover sheet can be quickly queued for printing right along with the document you want to fax. If that's important to you, then use a word processor for the layout. Here are the steps:

1. Create a new letter-sized document (8.5-by-11 inches) in portrait orientation. Give the page 1-inch margins.

2. Since a fax page generally comes out of the fax top first, let's tell the receiver what this page is as early as possible by positioning the name of the company at the very top of the page and the words *Transmittal Sheet* directly under the name. For this example add the company's logo first, and the transmittal title force-justified across the page, as shown in Figure 9.2 on the next page.

3. Now that we've told the receiver what this piece of paper is, the next most important item is the person to whom this fax is addressed. Add the text *Please route this fax immediately to:* on the next line of the form.

4. Add *From:* so the addressee knows who is sending the fax.

5. Add several *Subject:* lines so an adequate description can be included, if necessary.

Figure 9.2   *The beginning of a fax cover sheet design.*

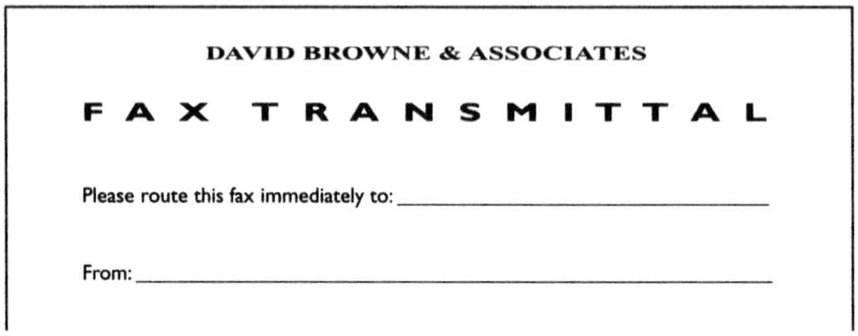

DAVID BROWNE & ASSOCIATES

F A X   T R A N S M I T T A L

Please route this fax immediately to: _____

From: _____

---

6.   To create the lines for the subject area, use the underline character on your keyboard rather than adding graphic lines.

Refining

To improve this form, let's add a line toward the bottom of the page that indicates either the total number of pages in the transmission (including the cover sheet) or the number of pages to follow (not including the cover sheet). In either case, include a telephone number to call in case any of the pages did not transmit. This number should not be the fax machine number, but the number of the person responsible for fax operation.

Finally, think about making the cover sheet more effective by including information the receiving party may want to jot down, such as the date and time the fax was received (many fax machines and fax modems record the date and time of transmission at the top of each page). Routing information is also handy.

Printing

Print a master of the form on your laser printer, then make as many copies as you need on a good copier. Distribute the form along with your other stationery supplies. If you created this form with a word processor you can create a macro that prints one copy of the cover sheet each time you print a document to be faxed. Of course, if you are using a fax modem the cover sheet is actually just a graphic file which is sent automatically. To make the cover sheet a fax modem graphic cover sheet, simply capture the screen to the Clipboard by displaying it in the program that created it and pressing the Print Screen button on your keyboard. Then paste the Clipboard image in an art program that saves files in a graphic format your fax modem software requires (such as TIF, PCX, or WMF).

Specifications at a Glance

Page Size	Margins	Orientation	# of Pages	Guide Settings	Columns
8.5" by 11"	all 1 inch	portrait	1	1st line at 1" 2nd line at 1.5" 3rd line at 3" 4th line at 3.5" 5th line at 4"	1

Font	Size	Leading	Indents	Space above/below	Align	Hyphen
Title set Gill Sans Bold	14pt	17pt	none	none	Force	n/a justified
Body set Gill Sans Cond.	12pt	14.5pt	none	none	Left	n/a

Letterhead, Business Cards, and Envelopes

Commonly known as a corporate identity package, the design of your company's letterhead, business cards, and envelopes is the single most personal design you'll come up with in business. I can't hope to do that for you in this book; I can give you some suggestions that may point you toward a unique idea.

Planning

Whatever you come up with, the design of the business card, letterhead, and envelopes should be as identical as possible. Here's a trick mentioned in an earlier chapter: Create the business card first, the letterhead, and envelopes will fall into place. The business card is always the hardest to design because of its size. Fitting all the information in a 2-inch by 3.5-inch area can be a major headache. First of all there's a lot to go on a business card:

- Company name
- Company address
- Telephone numbers and fax numbers
- Corporate logo or service mark
- Name of employee
- Title of employee
- Advertising, lists of products or services, graphics, and more.

If you have a lot of information to add, consider using a larger card size. For example, design the card 3.5 inches wide, but 4 inches high and fold it down. This gives you a front cover to carry the company information; open the card up and you have plenty of room for information about products and services, plus the employee's name and title. Another variation is to have the cover a bit short, so the employee's name shows at the bottom when the cover is closed.

The size of the card, and the orientation of type on the card are relative to

Sam Bellows

the size of the company name, and possibly the logo. Short names and narrow logos are easier to fit if you turn the card from its more traditional orientation where text runs along its wide edge, making a vertical card. Longer names suit a horizontal card. If the company has a long name but a narrow logo, consider prominently displaying the logo on the card but use the company name and logo on the stationery. Once you get the business card nailed down, the stationery designs itself. Some card/name orientations are shown below.

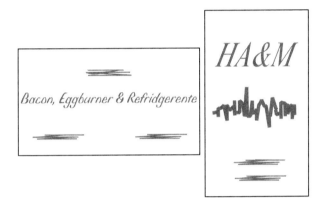

Layout

Again, the way you lay out the business card is decided by the visual shape of the company name. But you can do a lot in very little space:

- Use a condensed typeface to close up a longer name to make it fit comfortably on the card. In the first example shown below, 24-pt Gill Sans is much too wide for the width of the card:

- By changing the font to Helvetica Condensed, and further reducing the text by setting horizontal spacing at 90 percent, yields a more reasonably-sized proportion.

Hamstring & Crumdinger
Attrorneys at Law

- Focus the reader's attention. If you don't have a corporate logo, or if there isn't room, use a graphic flourish to center the eyes on the card. Here the ampersand is enlarged to 36 pt to achieve some focus on the large name. The font for the ampersand is changed to Times Roman which has a much more attractive ampersand, and the baseline for the character is dropped down by 3 pts:

Hamstring & Crumdinger
Attrorneys at Law

- If the type looks too small, it's probably about right. The name on our card is impressive, but there's not much room left for the remaining information. Let's see what we can fit in. First add an information line noting the type of practice for the law firm. Set it in 10 pt-Gill Sans:

Personal Injury and Product Liability

Hamstring & Crumdinger
Attrorneys at Law

- Notice that with these two lines of type you have defined the margins for the business card. As shown below, once you have one corner defined you can set guides for the other corners:

- Remember to maintain balance. I find myself visualizing that the card is balanced on the point of a pencil, and the type I add has to keep the card stable. Let's add the individual's name, address, and telephone number. Soften the information line by making it italic:

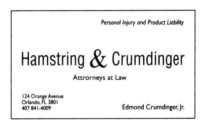

To reduce the bulk of the address, run the telephone number in with the city and state line. Finally, add a second color to jazz up these stuffy attorneys. Color should be balanced just like the layout; try to weave the second color into the design of the card. For instance, it's logical to make the names of the two partners the same color as the line *Attorneys at Law*:

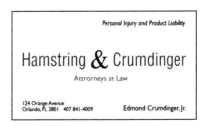

Attorneys don't ordinarily use color on business cards because they usually have them engraved, but with names like these guys have, they need all the help they can get. Once you have nailed down the final layout for the business card, transfer the same design to the letterhead (removing any employee names and titles), and to the envelope (removing the telephone and fax numbers as well). A normal business envelope (#10) is 9.5 inches wide, so to create the setup for the envelope, create a landscape page 4.25-by-9.5 inch. By turning the page, you are able to print crop marks on your laser printer.

Refining

If you are dealing with one particular foreign country, it's a good idea to include both languages on the business card and stationery. If you work in Japan, create a Japanese-language version of your business card, or put English on one side and Japanese on the other. These days it's common to find e-Mail addresses, international telephone numbers, satellite paging numbers, even cellular phone numbers on business cards and stationery.

If you add a second color to your design, try to carrying the same two-color theme to the envelopes. I've often heard the argument not to add color to envelopes because they're just thrown away and no one sees them. I disagree. Envelopes are an important part of the corporate identity package, and two-color envelopes (although they cost twice as much as a single color) are a sign of affluence and professionalism.

Printing

I've always produced my own stationery, had a service bureau create high-resolution negatives, which I've taken to my commercial printer to print. Once I was rushed to get stationery printed for a new business venture, and I bypassed the service bureau, delivering pages directly from my 30 dpi laser printer to my commercial printer. Guess what: There was so little difference between that stationery and the high-resolution stationery, only I could tell which was which. I'm not saying you don't need the best resolution you can get, but in a pinch, 300 dpi will reproduce amazingly well, depending on the typeface and size of type used.

Normally, if you have the time, get the document containing your stationery design printed at a service bureau, with crop marks in place. Select a good quality, cotton-rag bond and have your commercial printer do the printing for you.

NOTE

If you have several branch offices you need to produce stationery for, or if your offices are moving in the near future, here's an idea to save money by using your laser printer and your commercial printer:

1. Design your stationery with the name of the company (which doesn't change between locations) in a color other than black. Leave off the specific street addresses, but add anything else you want in the color, not in black.

2. Collect the printed stationery and use your laser printer to add the addresses in black. Now you have two-color stationery for a number of locations, for the cost of printing one-color stationery for only one location.

Press Releases

A press release contains newsworthy information for the press to use as the impetus for a story. Press releases must be timely to be effective and need to state the facts as clearly and quickly as possible. The best press releases are those written in the same voice and style as the news agencies they are targeting. The less rewriting required, the more likely your press release will be used.

Planning

A press release should clearly state, who you are (the company issuing the press release) and the news tag (the reason for the press release). It should tell the reader who to contact at your company for more information (preferably in public relations) and should have telephone numbers and fax numbers where reporters can call for more detailed information. If you are issuing a press release in conjunction with your company's attendance at a trade show or conference, you should provide contact names and phone numbers at both your offices and at the location of the event. The easier it is for reporters to get information, the greater the chance of their using your material.

Press releases should rarely be sent by themselves. You should generally plan a complete *press kit*, that includes the release (or releases if you can think up sidebar stories that the reporters would also be interested in), background information, bios on employees involved with the news event, a glossary of specialized terms, glossy black and white photos, and

35mm Kodachrome slides. The press kit should be assembled in an attractive folder and sent out in an appropriate envelope indicating that this is urgent material for the press. If you assume that the press does not understand your business, and needs to be spoon-fed everything necessary to create a story, your press kit is complete, and probably successful.

Layout

To see how we can develop an easy format for a press release:

1. Open a page composition program and create a new document. Set up a normal page size, with portrait orientation. Set the left margin wide at 1.5 inches, the right margin at 1 inch, the bottom margin at .75, and the top at 1 inch.

2. Create a text block. Set the words *Press Release* in 96 pt Times New Roman. Then rotate the text vertically so it runs up the page. Adjust the position so the baseline of the type is 1.25 inches from the left edge of the page.

3. Create a text block. Set the words *FOR IMMEDIATE RELEASE* in Gill Sans Bold 14 pt. Position the text block at the corner of the left and top margins.

4. Now add your company's logo in the upper right corner. Under the logo, set right-aligned to the right margin, the line *For Further Information, contact:* in Gill Sans Bold 14 pt. Under that, right-aligned to the right margin, set the name and telephone number of the contact person. The top of your press release should now look something like this:

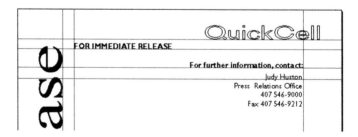

5. All we need to do is to add the company name and address to the form. Move to the bottom and add a 1-pt line to separate the footer from the text of the press release. Under the line add

the name and address, with enough horizontal spacing to fill the length of the text line, margin to margin. The bottom of the form should look like this:

Refining

There's very little else we can do to this form. We can reduce the darkness of the huge Press Release title, by shading it in a 20 percent screen of black. We could also create second sheets for the press release form by adding just the large, vertical title to the second sheets, with nothing more. The finished press release should look like this:

Printing

You can print a master of this form on your laser printer and make copies on a good office copier. If you want a sharper, more impressive form, have it printed on a high-resolution imagesetter—the 20 percent screened title comes out a very nice light gray, and have your commercial printer run off sets of the release and the second sheets. If you print the release on a lightly colored stock you essentially have a three-color form—the gray title, the black remaining type, and the color of the paper stock—for the slightly higher cost of the stock.

Specifications at a Glance

Page Size	Margins	Orientation	# of Pages	Guide Settings	Columns
8.5" by 11"	left 1.75", right 1", top 1", bot 1"	portrait	1	Hor. guides 1 at 4.5, 6, 9, and 10.5 picas	

Font	Size	Leading	Indents	Space above/below	Align	Other
Title set Times New Roman	96pt	96pt	none	none	centered	130% hor. scale
"For Immediate Release" set Gill Sans	14pt	17pt	none	none	Left	
Logo set AG Old Face Outline	36pt	40pt	none	none	right	150% hor. scale
"Further info..." set Gill Sans Bold	14pt	17pt	none	none	right	
Contact name set Gill Sans Plain	14pt	17pt	none	none	right	
Co. Name set Gill Sans Plain	14pt	17pt	none	none	center	105% hor. scale

Mailing Labels and Diskette Labels

Printing mailing labels on a laser printer used to be a royal pain; it took precise alignment to get it right and you invariably wasted a lot of expensive labels in the process. Then Avery and other label manufacturers got into the act and came out with software that configured the labels for you (Avery has an application called *LabelPro* that does just that). About the same time WordPerfect, Microsoft, Aldus, Quark, and others began supplying templates for Avery labels. Using a template is a breeze, and gives you professional looking labels.

Before you go to the trouble of designing a label, be sure your laser printer is capable of printing labels. Some printers apply too much heat when fusing the toner to the page, which melts the label adhesive. Read the user manual that came with your printer to find out the specification for labels it can handle. Having said that as a disclaimer—melted labels stuck to the fusing element isn't the best thing for a laser printer—most laser printers can handle Avery labels.

Planning

Avery laser printer labels come in a variety of sizes; you can find them at any good office supply company. The sizes most commonly used are:

Type	Size	Avery Product Code
3.5-inch diskette	2-3/4" by 2-3/4"	5196
5.25-inch diskette	1-1/2" by 4"	5197
Large mailing	3-1/3" by 4"	5164
Medium mailing	2" by 4"	5163
Small mailing	1-1/3" by 4"	5162
Clear large mailing	2" by 4-1/4"	5663
Clear medium mailing	1-1/3" by 4-1/4"	5662
Clear small mailing	1" by 2-5/8"	5660
Large file folder	1" by 4"	5161
Medium file folder	1" by 2-5/8"	5160
Small file folder	1/2" by 1-3/4"	5267

The larger size labels (5196, 5197, 5164, and 5663) lend themselves easily to designs. Let's look at creating a mailing label. You can apply the same techniques to any other size.

Layout

In one of the many Windows applications that support Avery labels, open the template for the large mailing label 5164. If you are using WordPerfect for Windows, open the Macro menu and choose Play to display the Play Macro dialog box. Choose the Label macro and choose Play. Pick the Avery label from the list displayed, and WordPerfect configures the page for you. In Microsoft Word for Windows, choose the MAILLABL template when creating a new document and answer the questions that the label macro asks.

1. Open the template for the 5164 label or set up a new page size as 3-1/3 inches wide by 4 inches high, with very narrow margins, say a 10th of an inch.

2. Divide the page by adding a vertical guideline 1.25 inches in from the left side of the page and a horizontal guideline 1.25 inches down from the top margin. Your label should look like this:

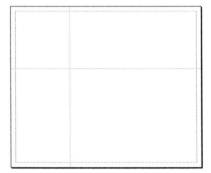

As you can see, the label is divided into four unequal-sized quadrants. Reserve the upper left quadrant for a corporate logo; the upper right for the company name and address; the lower left is normally blank (reserved for specific instructions) and the lower right corner contains the addressee's name and address.

3. Add your logo to the upper left quadrant. Then set your company name and address in the upper right quadrant. Your label is starting to take shape:

Refining

I usually feel the need for a line between my company name and address and the name of the addressee; add one if you agree. You might want to add a pointing finger dingbat, or an arrowhead dingbat to show the addressee area of the label. Zapf Dingbats and TrueType Wingdings have a wide variety of choices.

Once you have the single label the way you want it, choose the Select All command from the Edit menu to select all the elements in the label. With the elements selected, choose Copy to copy the label to the Clipboard. Move to the next label and use the Paste command to paste the label where you want it. Do that for each of the labels on the Avery label page.

Printing

To fully appreciate your laser printer, just give your commercial printer a call and ask how much it costs to print labels. Labels are very expensive to print, mostly because it requires a special press to handle them. Avery labels certainly aren't cheap, so before you begin printing, test the label on blank paper, line the paper up with a blank sheet of labels and hold both up to the light. You should be able to see if your labels print correctly on the Avery sheets. If so, put one sheet in the manual slot of your laser printer and try it out.

Corporate Logos

Corporate logos are very personal things, they are there to protect the name of the company or product with a unique, identifiable look. Often, logos are trademarked, and some logos have registered trademarks. So the design of a logo is important, not only to create and build name recognition with a product, service or company, but for legal protection as well.

Logotypes or typography altered specifically to create a unique look used to be created manually by an artist. Press type letters would generally be used, then altered with India ink to get a unique look. Once the logotype was finished, stats (high-quality photographic copies) were made at different reductions and magnifications to fit the expected use for the logotype. However, if the stats and art work were lost, the logotype would have to be recreated from scratch—an expensive undertaking. Luckily, now there are page composition programs that offer sophisticated typography; as well as specialized programs, like FontMonger, shown Figures 9.3 and 9.4, from Ares Software (415-578-9090) that allow you to alter the shape and characteristics of a font.

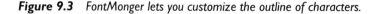

Figure 9.3   *FontMonger lets you customize the outline of characters.*

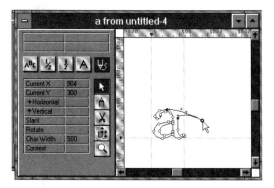

Figure 9.4 *The results can give you a unique logotype.*

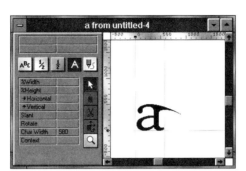

Planning

You can do a lot with page composition software in creating that unique look. For example, just altering the letter space between letters, adjusting the baseline of some letters, reversing type out of another color, adding a reflection, or rotating text can all contribute to a unique logo.

Layout

It's hopeless to try to develop a logo in this book that serves everyone's purposes. Instead, let's run down some hints that may lead to the right logo design:

> ♦ Be aware of size. Use the relative size of words to their advantage.

- Use space to create uniformity. Keep the spacing between words the same width as another element used in the logo.

all the same size

- Keep it simple; the simpler the better.

- Keep in mind that the logo must be able to be reduced small enough to fit on a postage stamp, large enough to fit on a billboard, and still communicate in both extremes.

- Use italics or a script typeface to add a human touch to the logo. Consider overlapped italic initials or an italicized corporate name:

- Or add a shadow to give a more floral effect:

- Combine type with other graphic elements to create a unique effect. Use reversed lines over the initials of a company to accentuate the shape of the letters, like this:

♦ If the first letter of a word lends itself to modifications, then experiment: reverse the letter, rotate the letter on its back, try effects you might guess couldn't possibly work and you may be surprised with the results.

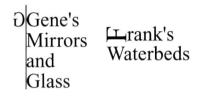

Refining

There are any number of opportunities to refine your basic design; just don't get carried away. You might use color on only one letter in a word; you might substitute a letter with a symbol that fits the shape of the letter and relates to the logo (a basketball substituted for the letter O in a logo for the Chicago Bulls, for example). You might add a gradient fill to an initial cap for a word in the logo. Using page composition software and your Windows computer, your choices are endless.

Printing

Print often to see the effect you are creating. Use your laser printer to print proofs as you develop your design. When it is finalized, send the file to a service bureau for imagesetting, and save the file as an encapsulated PostScript file. Then whenever you want to use it, you can place it on the page like any other graphic.

CREATING MARKETING INSTRUMENTS

Practically every business, regardless of its products or services, has a need for marketing material to send to prospective customers. These days it seems that retail business has slowly declined in favor of direct sales avenues through 800-telephone numbers and catalogs, which only increase the need for more marketing and sales communications. For companies selling through the mail a constant barrage of literature is needed to help convince prospective customers to buy.

Let's take a look at some of the different documents that can help sell your goods and services. They are arranged on the following pages in order of expense, from the least costly and quickest to produce, to the more expensive documents.

Flyers and Slimjims

The terms *flyers* and *slimjims* cover a multitude of documents that can be produced quickly and mailed out to a base of customers or potential customers. A flyer may be a single sheet of paper hand delivered or folded and mailed. A slimjim is a two or four panel folded flyer on stiffer paper stock, costing a little more to produce than the flyer. Each type of document advertises a particular product or service. The advantage of either is inexpensive production in large quantities, so they should be used on a regular basis, almost like issues of a newsletter. Each *issue* should concentrate on a single idea, product, or item.

Planning

Think of flyers and slimjims like ads on radio or TV, they are there for a brief moment, then gone forever. They will be glanced at and thrown away, so the message has to grab the readers, hold their attention, and be remembered. If you send these documents at the bulk mail rate they are bundled in with all the other junk mail that comes to us all—they may be lost entirely—so send these pieces first class mail if possible. As such, they must meet minimum stiffness requirements of the Postal Service.

Leave lots of room for an attention-getting headline—if it isn't noticed and read, the flyer or slimjim has died. Back up the headline with only the supporting details necessary to prove your point. Be sure to offer addresses, telephone numbers, fax numbers—every means for the customer to reach you for more information.

Layout

Use a page composition program or a Windows word processor will do in a pinch. Here are the steps:

1. Open a new document, 8.5-by-11 inches. Choose a 1-inch margin all around for a flyer, but .25-inch margin if you want to create a slimjim. You will have two pages for either document.

2. If you are creating a flyer, configure it with only one column the width of the page (the top of the flyer is folded down over the bottom with the fold horizontal). If you are creating a slimjim, set up 2 columns (the fold for the slimjim is vertical, with each column making a panel).

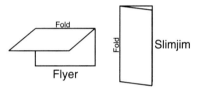

3. To add text to the flyer, divide the page into two halves with a horizontal guideline across the middle of the page (where the page eventually is folded).

4. Now treat the flyer as basically an ad on page 1—using the portion above the fold as an attention-getter or teaser, and the portion below the fold for the details.

5. On page 2, use a teaser line above the fold that encourages the reader to open the folded page. The area below the fold is the *front* of the mailed document. It holds the mailing address, the return address, and any postal information. Finally, go back to the teaser line above the fold and rotate it upside down (this is the back of the mailed document and the text must be rotated so it is read correctly (the fold should be at the top). The configuration of flyer pages looks like the example on the next page.

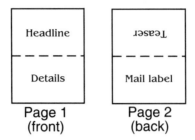

6. To create the slimjim, which can either be mailed in an envelope or by itself, set a gutter width for the two column format at .5-inch (so you continue the .25-inch margin for each panel of the document).

7. On page 1, add the body of the sales message to the two columns. You might use a headline at the top that runs across both columns. On page 2, the left column contains postal information (rotate the text on this page vertically so the fold is at the top); the right column holds the headline or teaser for the slimjim. The configuration for a slimjim looks like this:

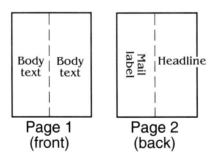

Refining

You needn't worry too much about these types of documents; it's better to get them out quickly than waste time with intricate details (which probably won't be noticed). Use color, by all means for headlines or body copy, and choose a colored stock. Use clip art or scanned photos if available, but keep the message simple. The idea is to attract attention and have the reader either visit the store or call for more details.

Printing

The flyer is meant to be handed out, delivered to home addresses, or mailed. If you intended to mail the flyer use the heaviest paper stock your laser printer can handle. The Post Office needs a certain weight paper for mail handling, so use a card stock weight paper (such as business cards are printed on).

N O T E

If your laser printer has a straight-through paper path (such as laser printers that use the Canon SX engine like the Apple LaserWriter II, IISC, IINT, IINTX, IIf, IIg; the HP LaserJet II series, the QMS PS810; the NEC 990; and many others) you should be able to handle up to a 67# card stock. Contact a paper company specializing in laser printer paper (like PaperDirect 800-272-7377, see below) for supplies. While your laser printer can handle card stock weight, most office copiers can't, because of the complicated paper path, so don't try to run heavy paper stock through your copier unless it's approved by the manufacturer.

The slimjim is simple to print; however, it too needs a heavier stock for mailing unless you stuff the document in an envelope. If you decide to use an envelope, you need to reset the page size to 8.5-by-9.5 inches, and have your quick print shop trim off the excess inch and a half to fit in a number 10 business envelope.

Finally, if you do choose to print these marketing pieces on card stock for mailing, don't try to fold them yourself. Instead, take them to a commercial printer, who will score and fold the pages properly on equipment designed to handle the heavy paper.

Specifications at a Glance

Page Size	Margins	Orientation	# of Pages	Guide Settings	Columns
Flyer 8.5" by 11"	all 1"	portrait	2	set hor. fold at 5.5	1
Slimjim 8.5" by 11"	all .25"	portrait	2	set vert. fold at 4.25	2

Font	Size	Leading	Indents	Space above/below	Align	Hyph
head/teaser set at Gill Sans Bold	36pt	42pt	none	none	Center justified	n/a
Body set Times Roman	12pt	14.5pt	none	none	Left	n/a

Product Fact Sheets

For certain types of related products, individual product fact sheets are a simple, easy way to distribute information. The problem with including all the products in a brochure is your prospective customers may want to buy only one of the products. Fact sheets allow you to tailor an information package to the exact needs of each customer. Combine just the fact sheets the customer requests in an attractive folder with a cover letter and price list and you're on your way. The general brochure can come later.

Planning

There are a number of advantages to using fact sheets as the main source of marketing literature:

- Fact sheets are easy and quick to produce. If you are constantly adding new products to your line of goods, product brochures need constant revising. Producing new product fact sheets is much more cost effective.

- Fact sheets contain just the facts and nothing but the facts. Specifications, sizes, weights, installation dimensions, voltages, and more should be included. The customers that need fluff and promises probably won't be interested in your fact sheets; the customers that need specific facts to reach a decision will be.

- Fact sheets are easy to file, easy to save. They provide reference material that customers can use in making a buying decision.

- Fact sheets aren't perceived as marketing hype, so you can sneak in some hyperbole about your company and its products with less interference than with brochures.

- You can print up the basic information that all fact sheets share in advance, store the *blank* fact sheets in large quantities, and over print the specific information when you need a new or revised fact sheet, with your laser print. The larger printing runs for the *blank* sheets saves you money by lowering the per-unit cost; over printing specifics on just the number of blanks you need with a laser printer costs virtually nothing.

Layout

Here's a formula for successful, easy-to-read fact sheets:

1. Open a new 8.5-by-11 inch document in a page composition program (you could also use a Windows database, like Microsoft Access to produce your fact sheets as individual reports). Set the margins at 1 inch all around, one column, and two pages (configured front and back).

2. On the first page (front) set horizontal guides in equal thirds across the page. The top third contains the product name and model number, and a photo or drawing of the product. The second third holds a brief description of the product and one paragraph that sums up its use and advantages. The bottom third holds easy-to-read bulleted lines describing the product in more detail.

3. On the second page (the back) set a horizontal guide about one-quarter of the height from the top and another the same distance from the bottom. The top area holds the name of the product and the model number. The large half-page section holds technical specifications, dimensions, installation measurements, and any other data about the product. The small bottom area can hold a warranty statement, minimum requirements for the product to work correctly, a disclaimer that specifications and price are subject to change without notice, and the name, address and telephone numbers for the company. The two pages should now look something like this:

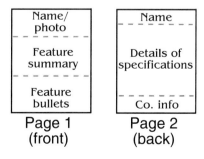

Refining

When you compose the Name/photo area on page 1, set the product name and model number at the very top. Then set it again in smaller type rotated vertically on the right side in the upper-right-hand corner. If the fact sheet is either filed in a file folder, or three-hole punched and stored in a three-ring binder, the vertical model name and number will be immediately visible. The top of the fact sheet might look like this example:

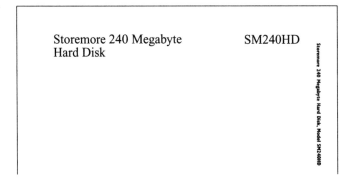

Make the feature summary area on the first page an easy-to-read one-column paragraph in a fairly large type size. Create two columns for the feature bullets on the first page (two columns of bullets look more balanced than one column). If you are expecting orders via telephone, include the number on both sides of the fact sheet. Use color sparingly (these are supposed to be inexpensive to produce) and leave lots of white space.

Printing

Two colors (black and an additional color) work nicely for this layout. Choose a colored stock to add a third color. You could probably use your laser printer to produce the final mechanical; for a little more money have the pages imageset by a service bureau. Have a commercial printer print the color and add the black text yourself with your laser printer as you need fact sheets.

Specifications at a Glance

Page Size	Margins	Orientation	# of Pages	Guide Settings	Columns
8.5" by 11"	all 1 inch	portrait	2	front hor. guides at 4", 8" back hor. guides at 2", 9"	1

Font	Size	Leading	Indents	Space above/below	Align	Hyph
Heads set Gill Sans Bold	24pt	27pt	none		Left and right	
Vertical head set Gill Sans Bold	10pt	12pt	none		Left	
Feature summary set Times Roman	14pt	17 pt	none		Justified	
Feature bullets set Times Roman	12pt	14pt	none		Left	
Back specs area set Times Roman	14pt	17pt	none		Left	
Co info set Gill Sans	10pt	12pt	none		Centered	

Print Ads

We call them print ads because they're printed in magazines and newspapers, but it would be more accurate to call them picture ads. It's the product photo that is predominant in almost all ads, the proportion is usually three-quarters photo to one-quarter words. If you don't have a photo (for example, your product hasn't yet been manufactured) leave the same amount of space blank; the massive white space is almost as effective as a photo.

Planning

The formula for ads seems to be a dominate color photo, a catchy headline that is usually a play on words of the photograph, and a small area below or to one side of the photo for body copy. At a glance, the photo, headline, and company logo all get noticed, which may be all the attentionn the ad gets as readers thumb through magazines.

In planning your ads keep in mind a few key points:

- Keep the ad simple. An ad is much like a roadside billboard; it must attract attention and leave you with the correct impression in the glance of an eye. Make one point clearly in your ad and it has more chance of success. If you have a number of important points to make, plan on a number of consecutive ads.

- Give the ad a chance. Don't change ads each issue. Ads need time to sink in. So does the name of your product—and the more name recognition the more likely it is that customers recognize your product when they see it. Figure on leaving the same ad in for three issues of the publication before changing it.

There are some exceptions to this rule. For example, if you are planning an introduction, you might want to count down the days (weeks or months) by having a different ad in each issue. You also might want a different picture but the same copy (or vice versa) in subsequent issues. And, you might want to vary the ad to changing conditions in the weather, stock markets, real estate values, or other fluctuating standards.

- Color photos are almost always more effective than black and white photos. One large photo is better than several smaller photos.

- One large ad is usually more effective than two or more small ads (just as a huge billboard is more noticeable than little billboards).

- Give ads a chance to work. Run them in the same publications long enough to measure the results. If you can't afford to give them a decent run, then postpone the advertising until you can afford it.

◆ Measure the results of the ads. Use a special telephone number, a made-up department name, or a specially-assigned Post Office box number in the ad so response from the ad can be measured, and the effectiveness of the ad can be honestly judged.

Layout

Let's lay out a full page ad for a magazine. Here are the steps:

1. Open a new document in a page composition program the size of the trimmed dimensions of the magazine page.

2. Place or import the photo you want to use. Size it to fill the top three-quarters of the page shown in Figure 9.5. Bleed the edges of the photo past the left, top, and right edges of the page.

Figure 9.5   *Photo added to ad page with a bleed on three sides.*

3. Add a headline to the ad, see Figure 9.6. The head should be set in large type (36 points or more), either across the photo or under the photo. The headline should be catchy, but not wordy (no more than five words).

Figure 9.6   *Head attracts attention and relates to the subject of the photo.*

4. Now add two columns of body copy under the photo, as in Figure 9.7. Make the copy relate back to the photo. Sell one or two points only. Leave room for a logo and telephone number.

Figure 9.7   *The body copy and logo are added.*

Cloudless, cobalt blue skies, endless pure white beaches, sunsets under the shade of gentle palms, moonlight strolls and moments stolen from paradise. The Bahamas has it all. The most gracious dining this side of Palm Beach, yachting, sport fishing, scuba diving, spear fishing, and swimming in some of the most beautiful waters in the world. Yet we're a 10 minute flight from Miami, 30 minutes from Walt Disney World. So don't bother packing, just come as you are.

Best in the Bahamas
800-545-9000

Refining

You can create a vertical format with the text to the right of the photo if your photo lends itself more to a vertical. Remember not to have people looking off the page (on the right side of the photo with their head turned to the right, for example). Leave enough room in the photo for the subject to move into—the couple in the Figures 9.5 to 9.7 need to have that beach to the right to walk into, cars need space to drive into, and so forth.

Use color to pull the elements of the ad together. If the ad in the figures above were in color, I'd probably color the headline text a deep blue, and add the same color to the logo and telephone number.

Printing

Print ads obviously need the highest resolution you can get, so send these jobs out to your service bureau. Most Magazines require right-reading emulsion-side down film (in PageMaker, you would leave the Mirror and Negative check boxes unchecked). Check with the magazine before sending the job to the service bureau.

Also check with the magazine to see how high a line screen the magazine's paper will allow (probably around 150 lines per inch). If extreme resolution is important, you can normally have full page ads printed on a higher quality paper which allows screens up to 300 lines per inch.

Brochures

Brochures are the mainstay of any marketing communications effort. They provide information about your company, its goods, and services. But brochures do more. Just like your stationery, brochures are a symbol of your company's success. A poorly done brochure, printed on cheap paper, with pitiful photos, and a disheveled layout speaks badly about your company and offers proof positive that if you can't create a professional brochure you probably can't do anything right. Clearly, a neat, clean, orderly brochure that communicates and exhibits the class and style of your organization can have an opposite, positive affect.

Planning

Think of the brochure in terms of the number of pages needed. The smallest brochure has four pages, created from one sheet of paper, folding in the middle and printed on both sides. If you want an 8.5-by-11 inch brochure, that means you fold one 11-by-17 inch page to create the brochure. The next size up from four pages is an eight-page brochure: two 11-by-17 inch sheets folded to 8.5-by-11 inches and bound (stapled or saddle-stitched) in the middle. And so on in additional folded and bound sheets (or sets of four pages). If you think about the brochure opened at the fold, you realize, as displayed in Figure 9.8, that the page order is different than for documents bound along the left edge. The arrangement of double-sided pages that are folded and bound is called an *imposition layout*, which is different than the order of pages normally used to lay out a brochure in a page composition program.

Figure 9.9 *The order of brochure pages printed on both sides and folded in the middle.*

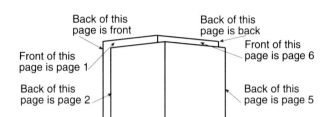

Remember, that if you have a four page brochure, you have a front, a back, and two text pages—not much room to explain what you're selling. Also, since most brochure covers are a heavier stock than the inside pages, printing a four page brochure means you either are printing the whole thing on cover stock (like creating a menu), or on text weight pages (very flimsy). Therefore, the smallest brochure you can get away with, (and maintain the image of a real brochure) is eight pages, a front, a back, and six text pages. Once again, to get all six pages, you must add text to the inside of the front cover and the inside of the back cover. Leave the inside of the front and back cover blank, which is the more usual practice, and create a brochure with four text pages.

Layout

Since most laser printers can not handle an 11-by-17 inch paper, use the Tile option in the Print dialog box of your page composition program, which will print the larger page size in tiles for you to tape together. However, when you deliver this job to your service bureau, they can handle the larger page size and can print the pages without tiling. Here are the steps:

1. Open a new 11-by-17 inch document with one inch margins all around, in landscape orientation. Configure the pages as double-sided, printed on both sides. There are four pages in this document.

2. Go to the master page for the pages and divide the pages in half with a vertical guideline set at 8.5 inches on the horizontal ruler.

The guide marks, where the large pages are folded and stapled, create the individual pages of the brochure:

- Page 1 is the back cover and the front cover of the bound brochure.
- Page 2 is the inside of the front cover and the back cover of the bound brochure.
- Page 3 is page 4 and page 1 of the bound brochure.
- Page 4 is page 2 and page 3 of the bound brochure.

3. To mark the inside margins on either side of the fold guideline, add an additional guideline at 7.5 inches and one at 9.5 inches.

4. Divide each *page* into two columns. Add a vertical guideline at 4.25 inches and one at 12.75 inches on the horizontal ruler. To create a gutter between columns, add a guideline 1/8th of an inch on either side of the column guides.

Now you're ready to begin adding text and graphics to your pages.

Refining

Refining a full color brochure is based solely on how much money you want to spend. The biggest improvement is to add additional color other than just the color photos. A nice touch is to draw a thin box around your photos in a color other than black. Add captions to photos in the same color. Add rules between columns in color, perhaps gold or bronze (which are printed as additional spot colors on the page).

You might want to consider die cutting a window in the front cover so a photo on page 1 shows through (saving you the expense of a separate color photo on the front page). Another nice touch is to add a flap to the bottom of the back cover, which folds up from the bottom to form a pocket to hold fact sheets. Slit the flap and you can insert a business card.

Printing

Brochures require careful proofing before they're sent off to the service bureau. You need to proof not only the words but look for items noted in the wrong color. The best way to proof spot color is to print only items in a single spot color at a time; then you can be sure the right items are in the correct colors. Since you have 11-by-17 inch pages in this brochure, remember to use the Tile option in the print dialog box. When everything is correct, print a final set of tiled pages from your laser printer to accompany the file to the service bureau.

Using Preprinted Paper

Preprinted paper is sheets of laser printer paper that have already been run through a color press and printed with a variety of color designs. You run the sheets through your laser printer, adding the necessary elements to turn the pages into stationery, brochures, fact sheets, or whatever you require. The concept of preprinted laser paper takes your laser printer into the realm of a final printing device for your documents. The resolution is certainly good enough, and the price of the preprinted sheets is a fraction of what the color printing would cost if you designed the pages from scratch.

A company called Paper Direct (800-272-7377) is probably the largest supplier of preprinted paper stock. They offer a huge inventory of different designs, everything from marble borders to parchment, to presentation packages, to matching envelopes, and business cards. All you do is run them through your laser printer.

You can expect to see a number of Windows applications offer templates for Paper Direct paper stock. Paper Direct sells templates for many applications, including WordPerfect for Windows, Microsoft Word, Ami Pro, and PageMaker. However, version 2.0 of Microsoft Publisher already comes with Paper Direct templates. Let's take a look:

1. In Microsoft Publisher, open a new 8.5-by-11 inch document.

2. Choose the Page menu and click the Special Paper command. You'll see the Special Paper dialog box, shown in Figure 9.9 on the next page. Scroll down the list of paper types; you can see a sample of the paper's design in the Preview box. The Description box will show you the Paper Direct stock number to use to order the design you see previewed.

Figure 9.9 *Microsoft Publisher's Special Paper dialog box lets you choose a Paper Direct template.*

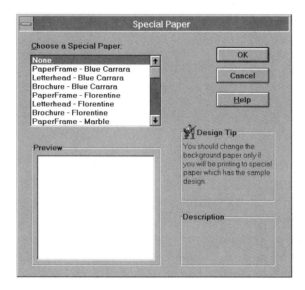

3. Double-click on the sample you want. For example if you needed a quick news release, click the Design Paper-News style, which is Paper Direct's stock DT1101, a Willow white speckled recycled paper with a bold box in the upper left, and the word NEWS in gold, as in the example to the right.

4. Add the text you want to the displayed page in Publisher.

Remember, the elements of Paper Direct's stock do not print, you must buy that stock, put it in your laser printer and print the text you've added in Microsoft publisher on top of the design.

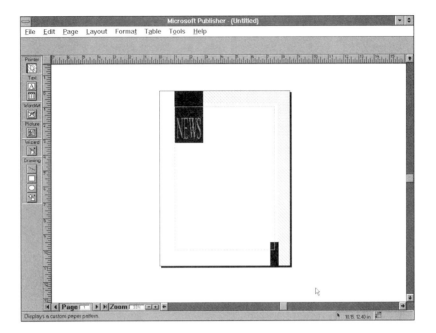

CHAPTER SUMMARY

At one of the companies I worked for we had a guy named Bert who we'd give all the design and printing jobs to. You've probably worked with a Bert too; somebody who brokers out everything—a middle man who tells you you can get it tomorrow regardless of what *it* is (and who never delivers on time). Our Bert was a walking nightmare. He never got anything right. Designs were wrong, work was printed in the wrong color, why he even messed up a simple three-hole punch job—none of the holes matched up! Bert was a mess but I'm eternally grateful to him; he forced us to get computers and start doing these projects ourselves. I hope this chapter has saved you from the Berts of the world, and encouraged you to take your communication needs in your own hands and create your own business and marketing tools.

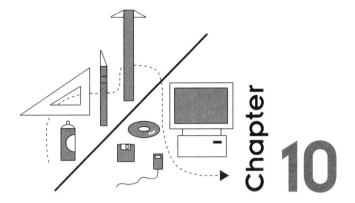

Chapter 10

Creating Newsletters that Sell

The proliferation of newsletters seems endless. Each year more newsletters are hatched: Every conceivable industry trade group seems to have a member newsletter; almost every consulting firm and non-profit organization publishes newsletters. Yes, there are even newsletters on how to write newsletters. Professionals appear pushed to publish newsletters. My family dentist, opthalmologist, accountant, family doctor and neighborhood hospital send out newsletters. City hall sends me a newsletter telling me about the new tax rates and the water department sends me one explaining the higher water rates. My various insurance companies all send out newsletters—one sent me a newsletter about how they keep premiums down the same day I received a premium increase notice!

The reason for all these newsletters is simple: they are great communication tools. If you sell things, newsletters can inform customers of new goods and services and give them warm fuzzy feelings. If you must raise money for charity, newsletters let you appeal for funds and explain where the funds go. If you are an employer, newsletters are a natural medium for internal communications, informing employees of company policy, promotions, new product lines, quality control procedures, and so on.

Yet this explosion in communicating through newsletters has brought some fairly awful examples to the marketplace. In the rush to get them out the door, many newsletter editors seem to have forgotten that if it isn't attractive it probably won't be read. And that's what this chapter is all about: producing newsletters that will be read, and hopefully remembered.

DESIGNING A NEWSLETTER OVER YOUR LUNCH HOUR

Grab your sack lunch, sit down at your Windows computer and let's knock out a newsletter. Here are the steps:

1. First open a page composition program, and configure a new 8.5-by-11 inch document, with 1 inch margins all around. The document consists of two pages. Set the measurement system to picas for this document.

2. Before we go any farther, let's create a grid of guidelines. This grid will be your cheat sheet and will save you a lot of time in laying out the pages. First set up six columns of guidelines on the page. If you have to position the column guides manually, set them to these positions, measured from the left margin (which include a 1 pica gutter for each column):

Column guide 1	5p8, 6p8
Column guide 2	12p3.95, 13p3.95
Column guide 3	19p, 20p
Column guide 4	25p8, 26p8
Column guide 5	32p4, 33p4

Now let's divide the page into 8 rows. Position horizontal guidelines at: 6p9, 13p, 20p3, 27p, 33p9, 40p6, and 47p2. Your document page should look like the example on the top to your right.

3. Think about the placement of the lead story. This should be prominently displayed and easily identified as such. Traditionally, the order of importance for the front page began in the upper left corner and moved diagonally (as shown in Figure 10.1) down the page to the least important story in the lower right

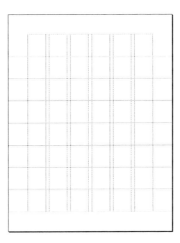

corner. Relative importance was judged by the decreasing sizes of headlines.

Figure 10.1   *Traditional front page places the most important story where you naturally begin reading.*

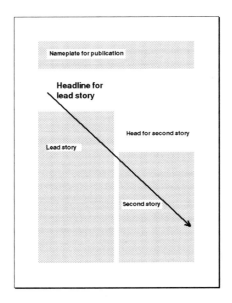

If you don't wish to be quite so traditional, you can make the lead story wider than other stories on the page to indicate its importance. Varying the width of stories gives a more modern look to the front page. Three examples are shown below.

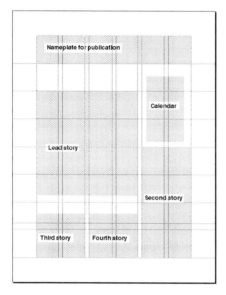

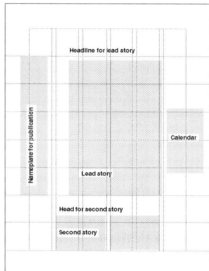

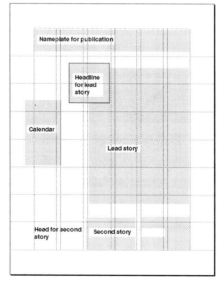

Adding the Nameplate

The *nameplate*, or *masthead*, is the name of the newsletter. The nameplate should consist of no more than one or two words, prominently displayed. You can set up the nameplate in a drawing program and import it as a graphic, or use your page composition software to create the name. Regardless of what you call your publication, do the nameplate in a bold scale to make it stand out. Let's say you want to create a desktop publishing newsletter called the *Desktop Counterpoint*. There's nothing wrong with setting the nameplate accordingly:

Desktop Publishing
Counterpoint

The trouble with this nameplate is it is visually uninteresting, it looks weak and doesn't illustrate anything about its subject. To spruce it up a bit, lets stretch the words *Desktop Publishing* wide enough to equal the width of the word *Counterpoint*:

Desktop Publishing
Counterpoint

That's a bit better. Juxtaposing the different sized type is a common design trick in nameplates and logos. Yet it still doesn't offer the reader anything interesting, it doesn't illustrate its subject, nor does it illustrate the concept of a counterpoint, or opposite.

To improve the nameplate, consider these steps:

1. Increase the size of the word *Counterpoint* and stretch it across the page, margin to margin. Then capitalize the *P* in *Point*, and set the word in small caps to get rid of the descender of the lowercase p in the previous example.

2. Reduce the size of the words *Desktop Publishing*, choose a very bold typeface, like Gill Sans Extra Bold, which is still readable in

smaller sizes. Fit the words between the Large *C* in *Counter* and the *P* in *Point*. Add a line between the two lines of type to separate them and you have something like this:

Now we're starting to get a distinctive look that has the elements we want.

3. To illustrate the idea of opposites, let's delete the line, replace it with a black box and reverse out the words *Desktop Publishing*.

COUNTERPOINT

4. To add some scale and color to the nameplate, click on the top of the box and drag it up off the page. The final nameplate looks something like this:

Adding the Main Story

The main story will be positioned across four of the columns in our grid, flush against the right margin. It will be the predominant story on the page.

Because the line measure of the story will be almost 26 picas, add more leading between lines that would be normal for the 11-point type. Here are the steps:

1. Choose the Place or Import command and select the text of the main story you want to import. In PageMaker, you see a loaded text icon; use it to define the width (four columns) and depth (about 32 picas) of the story.

2. Once placed on the page, choose the Select All command and give it the following type characteristics: 12 point Palatino font, with 17 points of leading, and justified alignment.

3. Add a byline above the story, flush right. Set the byline in Gill Sans 10 point on 12 points of leading. Add a 1 point line under the byline, flush right with the name, and extended to the left one and one-half columns.

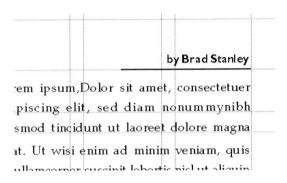

4. Finally, left-indent the first three lines of the main story the width of one column to make room for the story's headline. Set the headline in 12-point Gill Sans Extra Bold on 17 points of leading, the same leading as the story. Align the head so the first line begins one line above the story and the remaining baselines for the story and head are aligned. Make the length of the headline two columns and up to four lines above the baseline for the first text line of the main story. Add a 10 percent screened box behind the headline. See the example on the next page.

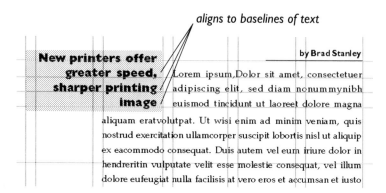

aligns to baselines of text

Jumping the Main Story

If the main story is longer than its 32 pica-depth on the front page, *jump* (or continue) the story on the back page (page 2). Again, the prominent position on the page is the upper left corner. Create a text block three columns wide and run the story down the page as far as it can go.

At the bottom of the main story add a *continued-to* line. Set it in 9 point Times Roman italic with 11 point leading, flush to the right margin. Add a 1-point line above the length of the text to separate the jump line from the text above.

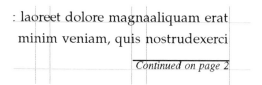

Continued on page 2

At the top of the back page, add a *continued-from* line set in the same style as the continued-to line. Add the 1-point line below the text to separate it from the story text.

Continued from page 1

tation ullamcorper suscipit lobc
aliquip ex eacommodo consequat. L

Adding a Second Story

According to our layout, the second story on the front page is positioned directly under the first story; but set up as two columns of text. Use the Place or Import command to import the story you want. Position the beginning of the story 45 picas down from the top margin. Set the story in the same style as the first story, but instead of 11-point type with 17-point leading, specify 10.5 points with 13-point leading.

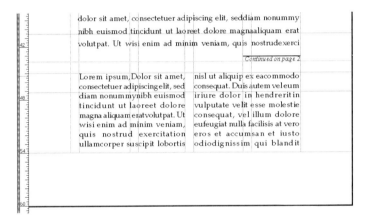

Once you have positioned the story where you want it, let's add a headline:

1. Create a text block to the left of the story, filling the two columns and even with the top of the story, 45 picas from the top margin.

2. Set the headline flush left in the same style as the head for the main story, or in a similar style (in this case use Helvetica Black, 14 points on 16 points of leading).

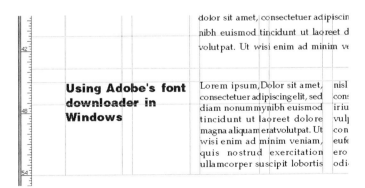

3. Finally, add the byline, like this:

1. From the end of the headline, press **Enter** twice to move down two lines. Choose the style for the byline (flush right Gill Sans Bold in 10 points, with 12 points of leading).

2. Add a line under the byline, one and a half columns long, set flush with the byline. The results should look like this:

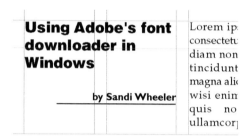

Add the finishing touches to the story, such as continued-to and continued-from lines, and you're just about finished.

Adding the Final Touches

Just a few more steps to go. The newsletter still needs volume and date information, some sort of descriptive line under the nameplate that explains what this thing is all about, a copyright notice, and headers and footers.

The descriptive line under the nameplate can be anything you want it to be. It can be a slogan, a famous saying, or a further definition of the newsletter, such as a division name, or school name. It should be set in relatively small, but readable type so it doesn't compete with the nameplate. Set a line explaining the newsletter in 10 point Copperplate 33, an attractive, highly readable small caps typeface, centered on the page.

Now, let's set up a volume, number, and date. The volume usually indicates the number of years the publication has been published; the number indicates the number of the issue within the current volume. If the newsletter is monthly, it was published for three years and this is the November issue, the volume information looks like this (set in Copperplate 33, 9 point type):

VOLUME 3
NUMBER 11
NOVEMBER, 93

While we're working in the upper half of the newsletter, let's add a registered trademark symbol to the nameplate. The *R* inside a circle can be created in PageMaker by pressing Ctrl-Shift-G, in QuarkXPress by pressing Alt-Shift-R. The symbol is also a part of most fonts, which means you can copy the character to the Clipboard using the Windows Character Map. Make the symbol small, but readable—set it in 8 point Helvetica Light. Position the symbol at the top of the trademarked name like this:

Adding a copyright notice to the publication is a further form of protection. Copyright notices should contain the word copyright, the copyright symbol, and the year of publication. It should also contain words to the effect that all rights are reserved and the copyrighted material is printed in the United States of America. You can create the copyright symbol in PageMaker by pressing Ctrl-Shift-O, or in QuarkXPress by pressing Alt-Shift-C. You can also use the Windows Character Map to copy the symbol to the Clipboard and paste it in your document.

Draw a footer line at the bottom margin and add the copyright information in 8 point Helvetica Light:

by Sandi Wheeler

wisi enim ad minim veniam,   eufeu
quis nostrud exercitation   eros
ullamcorper suscipit lobortis

You've added a footer line to the first page. Now set up headers and footers for the second page:

1. Move to the second page and draw two lines across the page, margin to margin to hold header text. The lines can be in any style, but lean toward light rather than heavy lines.

2. Add whatever text you want for the page header. This should probably be the name of your newsletter, or as in the example, the descriptive line from the nameplate:

NEWS AND VIEWS OF DESKTOP PUBLISHING HARDWARE AND SOFTWARE

Printers

Continued from page 1

tation ullamcorper suscipit lobortis nisl ut aliquip ex eacommodo consequat.Lorem ipsum dolor sit amet, consectetuer adipiscing elit, seddiam nonummy nibh euismod tincidunt ut

volutpat.Lorem ipsum dolor sit amet, consectetuer adipiscing elit, seddiam nonummy nibh euismod tincidunt ut laoreet dolore magnaaliquam erat volutpat. Duis autem vel eum iriure dolor inhendrerit in vulputate velit esse molestie consequat, vel illumdolore eu feugiat nulla facilisis at vero eros et accumsan etiusto odio

---

3. Add the same style line to the bottom of the page as a footer.

That's it; a two-page newsletter, created over lunch.

Adding More Pages

You can add as many pages as you want with the format described in this chapter. However, you must first consider how you will bind the newsletter. If the pages are individual sheets that are creating more front and back pages—bind them by stapling the corner. If you want to three-hole punch the page but still keep them separate, not folded, remember that other than the first page, the additional pages are opened sets (bound in the middle by the three-ring binder). Finally, if you want the page folded and bound in the middle, like a book, remember that the order of printed pages is different than the order of laid-out pages (see "Planning Brochures," in Chapter 9).

Figure 10.2 *Front page of the lunch-hour newsletter.*

COUNTERPOINT

NEWS AND VIEWS OF DESKTOP PUBLISHING HARDWARE AND SOFTWARE

VOLUME 3
NUMBER 11
NOVEMBER, 93

New printers offer greater speed, sharper printing image

by Brad Stanley

Lorem ipsum,Dolor sit amet, consectetuer adipiscing elit, sed diam nonummynibh euismod tincidunt ut laoreet dolore magna aliquam eratvolutpat. Ut wisi enim ad minim veniam, quis nostrud exercitation ullamcorper suscipit lobortis nisl ut aliquip ex eacommodo consequat. Duis autem vel eum iriure dolor in hendreritin vulputate velit esse molestie consequat, vel illum dolore eufeugiat nulla facilisis at vero eros et accumsan et iusto odiodignissim qui blandit praesent luptatum zzril delenit augue duisdolore te feugait nulla facilisi.Lorem ipsum dolor sit amet, consectetuer adipiscing elit, seddiam nonummy nibh euismod tincidunt ut laoreet dolore magnaaliquam erat volutpat.Lorem ipsum dolor sit amet, consectetuer adipiscing elit, seddiam nonummy nibh euismod tincidunt ut laoreet dolore magnaaliquam erat volutpat. Duis autem vel eum iriure dolor inhendrerit in vulputate velit esse molestie consequat, vel illumdolore eu feugiat nulla facilisis at vero eros et accumsan etiusto odio dignissim qui blandit praesent luptatum zzril delenitaugue duis dolore te feugait nulla facilisi.Lorem ipsum dolor sit amet, consectetuer adipiscing elit, seddiam nonummy nibh euismod tincidunt ut laoreet dolore magnaaliquam erat volutpat. Ut wisi enim ad minim veniam, quis nostrudexerci

Continued on page 2

Using Adobe's font downloader in Windows

by Sandi Wheeler

Lorem ipsum,Dolor sit amet, consectetuer adipiscing elit, sed diam nonummynibh euismod tincidunt ut laoreet dolore magna aliquam eratvolutpat. Ut wisi enim ad minim veniam, quis nostrud exercitation ullamcorper suscipit lobortis nisl ut aliquip ex eacommodo consequat. Duis autem vel eum iriure dolor in hendreritin vulputate velit esse molestie consequat, vel illum dolore eufeugiat nulla facilisis at vero eros et accumsan et iusto

Continued on page 2

Consider reserving half the back page of the newsletter for mailing information (unless you are sending the newsletter in an envelope). Simply draw a box inside the margins about half the size of the page. Set up the box like an addressed envelope, with the return address in the upper left corner, postal information (bulk permit number, for example) in the upper right corner, and space for mailing labels in the center.

Getting Free Color

Yes, there is such a thing as a free lunch when it comes to printing color. As I've explained earlier in this book, a screen of a solid color produces a lighter tint of the color. The screen is a dot pattern of the solid color. The more dots you have in close proximity the darker the tint and the closer the color is to the solid color. The fewer dots (and more white space between the dots) the lighter the tint. So, a 90 percent screen of black produces an extremely dark gray; a 10 percent screen of black produces a very pale gray. The same is true for any color: a 50 percent screen of red produces a medium pink, for example.

Now, here's the free part. If you use a color other than black in your document, you pay an additional charge to have the color mixed and the press cleaned after your job is printed. Neither the commercial printer nor the printing press care whether the color used is solid, or a screen of the color. If you create the screens in a page composition program like PageMaker or QuarkXPress, when the color ink is printed through the screen, another (free) color is printed. So if you choose a dark forest green as the solid color, you might get two very nice free colors by using a 60 percent and a 30 percent screen of green—three colors for the price of one.

The screens that the page composition programs produce are excellent as long as you have your service bureau provide film, not paper to your commercial printer. If the service bureau outputs your newsletter to paper, the commercial printer will be to replace the screens on the paper with new screens when the negatives are made, for which you are charged.

CHAPTER SUMMARY

Newsletters can be most effective vehicles for winning support, gaining customers, garnering contributions, and satisfying employees. They can be an important part of a marketing campaign. They can carry profitable ideas and opinions to loyal readers. Newsletters are pretty much instant print communications, and with a little practice, are easy to produce with your Windows computer on any number of page composition applications. To have newsletters read and remembered you must set an attractive table if your readers are to feast upon your words.

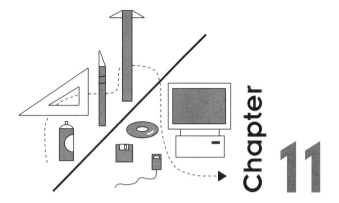

Chapter 11

First Aid for Visual Aids

At one time I worked for a company that used more than 65,000 visual aids in a single year. Visual aids were a way of life there, and were used for every presentation and every meeting. If you worked for this particular company, you learned a lot about visual aids.

Visual aids are either important to you or they're not. If you never give presentations, speak before the public, teach or train groups of people, you have no need for visual aids. But if you do present information in person, visual aids can be a great help (or a great crutch). All too often we rely on the visual aid to provide the message, instead of enhancing the message. If you have ever jammed your talk onto overhead transparencies or slides, and repeated what's on the screen to your audience, your visual aids need some first aid, and that's what this chapter is all about.

There are a number of Windows applications that virtually design your visual aids for you—chief among them are Aldus Persuasion and Microsoft PowerPoint. Both can give you professional-quality visuals, identical to slides and view foils costing many times the price of the software. You don't need specialized software to create your own visuals, you can do just as well using a Windows word processor, an art package like Adobe Illustrator or Aldus FreeHand, or a page composition program. I won't try to explain specialized presentation software in this chapter, but rather give you some basic guidelines to use in developing your own presentation.

OUTLINING YOUR PRESENTATION WITH VISUAL AIDS

Well-designed visuals do not replace your presentation, they enhance it. Most problems stem from presenters copying their speech onto visuals. It goes something like this:

Presenter: "Our mission is to develop products that make a significant impact in the marketplace (they're popular) leading to increased revenue and decreased manufacturing expense (they're profitable) and major recognition as a long-term resource for the corporation (they make the boss happy)."

Supporting visual aid:

Division Mission Statement for New Product Development

> Develop products that make a
> significant impact in the marketplace

> Develop products that lead to increased revenue
> and decreased manufacturing expense

> Develop products that are recognized as a
> long-term resource for the corporation

Not a very useful visual aid is it? Yet, lots of visuals are just as obscure, just as wordy. When the audience sees that visual, they immediately read it instead of listening to the speaker. Then they write down every word of it— while the speaker has moved on to a new topic. A better visual that supports the speaker's mission statement would look like this:

Our Goals for New Products

Universally accepted

Highly profitable

Improve our image with Corporate

Short, simple, to the point; and really what the speaker wants the audience to remember about the mission statement two months after the presentation. Visual aids should outline your presentation, not restate it on the screen. When you make your visuals short and to the point, you get the bonus of room to make the text a decent size so they can be read. If there is anything more annoying than a verbose visual aid, it's one with the type so small it can't be read even if you wanted to.

Visuals Show Your Key Points

Overhead view foils and 35mm slides have many similar characteristics. They are both projected onto a lighted screen, they both require reduced lighting—slides more than view foils—and both offer about the same viewing area, a width to height ratio of 3:2. You can only fit so many words or pictures onto either before they become unreadable. And regardless of which you use, they should contain some common elements, as shown in Figure 11.1. Both types of visuals have room for titles, subtitles (or body text), build titles, logos, and graphics.

Figure 11.1 *Elements necessary for an effective visual aid.*

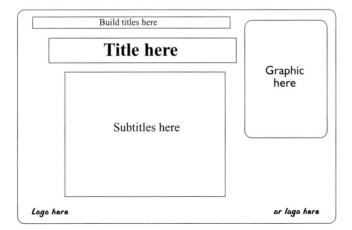

- **Titles.** Headlines for visuals that should be styled like headlines. No more than four or five words in length, titles should be set in the same bold typeface and sized no smaller than 30 point. Titles should contain active verbs. They should be in the active voice. Titles should relate to what you are saying but not necessarily duplicate your talk. Center titles in the title area of the visual.

- **Subtitles.** The body of the visual and should be treated like quick bulleted thoughts. Subtitles should be set in a slightly smaller size than titles, but no smaller than 24 point. They are often indented from the left edge of the title and left aligned. Both titles and subtitles should be set in initial caps and lowercase, which is easier to read than all caps.

- **Build titles.** Running headers that tell the viewer where you are in the presentation. Build titles are like chapter titles, explaining what major section of the presentation you're currently in. There are a number of ways to handle build titles effectively, which I'll get to in a moment.

Figure 11.2 An easy-to-read visual needn't seem crowded to be effective.

Interstate Banking Review, 1993
The Next 12 Months

Federal Restrictions

Reserve percentage increased

Insurance rate inceased

Tighening money supply

Secondary market restrictions

Decreased HUD participation

DB&A _____

- Logos. A nice touch for any visual aid. If you are giving an internal presentation at your own company the logo is less important (but more formal) than if you're presentation is outside your company. If you are selling something with your presentation, the company logo is important, providing another way for potential customers to gain more name recognition about your company and its products. Logos should be set in a manageable size, no smaller than 18 point (which is the smallest size type that is readable on a view foil or slide).

An attractive visual with all these elements in place, might look like Figure 11.2. Even though the type looks overly large, it simply can't be read in sizes smaller than 18 point—24 point is much better for slides that are generally viewed at greater distances than view foils.

N O T E

A word about consistency: Once you decide which of the elements you want to use in your visual aids, position them in the same place on each slide or view foil. Otherwise as you move through your presentation, titles, logos, and graphics will be jumping from place to place on the visual aids—a real distraction and a nuisance to boot. Remember the image area you have to work with: slides require a width to height ratio of 3:2, so specify a 9-by-6 inch page size. For view foils use a 4:3 aspect ratio (an 8-by-6 inch page size). If you're not sure whether you will use slides or view foils, work with the 8-by-6 inch page size and you can't go wrong.

Visual aids should contain only the key points of your presentation. Think of your visuals as the headlines and subheads of your talk. If you develop an outline of your presentation, that outline can serve as the basis for most of your visual aids. For example, if the outline for a new product proposal looks like this:

```
  I. Product definition
        A. Market analysis
        B. New market growth
        C. Future initiatives

 II. Product Competition
        A. Existing products
        B. Anticipated future developments
        C. Installed customer base

III. Comparative analysis
        A. Performance analysis
        B. Service analysis
        C. Residual sales analysis
        D. Cross-over sales analysis
```

Your visuals would use the same order:

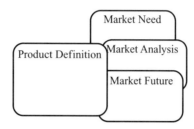

If your key points include the results of spreadsheet compilations, spare your audience visuals of the spreadsheets—they won't be large enough to be seen anyway. Instead, take the five seconds required to have Excel (or any other Windows spreadsheet) chart the spreadsheet, and paste the resulting chart in the program you use to create your visuals. As shown in Figure 11.3, add a title and your visual is done. Just remember to proportionally size the chart large enough to be read and understood.

Figure 11.3 *Chart drawn automatically by Excel and pasted into PageMaker.*

Visuals Keep Information in View

It's not the quantity of visuals you use for your presentation, but what they say. Visuals are a way to keep thoughts, views, subjects, or ideas in suspension while you continue your presentation. Good visuals keep an audience from loosing their place—they know where they are and pay more attention to what you're saying. An excellent way to keep everyone on track is with transitionary visuals that show where you are in your presentation. For example, as you finish discussing items germane to a particular visual, replace it with a *where are we visual*, such as in Figure 11.4 on the next page, that shows the major topics of your presentation. Leave it up until you're ready for the next visual that relates to what you're about to say. Then when you're through with that visual, go to the next *where are we* visual. Showing a progression of topics as a part of your visual aids keeps everyone (including you) on track.

Figure 11.4 *A transitionary visual that shows where you are in the presentation.*

Where are we...
Definition
Assumptions
Current year projections
Future growth
⇨ Cost savings
Increased efficiency
Competition
Product life cycle
Technical support
Proposed budget

Another way to keep information in view of your audience is to pick up the title from the previous visual to use on the next visual. For example, if the marketing portion of a presentation included the subjects of mass marketing, magazine advertising, direct mail marketing, marketing administration, and sales follow-up, titles for your visuals might look like:

Marketing Administration

Lead generation and distribution
Literature storage and distribution
Order receipt and build request

Marketing Administration
Lead Generation and Distribution

Lead Management

Key leads to territories
Enforce using sales report form
Feedback from sales reps
reevaluate lead quality

Marketing Administration
Literature Storage and Distribution

Literature Management

Stock literature in quantity
Enforce weekly inventories
Bring printing in-house
Preprint color to lower costs

Marketing Administration
Order Receipt and Build Request

Order Processing

Install toll-free order line
Tie order to processing clerk
Use master order number
Track via new online system

Visuals Build Your Talk to its Conclusion

Building visual aids are a way of controlling what the audience sees, forcing them to pay attention to only what you are saying. A build format hides each line of a visual aid until such time as you're ready to talk about it. Each successive visual duplicates the visual before, but adds another line of information, like this:

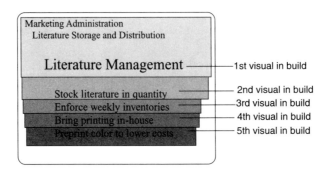

Builds work well for visuals with words, some types of charts, and illustrations. Pie charts, for example, can be broken down into individual wedges, with each successive wedge added to complete the pie. Organization charts, like Figure 11.5, can be displayed in a similar way, with each *leg* of the chart built upon the previously shown leg until the whole chart is visible.

Figure 11.5   *Progressively-built visuals for a new organization.*

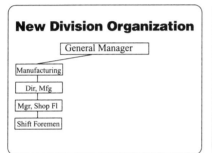
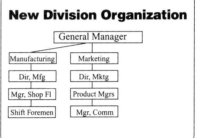

Visuals Should Have Contrast

Black and white is fine for visuals; color is equally as good but more expensive. The important thing is not so much the individual colors, but the amount of contrast in those colors that make your visuals attractive and highly readable. Dark titles and subtitles, using a bold typeface and large, readable sizes against light backgrounds are easiest to read, and most comfortable to look at. Often, the type on visuals are reversed out of a black or dark blue background. Reversing gives a rich look to the visual aids, but is hard to read—type in smaller sizes is more difficult to discern, and graphics and illustrations are more difficult to create in a reversed format. Stick to a simple, direct look, like the styles shown in Table 11.1.

Table 11.1 *Simple style guide for visual aids*

Style Name	Font	Style	Size
Title	Sans Serif	Normal (or bold if serif)	36pt (no smaller than 24 pt)
Subtitles	Serif or sans serif	Normal (or bold if smaller)	24pt (not smaller than 18 point)
Build titles	Serif	Bold (or normal if sans serif)	18pt
Logo			Equivalent of 18pt

CHAPTER SUMMARY

Effective visual aids needn't be fancy, colorful, or cost a lot of money to produce. You can do most of the work with practically any Windows application you currently own. You can print your own transparencies with your laser printer, use a desktop film recorder to make your own 35mm slides, or send a PostScript file of your visuals to a slide imaging service bureau. Regardless of the method you use to produce the visuals, you have the assurance of knowing they're what you want—because you made them—and you'll save enormous time, money, and aggravation to boot. Here are a few do's and don't's to keep in mind:

- Don't let the visual fight for attention.
- Don't put your speech on visuals.
- Don't have a lot of visuals. Your audience gets into the rhythm of seeing your visuals instead of listening to you.

- Don't read your visuals. Let them speak for themselves. Presenters who stand beside the screen and point to the sentences on the visual, then read them to the audience might as well go home and cut the lawn, they're wasting everybody's time.

- Do keep charts and graphs off visuals unless they are extremely simple—they usually can't be read anyway. If their data must be shown, summarize the charts as bulleted subtitles.

- Visuals should be so secondary to your presentation that if the projector dies, no one, least of all you, should take notice.

- To keep your audience from taking notes, instead of listening to you, tell them you'll have hard copies of the visuals available at the *end* of the presentation.

Above all keep in mind that visual aids are merely tools, no different than the speaker's podium, the public address system, or the auditorium or meeting room in which you're speaking. And, long after your presentation has been made, it is your words, not your view foils or slides that should be remembered.

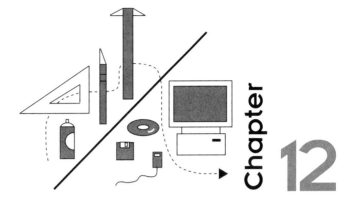

Tips for Long Documents

W hen it comes to creating long documents, desktop publishing can take on very different needs. Long documents generate special circumstances:

- Publications that comprise major sections or chapters
- Pages that include photos, illustrations, charts, graphs, and spreadsheets, all referenced to as the front matter
- Text notations that are cross-referenced among several chapters
- More pages than is typical of a booklet or brochure.

Book-length publications may have a variety of people contributing their best efforts. Chapters may be handled in the computers of writers, editors, editorial assistants, proofreaders, and others. Whether you're involved in a 50-page proposal or a 500-page technical manual, book-length publications can plague you with special demands, and wind up looking less than professional if you don't know some of the tips in this chapter.

WHAT'S THE MATTER WITH THE FRONT MATTER?

The front matter of a book or manual is traditionally anything preceding the first chapter. It includes the Table of Contents, Preface, Foreword, publication and copyright notices, special acknowledgements, and the title page. If the publication is technical in nature, you may also wish to add additional tables of contents, or lists, that itemize illustrations (List of Illustrations), figures (List of Figures), tables (List of Tables), and perhaps a revision system (List of Effective Pages) that notes where updated pages have been added. The pages of the front matter are usually numbered with Roman numerals. Each new section in the front matter usually begins on a right-hand (odd-numbered) page.

Creating Front Matter Lists

The table of contents, (TOC), is the most common list found in the front matter of a book. The TOC contains the page numbers for chapters, and the first, second, and sometimes third order headings. Most page composition software, as well as most Windows word processors can create tables of contents automatically. Headings are simply marked to be included in a TOC listing. Then the table of contents is compiled as text entries that you can correct or modify just like any other text on the page.

It is a bit more difficult to create various lists to add to the front matter—lists that show the page number of figures or tables, for example. While WordPerfect for Windows and Word for Windows can create front matter lists other than tables of contents, most page composition software cannot. Here's a way to fool PageMaker or QuarkXpress into creating any front matter list you need. Let's use PageMaker as an example. First, create the table of contents by following these steps:

1. Open the application, create a style for each of the chapter titles, and each level heading for your document. The styles might be named: *Chapter Title, First Order Head, Second Order Head,* or *Third Order Head.*

2. In the Edit Styles dialog box be sure to choose the Para button to display the Paragraph specifications dialog box, shown in Figure 12.1, and click the Include in table of contents check box.

When you use the Create TOC command, any paragraph (in this case our paragraph is only a one-line heading) with this style is included as a part of the table of contents. Choose OK to return to the Edit Styles dialog box, and OK again to save the style specification.

Figure 12.1 *PageMaker knows what to include in a table of contents based on the Paragraph specifications dialog box.*

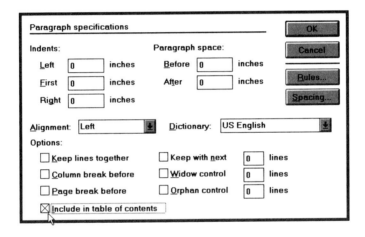

3. Repeat step 2 to create all the heading styles for your publication.

4. To generate the table of contents, insert a new page at the beginning of your publication, and choose the Create TOC command on the Utilities menu. Leave the default name *Contents* in the title text box. Choose OK and PageMaker will compile the chapter titles and headings in the correct order and present a loaded-text icon. Click the icon on the blank page to add the table of contents.

Now that you have the TOC, you can create a List of Figures (or any other list) by first removing the activated Include in table of contents check box from the chapter titles and headings. To create a Figure Caption style and activate the TOC check box for the captions:

1. Give the figures in the publication captions designated with the Figure Caption style.

2. Insert a new page at the beginning of the publication following the table of contents page you just created.

3. Choose the Create TOC command on the Utilities menu. Change the default name in the Title text box from Contents to List of Figures. Then click the Replace existing table of contents check box to remove the X (otherwise PageMaker will replace the table of contents you just created with this list of figures), like the example. Choose OK to create the List of Figures.

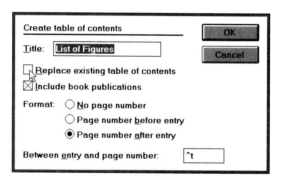

4. You will see the loaded-text icon meaning the List of Figures is ready to be flowed onto the page. Position the icon on the blank page and click the left mouse button.

You can create any front matter list that can be defined as a style in PageMaker, QuarkXPress, or any other page composition program that allows you to designate certain text in a style to be included in a table of contents.

Using PageMaker's Book Command

If you have divided your publication into separate chapters of individual files—as you should have for speed, simplicity, and security—you will have to compile the table of contents, and the various front matter lists on a chapter-by-chapter basis. This isn't as much trouble as it sounds, but if you have twelve chapters and three lists to combine, you can see it will take a considerable amount of time. If you use WordPerfect for Windows or Word for Windows you can link all the chapter files together into one massive document, called a *master document*. Changes made to the individual chapters are reflected in the master document but made only in the smaller chapter files. The compiled master documents of WordPerfect and Word are still monolithic files that are slow to work on.

A distinct advantage of PageMaker over Windows word processors as well as QuarkXPress is its method of combining chapter files. PageMaker creates *books* from the individual files, but never combines them into a huge master document. Instead, it simply sets up the links to each chapter file in the proper order, while you continue to work in the smaller, faster files. The Book command is the only step necessary to sequentially number the pages of your chapter files, to create front matter lists or indexes. The command works like this:

1. Choose the Book command on the File menu. You'll see the Book publication list dialog box, like in Figure 12.2.

Figure 12.2   *A PageMaker book combines all chapter files in the proper order.*

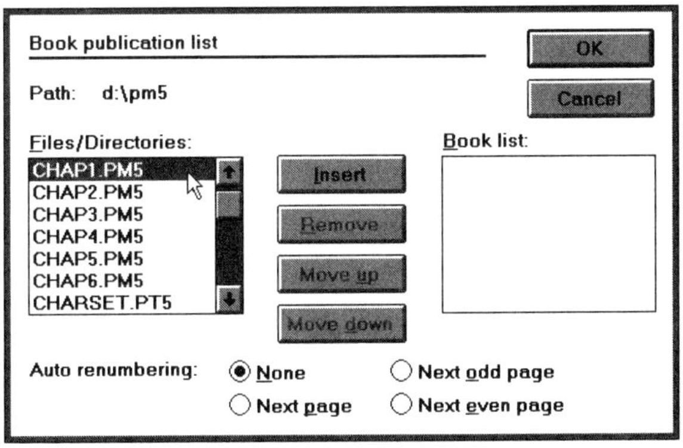

2. Choose each of the chapter files from the Files/Directories list box, and click the Insert button to move them to the Book List box. When complete, the book list might look like this:

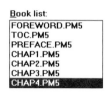

3. Use the Auto-Renumbering option buttons to sequentially number all the pages in your new book.

Controlling Front Matter with WordPerfect

Most Windows word processors can create tables of contents and front matter lists; however you must first generate a master document, in order to combine all the individual chapters. WordPerfect's approach to these functions is easy and straightforward; let's take a quick look:

1. As you develop your chapters, mark the text you wish to be included in front matter lists using the Mark Text command on the Tools menu.

2. To mark a heading or subheading for inclusion in a table of contents, highlight the text and choose Mark Text > Table of Contents. To mark text as a front matter list other than the table of contents, highlight the text and choose Mark Text > List to display the List dialog box:

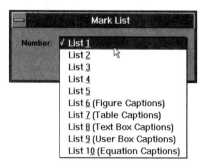

Notice that lists 6 through 10 are predefined as figure captions for the various types of graphic boxes you can create with WordPerfect; the first five are user-defined. It doesn't matter to WordPerfect which list you choose for a front matter list. For example, you can decide that list 1 will be tables that you compile into a front matter list called List of Tables. List 2 will be illustrations that become a List of Drawings in the front matter (you could even assign one of the list numbers to resumes, and compile a List of Project Resumes in the front matter of a proposal).

3. Use the Master Document command on the Tools menu to combine all chapter files (which WordPerfect calls *subdocuments*) into a master document.

4. Mark all of the text for your lists:

   ◆ Headings for the table of contents

   ◆ Figure captions for the list of figures

   ◆ Titles of tables for the list of tables, and so on.

   Position the insertion point where you want the first list—say the table of contents—and choose the Define command on the Tools menu. Then choose the Table of Contents command to define the TOC. To define each of the lists, start by choosing Define and the Lists command. You will see the Define List dialog box:

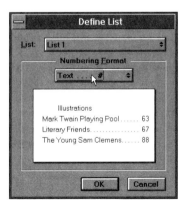

5. Choose the number of the list you want to define. If you decide that tables are to be List 1, and you have marked your table titles

as list 1's, position the insertion point on the page for the List of Tables, choose Define > List and select List 1. WordPerfect will place a hidden code at the insertion point position that will create the list. Now do the same for all the other front matter lists.

6. Finally, to generate all of these lists, choose the Generate command on the Tools menu. WordPerfect will collect all of the figure captions, table titles, drawing captions, and so forth, remember the page number they are found on, move to the hidden define code you created in step 5, and create the lists. Once created, you can edit the contents of the lists like any other text on the page.

If you make changes to a page that would change the page numbers in any of the generated lists, once a list is generated, you must regenerate the list before printing to change the page numbers. You need not delete the existing lists (and you certainly don't want to delete the hidden define codes for the lists). Simply choose the Generate command again, and the lists are updated. It's also a good idea to make the design and style of the front matter lists consistent. Use the same typeface, type style, and spacing for the text portions of the lists, and the same size and style for the page numbers.

TIPS TO CREATING AN EFFECTIVE INDEX

A good index is as much a requirement of a nonfiction book as correct spelling. I worry over the indexes in my books as much as the contents, and often find it harder to create the index than to write the book. Indexes are sorely mistreated in many books, considered a wayward step child of little importance. Indexes usually follow the completion of the manuscript and in the frenzy to get the book to press there's seldom time or patience to create a really good index. Here are some tips to keep in mind:

- The book's author should create the index. If many authors contributed their efforts, they should develop indexes for the parts they wrote and those indexes combined into one index. Who better than the author understands what the book is about? And who but the author really knows the knowledge level of the readers? To write a nonfiction book, whether it is a software user guide, a computer book like this one, a how-to book on brick laying, or a proposal for an in-flight navigation system, the author must understand the readers in order to write to them. Yet indexes are often turned over to persons who have no knowledge of the subject matter, and little, if any understanding of the book's audience.

- Look at your words from the eyes of the reader. How do you go about answering the questions readers will have? How are readers to find specific bits of information contained in the hundreds of pages? Try using this formula to start:

Reader's knowledge level + author's subject knowledge + author's familiarity with the book = index entry

It simply means that your index must be geared to the abilities of readers to find the index entries useful. It means, for example, a repair manual for automobile engines written to experienced auto mechanics will have radically different index entries than a repair manual written to the do-it-yourselfer. The description of rebuilding the fuel injection will be about the same, but the index must serve totally different experience levels. For the expert, an index entry on diagnosing starting problems might look like this:

> *Starting problems*
> > *airflow meter stop screw, adjusting 18, 48*
> > *air/fuel ratio sensor, replacing 32*
> > *Vehicle Control Module (VCM), replacing 130*
> > *emission testing 50, 54-56*
> > *fuel pressure bleed off, measuring 90*
> > *knock sensor, testing 28*
> > *vapor canister, cleaning and replacing 71, 73*

However, the same index entries for the book written to less knowledgeable readers must be more generalized, contain less technical vocabulary, and approach the answers to the readers' questions from more than a single perspective. The first two sub-entries are combined into a more generalized subentry:

> *Starting problems*
> > *adjusting air and fuel ratios 18, 32, 48*

Instead of referring to the control module, the term is simplified:

replacing the fuel injection control computer 130

In case the reader knows the correct name for the fuel injection computer, a second index entry is also added:

Vehicle Control Module (VCM)
    replacing 130

Finally, in case the reader doesn't know the exact name of the fuel injection computer, and isn't tracking down a starting problem, we'll create an entry that covers all the computers in the car, including the Vehicle Control Module:

Computer systems in vehicle
        Altitude Compensation Circuit (ACC) 276
        cabin temperature system 356-360
        electronic timing system 140-149
        Idle Control Module (IDC) 11, 97, 142-143
        On-board Driver's Computer 76-90
        Vehicle Control Module (VCM) 130

◆ Use sub-entries to give the reader starting points. It serves little purpose to create an index entry for this book called *Desktop publishing*, followed by a string of page numbers. First of all, since this book is about desktop publishing, you'd probably see a page number of every page in the book. Furthermore, you'd have no idea what is on each page; you'd have no starting point in your search for a specific answer to your question. Use sub-entries following the main entry, to offer clues to the reader about where to look. If you did away with the sub-entries in our automotive repair index above, you'd have an entry that looked like this:

Computer systems in vehicle 11, 76-90, 97, 130, 140-149, 276, 356-360

Not a very illuminating index entry, is it? In fact, it's a waste of time for its total lack of any information. Yet how many times have we all seen index entries just like this—forcing us to write

down all the page numbers and fruitlessly search through the
book looking for the answer to our question.

- Use action verbs in sub-entries. Adjusting, setting, arranging,
  modifying, changing, creating, all give the reader a sense that
  what they are doing relates to the index entries in the book. For
  example, the entry:

  Oil

  knowing when to change 34

Is more useful than:

  Oil

  characteristics of contamination 34

Creating Indexes Automatically

Using software to create your index is similar to the way you create tables
of contents and front matter lists. First the actual text is marked in some
fashion, then the individual markers are compiled to the index listing. There
hasn't been a program yet invented that can create an index without your
help and guidance. But once you know what the entries are, you can use your
Windows word processor to add an index marker to the applicable text.

Using a Concordance File

Windows applications allow you to automate some of the indexing process.
For example, WordPerfect for Windows can index entries based on a
concordance file. A concordance file is simply a list of words, preferably in
alphabetical order, that can be arranged using WordPerfect's Sort command. When you define the index, you can tell WordPerfect to use the
concordance file. It searches your document for the words in the concordance
file and adds the index markers automatically. Unfortunately, it does not add
sub-entries. But using a concordance file is a good first step in creating the index.

Creating Indexes with PageMaker

While PageMaker doesn't understand concordance files., it will allow you to
enter a word in the Find/Change dialog box and mark all instances of the

word with an index marker by entering ^; in the Change to text box. Again, you will generate the index entries without any sub-entries, but it is a useful place to begin developing an index.

Without a doubt, PageMaker has the most powerful set of indexing tools. For example, PageMaker can add cross references in index entries to other entries, such as:

Oil

  knowing when to change 34 (see also Lubrication requirements)

PageMaker can also show you the compiled list of all index entries and sub-entries, so that you can edit them prior to generating the actual index. Use the Show Index command on the Utilities menu and you will see the dialog box displayed in Figure 12.3., indicating two levels of sub-entries tied to the main index entries.

Figure 12.3 *PageMaker's Show index dialog box lets you edit index entries before the index is created.*

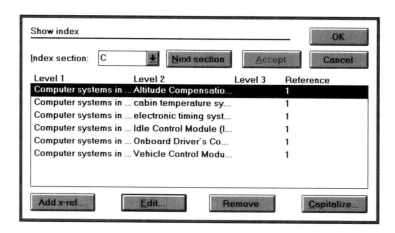

The dialog box lets you review entries alphabetically. Choose the Edit button to see the actual entry. You can change the spelling of any word in the entry, create more levels of sub-entries, or add cross references to other index entries.

UNDERSTANDING THE HIERARCHY OF HEADINGS

In a long document it is the chapters and headings that break up several hundred pages of words into readable and understandable segments. Chapters divide the book into logical units that cover the subject. Within chapters we use headings of different levels to further define the chapter. Usually, the hierarchy of headings includes two or three subheads. For example, if a chapter explains the preparation required to build a house, the major headings might break down the steps of preparation like this:

> *Collecting Bids and Estimating Costs*
> *Arranging Financing*
> *Pulling the Required Permits*
> *Preparing the Building Site*

Under the last major heading, you could have second-order heads that further define site preparation:

> *Preparing the Building Site*
>> *Arranging for Trash Removal*
>> *What to do About Trees*
>> *Insuring Adequate Drainage*
>> *Preparing for Utility Hook-ups*
>> *Positioning the House on the Lot*

And the last second-order heading could be further defined with these third-order headings:

>> *Positioning the House on the Lot*
>>> *Taking Best Advantage of a View*
>>> *What Will You See from the Road?*
>>> *Where is the Northern Exposure?*
>>> *Handling Shade and Sun*

The question arises, once you have all these headings, how do you tell them apart? If you were to open the book in the middle of this chapter and begin reading, how would you know where you were? As we mentioned many chapters ago, headings are the signposts that tell readers where they are going and where they have just been. You must have a consistent style for the hierarchy of headings so readers are always comfortable while deep in the midst of a discussion of construction planning.

Numbering Headings

One way to ensure that the reader understands your heading hierarchy is to number the headings, similarly to the way you number outlines. Numbered headings are usually reserved for government documents, or publications produced by government subcontractors. Generally speaking, if headings are numbered, paragraphs following the headings are numbered as well. Windows word processors usually provide an outline feature that can accommodate heading and paragraph numbering.

Rules for Effective Headings

It is difficult at best to make general statements about headings since they are the condensed subject areas of any book. But here are a few suggestions to keep in mind:

- Make heading styles distinctive. First-order headings should be distinctive from second-order heads. Once readers see the difference in headings they should be able to clearly differentiate between levels of headings throughout the book.

- Limit the book to at most three levels of headings. If you find you need an additional level, resist the temptation of adding a fourth level for the sake of accommodating a single chapter. Readers will notice the inconsistency and find it confusing. If you find yourself needing deeper levels of headings, consider creating numbered or bulleted items (like these).

- Make your headings interesting and informative. Headings should entice the reader onward. Make your headings short and to the point. Give them action—*Digging the Foundation* is better than *Preliminary Foundation Preparation*. Headings should not hold any secrets. They should give the reader a clear message of what the paragraphs following the heading contain.

- Stay away from cute headings. It may sound clever when you write it but headings that are overly cute, funny, or gimmicky get old and tiresome very quickly. Since headings are so fundamentally important to the reader's orientation and understanding of your chapters, you don't want them rolling their eyes at your headings.

- Try to have at least two of any level subhead. If you have enough to say to create another level of headings, you should also have enough to say to create two headings. A single subhead looks like an afterthought you couldn't find another place for.

CONTROLLING WIDOWS, ORPHANS, AND OTHER DISTANT RELATIVES

When a paragraph falls at the bottom of a column or page and the very last line is bumped to the next column or page, that solitary line is called a *widow*. Likewise, when a paragraph is begun at the bottom of a column or page and all but the first line is bumped to the next column or page, the first line that remains all by itself is call an *orphan*. Orphans and widows are common signs that a publication was produced by a word processor rather than a professional designer (even though most word processors can control the wayward lines if allowed to). The cure for widows and orphans is to break the paragraph with two or more lines at either the top or bottom of the column or page. Two or more lines look more natural and less haphazard than a single line.

PageMaker, QuarkXPress, WordPerfect, and Word, all control widows and orphans quite well. PageMaker and QuarkXPress allow you to set the minimum number of lines that can remain at either the top or bottom of the page. The wrong way to control widows and orphans is to create the page breaks artificially, instead of letting the application decide where it needs to break the page. Deciding for yourself where the pages break is something we all do with letters and correspondence, and while it may work for a three-page letter it won't work for a 50-page chapter.

Widows and orphans are generally controlled as a paragraph formatting function. Both WordPerfect and Word control the single lines automatically (although you can turn the options off if you so choose). PageMaker, for example, gives you specific control through its paragraph formatting offering several options for controlling the relationship between paragraphs and page breaks. Use PageMaker's Paragraphs command on the Format menu to open the dialog box, shown in Figure 12.4. In the Widow Control and Orphan Control text boxes, enter the minimum number of lines to retain at either the top or bottom of your pages.

Figure 12.4 *PageMaker's Paragraph specifications dialog box controls widows and orphans.*

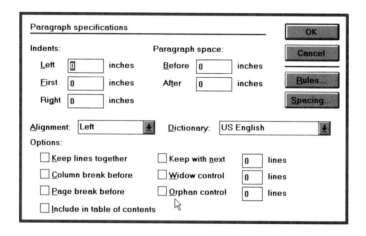

NUMBERING FIGURES, HANDLING CAPTIONS, AND HOLDING THE READER'S ATTENTION

Figures in books are normally numbered. This is done so authors can make in-text references to the figures and the figures needn't fall so close to the reference. The layout of the page, and the care needed in breaking pages to prevent widows and orphans makes it sometimes difficult to add figures close to their in-text reference. Consequently, the figure caption is needed to explain the figure; the caption should be able to stand alone, giving the figure adequate explanation.

Figures must always follow their in-text references, but because of layout difficulties, may turn up several pages later. And, while the figure caption should explain what is shown in the figure, the in-text reference makes it easy to find a further explanation: note the figure number and look backwards through several pages until you spot the same figure number in the text. Figures that immediately follow an explanation don't necessarily need a figure number or a caption; but be doubly sure it stays with the text explanation or the reader will be thoroughly confused.

While short, one-line figure captions are attractive on the page and easy to lay out, there should be no limit to the size of captions. As a matter of fact, if it is an important illustration, it deserves as much explanation as needed. Captions should make interesting reading, for the figures they pertain to are often the center of focus on the page.

USING SEARCH AND REPLACE, SPELLERS, AND GRAMMAR CHECKERS AS AIDS

Be careful when using software aids like search and replace, spellers, and grammar checkers. Remember they are no substitute for well-written pages carefully read and proofed. The search feature probably has the most use in a large document. It can move you quickly about your pages and chapters. Type in a bit of text unique to the sentence or paragraph you're looking for and tell the search feature (often called Find) to do its thing. Search and replace (or Find and Change) is a more serious command and should be used with a great deal of respect. Search and replace looks for one thing and replaces it with something else. Word for Windows has one of the most sophisticated Find commands, which can look not only for words but specific type and font characteristics, paragraph formatting, and styles. Choose the Find command on Word's Edit menu to open the dialog box, shown in Figure 12.5 on the next page. Enter the word or words you want to find in the Find text box. Use the Character, Paragraph, and Style buttons to define elements, type, paragraphs, or styles to look for. You could, for example, search for only the words desktop publishing, which are set in 12-point Avant Garde, within paragraphs with one-quarter inch left indents and left-justified alignment. By using the Replace command, you could look for the same words and replace the indented paragraphs the words appear in with hanging indents instead.

Figure 12.5 *The Find dialog box in Word can search for virtually any type of formatting, including fonts, paragraph specifications, and styles.*

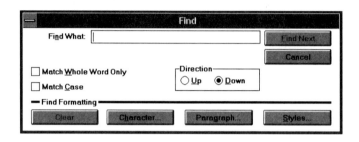

Spellers are useful for some kinds of spelling problems, but at the expense of a false sense of security that all the words are correct. In fact, with only about 100,000 words in their dictionaries, spellers don't know nearly as many words as we do. Spellers don't understand many of the typing mistakes we sometimes make, such as transposed words (*are they* for *they are*), and misused words (*they're* for *their*). Since most spellers have the ability to add specialized vocabulary to specialized dictionaries, you can create a dictionary of correctly spelled terms that you might not want to add to a dictionary for general use. (You might, for instance, want to keep medical terms and agriculture terms in separate dictionaries.) The ability to add new words to a dictionary means that you can add the correctly-spelled names of people, and use the speller to double check all the instances of the names in a chapter or book. Word for Windows dictionaries end in the extension .DIC, WordPerfect dictionaries are .SUP files, and QuarkXPress dictionaries end in .QDT. Unfortunately, PageMaker doesn't allow you to create your own customized dictionaries.

WordPerfect and Word for Windows both come with grammar checkers. A grammar checker looks at a document and compares the structure of the words against rules it has been programmed with. If it finds differences, it tells you what the possible problems are. They seem to bog down on unimportant details and ignore more glaring deficiencies in writing. I don't advocate using them, but if you're looking to be criticized by a machine you can't argue with, be my guest.

CHAPTER SUMMARY

A commercial printer, and good friend called recently to ask if I could create a PostScript file of a 350-page technical user manual done in WordPerfect for Windows. It had no headings and subheads, and only four chapters. It had no front matter, nor a glossary and index. It lacked a title page, an introduction and a table of contents. It was merely a collection of words that would eventually share a book cover. It was a lonely looking document without any of the trappings that give life and warmth to books.

Books should be inviting places to visit, regardless of the subject matter. They should be easy to reference, quick to use, and comprehensive in presentation. A book is neither a report nor an article. It will not be read in one sitting. It may possiblely not be read cover-to-cover at all, but used entirely as a reference tool. It's important, therefore, to give readers all the help they can get, by establishing a sensible hierarchy of headings and subheadings; chapters that divide the subject into logical bites, and front-matter and back-matter tools to make the book as easily referenced as possible.

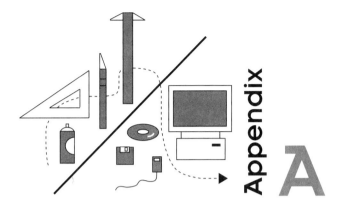

Nuts and Bolts of a Desktop Publishing System

In the first chapter of this book, I stated that you don't need a high-powered Windows computer to handle desktop publishing. I'll repeat it again here. But while you don't need the most expensive system you can buy, you do need a basic system with the capability to expand in the future, as your skills improve and your design requirements grow.

A fellow I met recently asked me about Pentium computers. He wanted to configure an extremely high-powered system with 64 megs of RAM, a gigabyte of disk space, capable of displaying 32-bit color. He wanted to buy a $15,000 computer to use in producing his company newsletter. I asked him if he had figured out his ROI or return on investment—how many newsletters would he have to create to justify the cost of the system. He hadn't considered the return on his investment. I asked him about color in his newsletter; he wasn't sure he could afford four-color printing. Then why the need to display extremely high-definition color? I asked why he wanted a Pentium computer; he didn't know exactly, but felt he should have the best. Here was a perfectly rational business owner who was buying a computer like he bought his last car (with the larger engine in case he had to pass a truck on a hill).

Before I explain what you need in a Windows computer system, let me mention what you don't necessarily need. These days, Windows computers are sold like automobiles. Speed, handling and horsepower are the claims raved about in magazine ads. And, like automobiles, manufacturers would like nothing better than for you to trade up to the newer, faster model every six months. Don't fall for the hype; don't step into a marketing trap that assures ease-of-use through faster processors. There is no doubt the Pentium is a powerful CPU, but the Pentium is also very expensive, and its added power may not be recognized in desktop publishing applications. Likewise, there is much advocacy for extremely fast, ultra high resolution video adapters (sometimes called Windows accelerators), capable of displaying 16.7 million colors, or more, simultaneously at very high scanning rates. These adapters can cost well over $1000. Unless you are using Adobe Photoshop or Aldus PhotoStyler to do professional-quality color correcting to scanned color photos or Photo CD images, you do not need this sort of high-resolution video adaptor. That's not to say if you have a thousand dollars burning a hole in your pocket don't buy such an adaptor, but there are much better ways of spending your money, which I'm about to do.

A TYPICAL WINDOWS COMPUTER SYSTEM

Let's go shopping for a desktop publishing computer. Any computer capable of running Windows with an 80386 or 80486 processor is fully capable of handling your desktop publishing needs. Entry-level 486 systems are now so inexpensive that it makes sense to start with an up-gradable 25Mhz 486. However, if you have already purchased one of the faster 386 systems, such as a 33Mhz or 40Mhz system, it is certainly fast enough to handle the added burden of desktop publishing.

Selecting the Processor

Starting with a computer sporting a DX-486 processor means a faster processor can be added in the future. SX processors, such as the Intel SX 486/25 (a 25Mhz processor) are not usually upgradable, nor are they as fast as their DX brothers. While a 486 DX computer is upgradable, many systems now carry the processor in a special socket on the motherboard called a *zero insertion force* (or ZIF) *socket*. A ZIF socket means the old processor can be removed without any special tools or the risk of damaging its delicate pins, and a new, faster processor can be plugged in with equal ease. In shopping for a computer, check to make sure the motherboard carries a ZIF socket. Then your 25Mhz 486 can one day become a 33Mhz or 50Mhz system.

There is one final feature to consider in getting a fast Windows computer: that's the case for *local bus architecture*. A local bus is not the city transit service you pick up at the corner. The bus refers to the slots in your computer which hold circuit boards, including the video adaptor board, the hard disk controller board, perhaps an internal modem, and probably an I/O board that contains serial and parallel ports. The speed that data can run over the bus is usually around 10Mhz (some buses can handle speeds of 25Mhz). It's obvious that if you need lots of video data or large chunks of data moved to and from your hard disk (as you do with Windows) the bus should run as quickly as the processor. Local bus is a way to do just that.

Some computers offer one, two, and sometimes three slots in the bus that operate at the same speed as the processor. So a 33Mhz processor would be able to move data over the local bus at a speed of 33Mhz, instead of 10Mhz. For video and hard disk controllers, local bus systems can make a marked improvement in Windows' performance, at a cost of about $100 more than a non-local bus system.

Recommendation: Start with a local bus DX 486 25Mhz system, and plan to upgrade with a faster processor and an OverDrive processor in the future. You can eventually move all the way up to a 66Mhz computer, which is really flying. There are hundreds of mail order manufacturers—many offer excellent products and support; others are fly-by-night garage operations which will not be in business a year from now. Consider comparison pricing from companies like Dell (800-247-5509), Gateway (800-846-2063), Zeos (800-554-7172), ALR (800-444-4257), PC Brand (800-722-7263), Compudyne (800-932-2667), Northgate (800-453-0129) Compaq (800-888-5903), NEC (800-374-8000), and Ambra/IBM (800-252-6272). All sell reliable products backed by first class technical support.

Choosing a Video Monitor

Next comes the video monitor. Good video monitors are worth the additional cost. Low-quality monitors are saturating the computer market, are short-lived, and have little factory support in the U.S. Some specifications to keep in mind are the dot pitch (should be no larger than .28mm) and the non-interlaced scan rate at 1024 by 768 resolution (should be no lower than 72Hz). The overall size of the monitor is an important consideration for desktop publishing.

Generally speaking, 14-inch monitors come standard with most computer systems these days. By the way, don't try to measure the screen with a tape measure; you won't get close to 14 inches. Monitor manufacturers are extremely liberal with their measurements (a 14-inch monitor, measured diagonally, might only be 13 inches and the actual image is usually smaller still). Don't be disappointed if your monitor doesn't measure up to what you believed you bought. If your budget allows, consider buying a larger monitor. A 15-inch monitor offers a sizable increase in work space—more than the inch increase in size would indicate—and the 17-inch size gives you enormous elbow room to lay out documents. A 17-inch monitor can add from $800 to $1,500 to the price of the standard 14-inch monitor, so do some comparison shopping. High-quality monitors you might consider include NEC (800-366-0476), Nanao (800-800-5202), Mitsubishi (800-843-2515), Sony (800-352-7669), and ViewSonic (800-888-8583).

How Much Hard Disk Space is Enough?

You can never have too much free space on your hard disk. Space on my hard disk is like space in my garage, loaded down with old German cars, irreplaceable parts, and boat stuff jammed into nooks and crannies. Occasionally Sally holds a secret garage sale and suddenly it's like I added another disk: more room to fill up once again. Don't let the fact that your system comes with a 250Mb or 350Mb drive scare you into choosing a smaller drive option. You'll fill up the space soon enough.

Systems with 250 megabytes seem common configurations right now. Remember that inexpensive disk compression software can effectively double the size of the disk (or you can use DoubleSpace that comes with MS-DOS 6). My favorite compression software is XtraDrive from IIT (408-727-1885) which compresses disks at the bios level, meaning Windows and DOS think you simply have a larger disk than you physically do. XtraDrive can compress Windows permanent swap files and can be used with virtually any disk utility (Norton Utilities, PC Tools, etc.). Based on the types of files in your system, you can increase the size of your hard disk by up to 800 percent (meaning you could get a 2 gigabyte drive out of a 250 megabyte drive).

How Much Memory?

You realistically need at least 8 megabytes of RAM to work comfortably in Windows with desktop publishing software. Even though most applications say they require 4 megabytes, you need to designate some memory to the font cache in Adobe Type Manager, and set an adequate cache size for the disk caching software you use (such as SmartDRIVE, Super PC-Kwik, or Norton Cache).

If you limit yourself to 8 megs, activate a permanent Windows swap file, if possible. A swap file is an area of your hard disk that Windows sets aside to store information currently held in memory. Only information that is held in memory the longest will be swapped to the disk, so it's likely that whatever you're currently doing won't be affected by the swap file. However, the swap file frees up more memory for your applications to use.

To create a swap file, open the Control Panel and double-click the 386 icon. Choose the Virtual Memory button in the dialog box to see the Virtual Memory dialog box. If Windows can't set up a *permanent swap file* (usually caused by configuring your hard drive with a third-party partitioning program like Disk Manager), create a *temporary swap file* instead. Permanent swap files are significantly faster since they are formed as a contiguous section of your disk. Temporary swap files are created each time you start Windows (meaning Windows takes longer to start up) and can become as *fragmented* as any other file on your disk. The more fragmented temporary swap files are, the slower they become.

By the time you read this book, memory may be very inexpensive, or very costly. Memory is as much a commodity these days as North Sea crude oil or pork futures, and the price can jump through wide gyrations. As you gain experience in desktop publishing and attempt more sophisticated designs, you will probably want to increase the amount of RAM in your computer—16 megs or 24 megs makes a significant impact in system speed. If you plan on using Adobe Photoshop, you might want to consider increasing RAM to at least 12 megs.

Be very careful when buying memory. It must match the speed of the existing memory in your system, as well as being of a compatible format.

There are two formats for memory: *SIMM modules*—*by-9 SIMMs* and *by-36 SIMMs*. Each is slightly different—the by-36 SIMMs have a notch in the middle of the pins—and they are not interchangeable in your computer. It is wise to purchase the highest-quality memory from the best source. I recommend starting with H.Co. Computer Products (800-726-2477) which manufactures its own memory chips, and provide a lifetime performance warranty for all the memory they sell. Many manufacturers and dealers buy their memory from H.Co. and they offer highly-competitive prices.

Don't Forget to Back Up

Backing up is a pain; there's no doubt about it. Messing with floppies, constantly formatting floppies, and storing the darn things can be a real nuisance. When you use a Windows system, everything—document files, applications, even Windows programs—are significantly larger than what you might have been used to in DOS. Backing up to floppies becomes a day-long event. It's time to consider using a *tape backup unit* instead of diskettes.

There are a number of inexpensive tape drives that connect in parallel to your floppy drives (they look like floppy drives to your computer). Called QIC (for quarter-inch cartridge) format drives, they are priced around $200 and can back up several megabytes per minute. While the largest cartridge holds 120 megabytes of data, the drives can compress files and store up to 250 megs on a single cartridge. Colorado Memory Systems (800-451-0897) was the initial developer of these low-priced tape systems, although there are now a number of competing brands available.

From low-end QIC tape units, the price tag climbs rapidly. DAT drives (Digital Audio Tape) can handle up to 4 gigabytes, but prices begin at around $1,000. Rewritable CD-ROM drives, called magneto optical (MO) drives, handle removable cartridges that look like a CD disc in a protective case. They are not compatible with CD-ROM drives. Each cartridge can hold 128 megs of data. The MO cartridges are fully rewritable and can be used over and over again, just like a floppy diskette. The drive units are priced at about $1,000 and cartridges cost about $60 each.

Another option for backup is to use optical floppy diskettes. Iomega (800-456-5522) makes a floptical drive that can read and write standard floppy diskettes, as well as 21 megabyte optical diskettes. Priced at about $500, the drive is three times faster than a standard floppy drive and replaces the 3.5-inch internal floppy drive in your system.

Choosing a CD-ROM Drive

If you plan to delve in Photo CD, as I hope you will, your system needs to include a CD-ROM drive. Most CD-ROM drives are compatible with Kodak Photo CDs, but you must double-check compatability before buying a drive, or a computer that includes one. Make sure that it is *multi-session enabled*, meaning it can read the multiple sessions of adding scanned images to the disc. Some manufacturers that offer multi-session drives include NEC (800-388-8888), Mitsumi (408-970-0700), Chinon (310-533-0274), Sony (408-434-6644), and Texel (800-886-3935). If you have any questions about multi-session drives, Kodak will send you a free catalog of drives they have found to be compatible (and they ought to know). You can call them at 800-242-2424, extension 53, and request the latest *Photo CD System CD-ROM Drive Compatibility Guidelines*.

Finding a PostScript Laser Printer

A PostScript laser printer is a PostScript laser printer. It is an independent device and as long as it contains printer ports compatible with your computer, it doesn't care whether it is cabled to a Macintosh or a Windows computer. There are a number of manufacturers who are dominant in the PostScript laser printer market, Apple (408-996-1010) being the most prominent (and one of the most expensive). Other manufacturers include Texas Instruments (800-527-3500), NEC (800-374-8000), and Xante (800-926-8839).

With the variety of 600 dots-per-inch printers on the market you may not believe me when I say that 300 dpi is enough resolution, plenty in fact with the latest generation of laser printers. Most have specific logic to sharpen and improve the resolution to the point that a new 300 dpi laser printer looks like the output of an older 600 dpi printer. If you think about what you will be printing, there are very few instances where you actually need more than 300 dpi: certainly not for type, and certainly not for most graphic situations. You may need higher resolution if you are printing screened, halftone photos with your laser printer; but for most situations that's a rare requirement. Generally, any document that contains screened halftones is destined for offset commercial printing, meaning you will have the document produced in film by your service bureau on a high-resolution imagesetter. And if you're using a service bureau, what do you need a 600 dpi printer for?

In fact, the current trend toward higher resolution laser printers is part and parcel to the type of marketing mentioned earlier in this appendix, in which hardware manufacturers would have you believe that more power, speed, and, in this case, dots per inch are always better. You might be better off spending the money you save, by not buying the higher resolution printer, on a library of fonts that can be stored on a hard drive subsystem that you can attach to your 300 dpi printer.

A PostScript laser printer needs about 2 megs of memory to process PostScript files. However, that much memory should be sufficient for just about anything that you will likely be printing. I printed color separation proofs for the eight color plates in this book, one of which was larger than 30 megabytes, on a PostScript laser printer with 2 megs of RAM. The files printed quickly and flawlessly. That's not to say you can't add more memory (some laser printers accept up to 16 megs of RAM) but you probably won't see any increase in performance. If you have a huge number of fonts in a document, a printer with only 2 megs may have trouble retaining all the fonts in memory necessary to print a page (but if you've been paying attention, by now you know you shouldn't be using that many different fonts on the same page anyway).

There are several questions you should ask in the course of searching for a PostScript laser printer:

- **Does it have a straight-through paper path?** This feature keeps paper from doubling back on itself so that you can use a much heavier weight paper in the printer.

- **What is the life expectancy of the printer?** Chances are you won't actually wear a laser printer out, but you may exceed the life of the laser (which is the most expensive part of the system). The life expectancy is measured in total number of pages printed. It should be higher than 100,000.

- **What is the cost of replacable materials?** Find out how much it costs to replace the toner cartridge, the OPC belt, or any other replaceable systems in the printer.

- **Does the printer come with specific Windows drivers?** The standard PostScript driver supplied with Windows is more than adequate, but it's always nice to have a printer driver specifically designed for the individual printer.

♦ **What support is offered?** You need to find out if there is onsite service available and toll-free technical support available.

Typical Software Tools

Windows is rich ground for growing graphic applications. Here are just a few for you to consider:

Adobe Illustrator

The leading vector drawing program for both Windows and the Macintosh. Illustrator can create .AI files or .EPS (encapsulated PostScript) files.

Adobe Photoshop

One of the leading photo enhancement programs, it can control the scanning of photos and art work, manipulate color, brightness, contrast, and apply special effects to color photos.

Adobe Streamline

Changes bitmapped images to PostScript images which can be modified in a vector graphics drawing program like Adobe Illustrator or Aldus FreeHand. Extremely handy for modifying parts of photos and enlarging bitmapped graphics.

Adobe Type Align

Replicates type along any line that you draw and allows you to apply masks of special shapes to type.

Adobe Separator

Prepares any color photo saved as an EPS file for color separation. Works mostly as a front-end program to control files sent to high-resolution imagesetters.

Adobe Systems, Inc.
1585 Charleston Rd.
Mountain View, CA 94043
800-833-6687

Aldus FreeHand

A program that competes head-to-head with Adobe Illustrator, FreeHand can read and modify Illustrator files.

Aldus PhotoStyler

Another high-end photo enhancement program, PhotoStyler includes tools to modify color characteristics, and apply a wide variety of special effects.

Aldus Gallery Effects

Lets you apply preset special effects to photos and illustrations saved in .TIF format.

Aldus IntelliDraw

One of a new breed of drawing programs to use intelligent objects and a host of detailed, specialized tools.

Aldus Persuasion

A presentation program that helps you design and create transparency and slide shows. Includes a presentation player that shows your presentation on your Windows computer.

Aldus Corporation
411 First Avenue South
Seattle, WA 98104
800-685-3540

Collage Plus

A simple-to-use Windows screen capture utility. Grab any window, dialog box, or portion of a window, and print proofs to any HP LaserJet printer.

Inner Media, Inc.
60 Plain Road
Hollis, NH 02049
603-465-3216

HiJaak for Windows

The most sophisticated Windows screen capture and graphic conversion program available.

Inset Systems, Inc.
71 Commerce Drive
Brookfield, CT 06804
203-740-2400

Kodak Photo CD Access
While not required for use with Photo CDs, Photo CD Access (not to be confused with Microsoft Access, a database program) makes it easy to see what's on your discs. Photo CD Access shows you a contact sheet containing thumbnail-sized photos. Click the photo you want and open it.

Kodak PhotoEdge
A photo enhancement application that can apply color correction to color photo images. PhotoEdge doesn't have the bells and whistles of Adobe Photoshop, but then it's a lot easier to learn as well.

Kodak Shoebox
A photo database that stores thumbnail-size images of photos, allows searches for photos based on key words, and makes photo retrieval easy.

Eastman Kodak Company
343 State Street
Rochester, NY 14650
800-242-2424

Designer
A vector graphics-based drawing program, similar in aspects to Adobe Illustrator. Comes with several Adobe products, including Type Align and a number of Type 1 fonts.

Picture Publisher
Another photo enhancement program that can do color correction to photos. Has filters similar to competing products. Picture Publisher is very fast and versatile in converting graphic formats.

Windows Draw!
A simple, inexpensive vector graphics drawing program I can't say enough good about. If you buy one drawing program for all your needs, this is the one.

Micrografx, Inc.
1303 Arapaho Road
Richardson, TX 75081
800-733-3729

PKZIP, PKUNZIP

The preeminent file compression and archival program. Versions have been around forever; it's used by everyone. Available as shareware on CompuServe, or by writing to the address below.

PKWare, Inc.
North Deerwood Drive
Brown Deer, WI 53223
414-354-8699

What Fonts Do I Really Need?

You do not need a huge number of fonts in your system. As a matter of fact, you probably won't use more than a dozen of your favorites. For service bureaus, and businesses like graphic designers that must have a font library available, I suggest two. First, Adobe Systems supplies fonts on CD-ROM called *Fonts On Call*. You get the entire Adobe Type I library on disc; however, you get the password to unlock the fonts only after you pay for them. So you could start out by only unlocking a handful of fonts, but if you get a job requiring fonts you haven't yet paid for, simply call Adobe (800-833-6687), purchase the fonts you need with a credit card, use the password they give you and *voilá*, you have the fonts you need in a matter of minutes.

For the rest of us, assuming you are using a PostScript laser printer that contains the standard 35 resident fonts (including Times Roman, Helvetica, Avant Garde, Bookman, Palatino, and Zapf Chancery), your primary needs are to acquire a couple of very bold headline fonts (the bold versions of your resident fonts just aren't bold enough for headlines). Some examples of heavy fonts include Helvetica Black, Colossalis, Gill Sans Extra Bold, and Rockwell Extra. The second group of fonts should be script or italic fonts, such as Berthold Script and Pepita. Finally, you need a couple of display fonts, like Biffo, Ironwood, and Lithos. These fonts will give you a wide margin of creativity in designing documents. Once you've acquired the basics, then you can pick up fonts for special projects as you need them.

Getting Help from Periodicals

If you subscribe to no other periodicals you might consider getting one of these. It's not a long list, but you will learn a great deal about Windows desktop publishing, as well as the latest in applications, fonts, and utilities.

Aldus Magazine
Aldus Corporation
411 First Avenue South
Seattle, WA 98104-2871
(206) 628-2321
Obviously a showcase for PageMaker and Aldus' other applications, *Aldus* Magazine is beautifully finished and very well written. If you work with PageMaker and FreeHand, this publication covers both expertly.

Before & After
1830 Sierra Gardens Drive
Suite 30
Roseville, CA 95661
(916) 784-3880
Publisher John McWade tells you "How to Design Cool Stuff" in this easy-going, informative 16-page newsletter. If you want to really learn how to use Aldus FreeHand, and create images you thought were impossible to do on a computer, subscribe. You won't be disappointed.

Byte Magazine
One Phoenix Mill Lane
Peterborough, NH 03458
(603) 924-9281
You've invested a sizable amount of money in your Windows system, and *Byte* keeps you current on hardware, software, and what is coming down the pike. The nice thing about *Byte* is that Windows and Macintosh news is covered equally.

Windows Magazine
600 Community Drive
Manhasset, NY 11030
(516) 562-7124
If you want to collect all the current news, opinions, knowledge about Windows, Windows applications, and the future of the operating system, it's here. It keeps you up to date with the fastest growing segment of the computer industry.

WordPerfect for Windows Magazine
270 West Center Street
Orem, UT 84057
(801) 226-5555
If you use WordPerfect for Windows, subscribe. The publication more than pays for itself with macros that save you time, tips for handling fonts, printing, and WordPerfect's advanced options. You'll also get the news on the latest enhancements to WordPerfect.

Getting Help from Professional Associations

Here are three associations geared to what you will probably be doing with your Windows computer system. They can be a great source of information and practical advice.

National Association of Desktop Publishers
462 Old Boston Street
Topsfield, MA 01983
(508) 887-7900
This is the oldest and largest organization of desktop publishing professionals in existence. Their member magazine, called the *Journal* is well worth the cost of membership alone. But NADTP is a great source for information, news, help, and major discounts on desktop publishing hardware and software.

Society for Technical Communications
901 North Stuart Street
Suite 304
Arlington, VA 22203
(703) 522-4114
If you work with technical publications, training manuals, on-line documentation or even technical brochures or proposals, the STC can be a great resource.

Windows Prepublishing Association
1804 Hayes Street
Nashville, TN 37203
(615) 320-9473
WPA is a fast-growing collection of Windows desktop publishers who share tips and tricks about publishing with Windows.

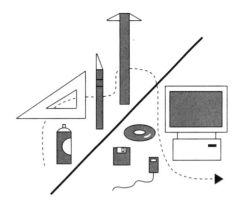

Glossary

A

accordion fold   Used for vertical brochures and slimjims, a wider page is folded like an accordion to create the pages of the brochure.

A4 paper size   The international page size equivalent of 8.5-by-11 inches.

ascender   The stems of lowercase characters which extend above the body of the type; such as *b*, *d*, and *f*.

alignment of text   How text compares to left and right margins: *left-aligned* is even on the left margin, but ragged on the right; *right-aligned* is ragged on the left margin and even on the right; *centered* lines are centered between each margin and are usually ragged on both sides; and *justified* is even on both margins.

B

backing up
To print on the back side of a printed page is backing up the page. *See also: work and turn*

bad break
Hyphenating the last word in the first line of a paragraph of type is considered a bad break. An incorrectly hyphenated word is also a bad hyphenation, or bad break.

baseline
An invisible line on which a line of type rests. To adjust one or more characters in the line up or down is to adjust their baselines.

basis weight of paper
A measurement system for the relative thickness of paper, the basis weight is the weight in pounds of a ream (500 sheets) of paper in a given size.

binding
Any number of methods of holding pages together to form a booklet or book that includes perfect binding, saddle-wire stitching, side-wire stitching, and edition binding.

bleed
To extend a color, photograph, or type off the trimmed edge of the page is to bleed it off the page.

brownline
Similar to a blueline, it is a brown photographic rendering of the final, camera-ready page, prior to printing.

C

calendered paper
During the process of making paper, the paper stock is sometimes rolled between heavy, extremely smooth rollers, called calenders, which produces a smoother finish on one side of the paper.

chrome
Refers to a color slide (or transparency), like Kodachrome or Fugichrome.

clip art   Black and white drawings that were traditionally clipped or cut out of large books by artists, desktop publishing clip art comes in a variety of formats. Included free with many applications, electronic clip art is also available from a variety of software companies.

coated paper   Refers to any number of methods for treating the surface of paper to give it a smooth, even finish. Coated paper handles the application of ink more uniformly and offers a truer rendering of printed colors because the coating keeps the ink from absorbing into the grain of the paper. Coatings can range from dull to extremely glossy finishes.

collate   To collect the printed sheets of paper in correct order for binding, collating is an added, but usually necessary, cost of commercial printing.

color bars   Used by printers as a guide to ink adjustments, color bars represent the four process colors, trapping values, and color densities. The bars should be included on all color separations, outside the cropped page size. Page composition software capable of separating colors print the color bars automatically.

color matching   To match preprinted swatches of custom-mixed ink to the colors you want. The most well-known color matching system is the Pantone Matching System (PMS). To retain the exact tint of the custom colors, they must be printed as spot colors, as opposed to including the colors in the three process color plates of cyan, magenta, and yellow.

condensed type   Characters and the space between characters have been narrowed horizontally, allowing you to fit more characters in a given line measure.

continuous tone print Reflective art (a printed photo as opposed to a slide or transparency) chemically processed to produce continued degrees of color. When you wish to print a continuous tone photo, the tones must be broken into a lined dot pattern, called a halftone, so that ink applied with a printing press can replicate the photographic image.

D

descender The *legs* of characters that drop below the baseline, such as in the lowercase *g* and *j*.

die cutting Any special cuts or trims given to printed paper must be done using a die (like a form or template). To cut a window in the cover of a brochure is called die cutting the window.

drilling When holes need to be punched in more than a few sheets of paper, commercial printers use a special drill that drills holes in the pages, neatly and uniformly.

dummy A very rough layout of a planned document.

duotone A photo printed in black, white, and a second color, usually a sepia or brown. Duotones are a way to add depth and contrast to a black and white photo without the expense of four-color printing.

E

electrostatic plate material Some PostScript laser printers (LaserMaster in particular) are capable of printing on special plate material that can be loaded in a letterpress printing press and printed, without the separate plate-making step.

em dash A dash the same width as the letter *M* in the font you are using. Em dashes replace the double hyphen (--) and indicate a pause or separate thought in a sentence.

embossing
Creating a raised relief of a type or an image on printed paper. A metal die is made of the image that will be embossed and paper is forced over the die. A notary public's seal is embossed in a document.

enamel
Refers to a type of coated paper, or to a coating applied to paper. A good finish for printing halftones and fine screens.

English finish
A term meaning a special, smooth finish for book paper—smoother than a machine finish.

en dash
A narrower dash than an em dash, the en dash is the width of the letter *N* in the font you are using. En dashes are generally used to replace the word *through* or *to* or when showing a group of two numbers (12:00-12:15).

expanded type
A term for type that is wider than a normal font—both the characters and the space between characters have been increased in width.

F

felt side
In paper terminology the top or smoother side of the paper.

flush left
Type is flush left when it is left aligned.

folio
Another term for page number.

footer
See header.

French fold
A type of fold used for formal invitations in which the page is folded both vertically and horizontally, resulting in a four-panel document.

G

gang or gang printing
A means of printing more than one page of a job at a time, thus reducing the cost per impression. Once

	printed, the larger sheets are trimmed to the correct size.
grain	Paper has a grain, much like wood. If a fold is placed against the grain of the paper, the fold breaks the finish of the page. Folds should always be specified with the grain.
gutter	The space between columns on a page.

hairline	The thinnest line you can print. In desktop publishing, hairlines are usually specified as one-quarter point lines (which is about the thinnest line a 300 dpi PostScript laser printer can reproduce). If you know you will be producing the pages on a higher-resolution printer, you can specify thinner hairlines.
halftone	The transformation of a continuous tone photograph into a printable form. The continuous tones are replaced by a dot pattern in which dark tones have more dots closer together and light tones have fewer dots further apart. For each dot a dot of ink is printed and the result is a printed rendering of the original photo.
header	Text and graphics added to the page above the top margin. Headers often indicate the title of the publication or the current chapter or section. Headers can also contain dates, files names, reference numbers, page numbers, and the like. Footers are essentially the same as headers only located below the bottom margin.
hanging indent	An arrangement of the left side of a paragraph of text in which the first line is further to the left than the remaining lines.

I

imposed film   Film from a PostScript imagesetter reflecting the arrangement of pages needed to print correctly so that they are in the proper order for binding. In creating large documents with page composition software, you should request imposed film from your service bureau.

indent   To move the left margin of a paragraph to the right by a fixed amount. A tabbed indent (or first line in-dent) at the beginning of the first line of a paragraph is moved to the right of the left margin, while the remaining lines are flush left. A double-indent indents both margins of the paragraph by an equal amount.

italic   A style of type in which characters with serifs form a script or cursive appearance. Sans serif characters are said to be oblique, rather than italic—instead of a cursive appearance oblique characters are usually slanted to the right.

K

kern   A term meaning to trim space from the right side of a letter. In desktop publishing, all Type I fonts contain a table of kerning values, indicating the amount of space which can safely be reduced. Most page composition software can automatically kern characters, by referring to the font's kerning table.

kicker   A subhead normally associated with a headline that teases the reader into reading further.

kiss fit   Instead of trapping the edges of colors that abut, a kiss fit (or kiss impression) fits the two colors exactly together and relies on the accuracy of the printing press to keep the colors adjoined properly.

kraft paper	Term for a strong brown paper used for wrapping, the word *kraft* derives from the German word meaning strong.

L

laid paper	Paper with a rough finish of raised lines, giving the impression of old-time handmade paper.
leading	Traditionally, thin strips of lead metal were added to the lines of type to increase the space between the lines. Now leading is specified in points. Where Auto Leading is available, it is normally 120 percent of the font size.
letterspacing	The space between the letters that form words; as opposed to word spacing. Letterspacing is adjusted by kerning the space tighter or looser. *See also kern.*
linen	A specific finish of paper or the type of covering for the bound cover of a book.

M

magenta	One of the four process colors, magenta is also called process red.
masstone	The color of an ink in large quantity, as opposed to the color of the ink when printed on white paper.
masthead	Traditionally the name of the newspaper or newsletter, positioned at the top of the front page. Also called the *nameplate*.
master page	Used in most page composition software to hold repeating elements that are exactly positioned on several pages. Master pages hold headers, footers, and page numbers, for example.

matte finish   Paper with a smooth, dull surface.

N

negative   In desktop publishing, a version of your pages that imagesetters produce on film instead of on resin-coated paper. Negatives can be either film-positives or film-negatives. Traditionally, the negative is a reverse of a camera-ready mechanical, created with a large-format camera.

newsprint   A type of paper reserved mostly for inexpensive, large press runs, requiring special printing presses. Newspapers are normally printed on newsprint, a very rough and absorbent paper. It is also used for large quantities of inexpensive flyers, such as newspaper inserts, or political brochures. A photo cannot usually be printed on newsprint any finer than with an 85-line screen.

non-scratch inks   Used where a lot of abrasion is expected to cover documents, non-scratch inks have a high resistance to marring and scratching.

O

oblique   See *italic*.

onionskin   A type of paper with a semi-opaque finish and a light weight.

opaque   The opposite of transparent. In desktop publishing opaque elements hide elements that are underneath.

overhang cover   In book binding, a cover larger than the pages bound inside, forming a lip edge.

P

Pantone Matching System   *See Color Matching.*

perfect binding   Pages are bound like a telephone book, in which the left edges are glued with a flexible adhesive.

pica   A system of measurement in which six picas equal one inch.

pinholes   In desktop publishing, a problem sometimes experienced with the film used in PostScript imagesetters. The output should be held to the light, where pinholes, or tiny spots, in the black sections of the film become obvious. If not corrected, the holes print similarly sized spots on your pages when the job is printed.

point   A measuring system primarily for type, in which 72 points equal an inch, 12 points equal a pica.

press proof   Normally used to proof four-color printed photographs by preparing the printing press and printing a small number of impressions. The only absolutely sure way to see what the printed results of your job look like. Also the most expensive form of color proofing.

process color   Recreating any color by printing a combination of the four primary colors cyan, magenta, yellow, and black. The degree to which each primary color is combined is controlled by the amount of screen of that color: the higher the screen percentage the more that color ink is laid down on the paper.

R

rag content or rag paper   Paper with some amount of linen or cotton fiber added for strength and quality. Normal percentages are 25, 50, 75, or 100 percent rag content.

ream	Five hundred sheets of any size paper is a ream.
register	Indicates that all the elements that are printed on a page are printed in the exact position they should occupy. Out of register printing means that colors overlap or don't print when they should.
registration marks	Are used to align negatives properly so the pages are printed in register.
right-reading	Meaning the image is read correctly left to right.
rule	A line of a particular weight or thickness.

S

scoring	Making a mechanical crease in a page prior to folding. All folds should first be scored.
screen	Printing a solid color through a fine grid that breaks up the continuous color into dots of color. The finer the screen, the closer and smaller the dots; the coarser the screen the larger and fewer the dots.
screen angle	When the screens of two or more primary colors are printed on top of one another to form a unique color, each screen must be at a precisely different angle, or unsightly patterns will be formed by the dots.
self-mailer	A document that can be mailed without an envelope.
set-off	When printed pages are stacked for drying. Ink from the top of one sheet can be transferred onto the underside of the next sheet.
show-through	A paper that is not opaque enough allows the printing on one side to show through the other side. Not desirable, especially in book printing.
spread	An open, two-page arrangement with the fold or bound edge in the middle.

T

thermography   A process that creates raised print, similar to but much less expensive than steel-die engraving. Thermography adds powdered resin to the wet ink and bakes the page until everything is dry. The resin dust creates the raised impression.

tooth   The texture of a paper or the amount of feel; as opposed to a smooth finish.

transparency   A colored film photograph as in a 35mm slide; as opposed to a color print.

trap   The steps required to minutely overlap colors that abut so that they print correctly, without showing the underlying color of paper between the edges of the colors.

trim marks   Indicate where the printed page is to be trimmed.

U

uncoated paper   Basic stock without any special finish.

upright   A binding orientation. A book or magazine bound along its long edge, as opposed to its short edge.

V

van dyke   *See brownline.*

varnish   A clear protective coating usually added to the printed covers of brochures and magazines to protect readers's fingers from smudging the ink. Varnish is also used to accent items on the page by creating a glossy appearance.

verso	The left side of a two-page spread, as opposed to the recto which is the right side.

watermark	An embossed mark created in the paper during manufacturing. You can order custom watermarks of your own design, but it is expensive to do so.
web press	One that can print on continuous paper, as opposed to a sheet-fed press. Web presses are reserved for large press runs, such as for printing newspapers.
wire side	The back side, or bottom side of a sheet of paper, also considered the wrong side.
work and turn	To print the front sides of all the pages, turn the stack over and print the back up (or back side).
wrong-reading	The opposite of right-reading, in which the image is a mirror image of its correct orientation.

INDEX

M

P